The Unifying Moment

The Psychological Philosophy

of William James

and Alfred North Whitehead

by CRAIG R. EISENDRATH

Harvard University Press

Cambridge, Massachusetts   1971

For My Mother

Yet mothers can ponder
many things in their hearts
which their lips cannot express.
—A. N. Whitehead

Contents

Preface

The philosophy of William James and Alfred North Whitehead is an attempt to answer the old Platonic question: how do
ideas work in the world? Put another way: how does mentality, which seems so insubstantial, come to characterize and
affect substantive reality?

This is the question which haunts Western thought. The
processes of the world, no less than God, are caught in its net.
It is the main question dividing schools of thought and ultimate attitudes toward life.

In answering this question, James and Whitehead force a
major reinterpretation of Western thought.

As for James, he often appears more a compiler than an
original thinker. His debt is immense to philosophers from
Plato to Bergson and to that small group of thinkers on both
sides of the Atlantic who in his generation were transforming
philosophy into psychology.[1] In 1890, James arrived with his
Principles of Psychology, like a guest with all his suitcases,
trunks, hatboxes, and pets, in a plethora of footnotes and
acknowledgments—there was practically nothing in the psychological writing of his time that James had not collected and
stuffed into his two-volume work. Its acceptance as a text was
immediate. Read again today, it emerges as a highly personal
philosophic document, *epochmachend,* as James would say, in
its representation of a new approach.

This approach was first outlined in an article James wrote
called "On Some Omissions of Introspective Psychology,"
which appeared in *Mind* in January 1884, and which became
part of the chapter "The Stream of Thought" in the *Psychol-*

ogy. In this article, instead of dealing with thoughts as the discrete accidents of a substantive mind, James looks exclusively to the thoughts themselves, and treats thinking as a continuous constructive process. Elsewhere in the *Psychology,* James says that thoughts, or thinking, elicit actions and alter psychic states, and so work in the world as final causes.

Whitehead saw the work of James as part of a decisive turn in Western thought: "The scientific materialism and the Cartesian Ego were both challenged at the same moment, one by science and the other by philosophy, as represented by William James and his psychological antecedents; and the double challenge marks the end of a period which lasted for about two hundred and fifty years." [2]

It was not James but Whitehead, with his background in mathematics and physics, who could draw the philosophic conclusions from the decline of mechanism.[3] James's view of the physical sciences was generally that of a push-pull materialism, "the belief that the hidden order of nature is mechanical exclusively, and that non-mechanical categories are irrational ways of conceiving and explaining even such things as human life." [4] James did grasp the statistical side of modern physical thought,[5] and he appeared to be familiar with the work of such physicists as Maxwell, Mach, Thomson, Boltzmann, and Planck.[6] Nevertheless, the more significant advances in physics which occurred in his lifetime, from the field equations of Clerk Maxwell to Einstein's special theory, seem to have had little effect on his basic thinking.[7] Their effect on Whitehead, however, was decisive: "There is not a single concept of the Newtonian physics which was taught as a whole truth, that has not now been displaced . . . This experience has profoundly affected my thinking. To have supposed you had certitude once, and certitude about the solidest-*looking* thing in the universe, and then to have had it blow up on your hands into inconceivable infinities has affected everything else in the universe for me." [8]

The new evidence from the physical sciences gave White-

head's thought a dimension which James's generally lacked.
Victor Lowe lists a number of developments in physics which
influenced Whitehead: "the development of *vector* physics, the
development of the theories of molecular and submolecular
energetic vibration, and thirdly the rise of *field* as a basic concept. Later come the statistical conception of physical laws, the
theory of relativity, and the quantum theory." [9] These elements are all apparent in Whitehead's most significant metaphysical work, *Process and Reality,* in which he extends his
thought into a complete cosmology. This system he called the
"philosophy of organism." Whitehead himself made it clear
that he arrived at this philosophy by way of mathematics and
mathematical physics, but that it would have been equally
possible to arrive at it by way of psychology and physiology.[10]
The latter was the path of James.

Together, James and Whitehead offer a philosophy which
represents an alternative line to that of Husserl, Heidegger,
and Merleau-Ponty on the one side and the logical positivists
on the other.[11] The James-Whitehead philosophy comes closest
to that point where real things are making themselves up out
of the materials of their own existence. It is an attempt to
analyze this unifying moment, both as a subjective fact for
the thing itself and as the introduction of a new objective fact
in the causal history of the world. With James and Whitehead,
we are back to that time of primal chaos which Plato writes
about when the forces of creativity are seen catching up the
world and guiding or persuading it into the organized forms
in which it appears. For Whitehead and James, this work is
taking place in every moment.

James writes of the organization of the conscious field and
of its development of the experiences of space and time. He
describes the creation of the self and the way it guides perception and action, and how the self is perpetuated, with its sense
of identity, from occasion to occasion. Here also James unifies
cognitive and dynamic schemes in psychology.

Whitehead shares much of this analysis, while elaborating

theories of space, time, and perception which take advantage
of modern physics. Both James and Whitehead are concerned
with the role of ideas in the processes of the world. James,
however, generally restricts his analysis to high-level experience. Whitehead goes beyond James in dealing with all
process, from electrons to human personality. He is concerned
with how ideas function in the process by which all occasions
or organisms constitute themselves, and with how aesthetics
and propositional forms guide the process and in so doing introduce novelty; finally he is concerned with how God interfuses
His being with that of the world to concretize His purposes in
history.

What is striking is that these men, so unlike in style and
temperament, and separated by a full generation, thought so
much alike. Whitehead was no doubt in part influenced by
James, but with the private papers of Whitehead unavailable,[12]
a tracing of this influence would be conjectural at best. What
is evident and more interesting is the similarity of content.

The precedents of Locke and Hume, or Kant and Hegel,
are not analogous. In these instances, the earlier thinkers are
the more adequate; the later thinkers are inexplicable without
the former. The relation between James and Whitehead is
perhaps less direct, but just as far-reaching: what James does
is to represent clearly a great body of evidence upon which
Whitehead grounds his thought. It is not all the evidence—
there are the findings of the physical sciences and of mathematics, of which James is relatively innocent. But the psychology which corroborates Whitehead's thought is as James
put it.[13]

Process and Reality is the kind of book James wished to
write: "I actually dread to die," he wrote in 1903, already a
sufferer from heart disease, "until I have settled the Universe's
hash in one more book, which shall be *epochmachend* at last,
and a title of honor to my children!" [14] He never wrote such a
work in philosophy. Perhaps such a systematic effort in philosophy was less a "live option" for a thinker of James's tem-

perament than a dream unlikely of fulfillment. Whitehead remarked: "So, when the rare balance of knowledge and perception appears, as in William James—one who could communicate so much more than most—it is perhaps an advantage that his system of philosophy remained incomplete. To fill it out would necessarily have made it smaller." [15] As James himself indicated, he ran out of time. But, less circumstantially, he felt uncomfortable in the rarefied air of systematic abstraction.

Nevertheless, scattered throughout James's work, and particularly in the *Psychology,* is a system *in posse.* Such a scheme is developed by Whitehead. [16] But an analysis of the two thinkers need not be all in one direction, for there is a fruitful complementarity between them: Whitehead is highly abstract and needs the exemplification which reference to James can provide. Conversely, Whitehead can be used to show the full sweep of general application implicit in James's ideas. Further, when James and Whitehead diverge, the differences illustrate alternative modes of thought within broad similarities of outlook: By and large, the two philosophers offer together a single philosophy. It is a line of thought which is alive to contemporary evidence and which speaks meaningfully of the universe.

In developing this topic, I have not resisted the temptation to assess the value of the ideas, their adequacy to the facts, or their aesthetic consistency. But, in general, my aim has been to make sense out of the writings considered and to show how they clarify major areas of human interest. When this requires imaginative extrapolation, however, I have not hesitated to attempt it. The problems are simply too exciting; and, in any case, the passivity of replication would be out of the spirit of the writers themselves. It was Whitehead who remarked, "The most un-Greek thing we can do, is to copy the Greeks." [17]

Acknowledgments

I am grateful to the following publishers for permission
to reprint passages from Whitehead's works: Atlantic-Little,
Brown, and Co. for the *Dialogues of Alfred North
Whitehead,* as recorded by Lucien Price (Boston: Little,
Brown and Co., 1954); Cambridge University Press for
Science and the Modern World (London, 1925); the
Macmillan Co. and Cambridge University Press for
Adventures in Ideas (New York and London, 1933; copyright
1933 by the Macmillan Co.), *Modes of Thought* (New
York and London, 1938; copyright 1938 by the Macmillan
Co.), *Process and Reality* (New York and London, 1929;
copyright 1929 by the Macmillan Co.), and *Religion in the
Making* (New York and London, 1926; copyright 1926
by the Macmillan Co.); and Philosophical Library for
Essays in Science and Philosophy (New York, 1927).

When Socrates insists that Theaetatus participate in the dialogue, the youth remarks that he would much rather be "a
listener while this subject is discussed." But such is not the
case and he goes ahead, for, as he says, "it would be a shame
not to do one's best to say what one can." I feel this applies
to my own efforts here, particularly to the critical and constructive sections.

While I have gone ahead and done my best, I have not been
entirely alone. I want to thank Dr. Richard J. Herrnstein of
Harvard University for his "behavioral therapy"; Professor
John Galloway of the Physics Department of Endicott College
and Dr. Gerald Stechler of the Psychology Department of
Boston University for their expert advice; Professor Morton G.

White of Harvard University and Professor Nathaniel Lawrence of Williams College for helpful criticisms in philosophy; Professor Joel Porté of Harvard University for his suggestions on style; and Betsy Eisendrath for her many insights into basic issues. In addition, I profited from a tutorial on William James which I conducted at Harvard in the fall of 1967 and from one on "thinking" conducted in the spring of 1968—I am particularly grateful to Daniel Whitman, Stephen Senter, and Steven Shea, who participated in both and contributed richly, and to Gregory Clark, who in the spring wrote brilliantly on the perception of time. I also want to thank Dr. Leslie T. Pennington, who first suggested to me the religious content of Whitehead's work; and the late Professor Henry Rago, formerly of the University of Chicago, who was my great teacher in philosophy. To Mrs. Nancy Clemente of Harvard University Press went the lugubrious job of editing; that she has done it so brilliantly is a testimony to her good humor and skill.

Finally, I owe most to my mother, who listened to me with her wonderful patience eighteen years ago, when I first read *Process and Reality,* and in a way I cannot describe is ultimately responsible for this undertaking.

Craig R. Eisendrath
Cambridge, Massachusetts
June 1970

Introduction

The books of all the great philosophers are like so many men.
Our sense of an essential personal flavor in each one of them,
typical but indescribable, is the finest fruit of our own accomplished philosophic education. What the system pretends to be
is a picture of the great universe of God. What it is,—and oh so
flagrantly!—is the revelation of how intensely odd the personal
flavor of some fellow creature is.[1]—William James

AD HOMINEM

SOCIAL BACKGROUND AND SOCIAL COMMITMENTS

Both Whitehead and James belonged to the relatively
comfortable middle class, the group which produced the
major theoretical thinkers of the last hundred years, the Dar-
wins, the Einsteins, and the Freuds. Erik Erikson connects
the identity formation of such men to the "cultural conditions
of a sedentary middle class." He suggests that it was precisely
the stability of their home and class, their associations and
their morality, which allowed them the psychic freedom for
innovation.[2]

Whitehead, born at Ramsgate, England, in 1861, was the
son of a vicar; James, more wealthy and socially prominent,
was born in New York in 1842, the son of a gentleman
scholar who had studied for the clergy.[3] In addition to stability, there were other factors conducive to novel thought:
social confidence, a certain obliviousness to immediate social
wrong, and an economic security that allowed them to be
intellectually disinterested. Which is not to say that they

didn't feel the press for money—both men had to work to eat; both came close to exhaustion at points in their careers striving to make ends meet, Whitehead teaching at Cambridge, James lecturing on the circuit. But the point was not to survive, but to maintain relative affluence. Nor did they ignore civic duties: Whitehead immersed himself in school administration in London for a period; James was an active committee member at Harvard and opposed United States involvement in the Spanish-American War and the ensuing grab for colonies. But neither man questioned basic social foundations. Whitehead said: "I am not suggesting that there were not a great many things which needed changing; but we intended to change them and had set about doing so." [4] Elsewhere, he wrote: "You have in me a typical example of the Victorian Englishman. I have been struck with the fact that every cause I have in any way voted for in England has finally reached such triumphs as a cause can reach. I have never been at final variance with the bulk of my countrymen." [5]

Whitehead's statement illustrates why he cannot be considered an engaged moral philosopher, like Sartre or even Dewey. In general, he was unconcerned with "issues." He wrote for the general understanding and for an exalted heart. The ideas which filled his mind were mainly atemporal, almost unworldly; the age went on; one thinks of Anselm or Bonaventura. Whitehead would not prescribe moral answers: conventionally they were given in the Victorian code; otherwise they came, without specification, from a general sense of things he tried to convey. He was, as he said when speaking of love, a "little oblivious of morals."

James was too, in his way. When he turned from his "profession" and mounted the popular podium, he became, in Perry's term, a "seer"—Emerson was his model. He was not a social critic, and, as did Emerson, he generally left popular causes to the reformers. But James's particular sense of public responsibility was, Santayana suggested, at least partially a function of his being a Harvard philosopher of that time:

"Now the state of Harvard College, and of American education generally . . . had this remarkable effect on the philosophers there: it made their sense of social responsibility acute, because they were consciously teaching and guiding the community as if they had been clergymen; and it made no less acute their moral loneliness, isolation, and enforced self-reliance, because they were like clergymen without a church, and not only had no common philosophic doctrine to transmit, but were expected not to have one. They were invited to be at once genuine philosophers and popular professors; and the degree to which some of them managed to unite these contraries is remarkable." [6]

In fulfilling this role, James spoke in a personal voice as one suffering man to his fellows; Whitehead was usually more impersonal and abstract. But neither was a technician, as the logical positivists often are; nor could either muster the detachment to consider social and ethical questions in the manner of Locke or Hume.

SECULAR RELIGIONS

For both, the religious backgrounds of their fathers were decisive; both sought a religious kind of grace in their secular thought. James's father, after renouncing the Calvinist clergy, achieved his "bundle of truth" in a mysticism derived from Emanuel Swedenborg. Many of the son's ultimate beliefs closely resembled his father's: the belief in an incomplete universe whose final goodness is dependent on man's advance of moral purposes; the transcendence of physical fact by spirit; the belief that truth is revealed to the heart and cannot be "reasoned into." [7]

But William was never a believer as was his father, and through his writings, one feels his desperate need for a faith he could not in honesty hold. He wrote to a friend: "I have no living sense of commerce with a god. I envy those who have, for I know the addition of such a sense would help me immensely. The Divine, for my *active* life, is limited to abstract concepts, which, as ideals, interest and determine me, but do so but faintly, in comparison with what a feeling of God might effect, if I had one." [8]

The religion of Whitehead's father was Anglican, and, Whitehead implies, principled and unemotional. At the base of the religion lie certain doctrines essential to Whitehead's thought: the present immediacy of a kingdom not of this world; the loving God into whose hands all spirit is received; God the creator, redeemer, and source of all good; and the dialogue of God with the world. But Whitehead, like James, found no comfort in the religion of his father. He once remarked that Christianity "did get some useful principles formulated, but in general it was too simple-minded and too ignorant." [9] Yet Bertrand Russell maintained that as a young man Whitehead had been all but converted to Catholicism by Cardinal Newman and that in later life he had tried to achieve in philosophy "some part of what he wanted from religion." [10] As one reads the final chapter of *Process and Reality,* Whitehead's favorite piece of writing, one sees transformed in Whitehead's cosmic abstractions the doctrines of a simple, almost conventional Christianity. Here all of Whitehead's boyhood beliefs are somehow justified. The chapter is ultimately touching as one realizes how personal it all is.

In the "conflict" between science and religion which raged after Darwin, James and Whitehead refused to take sides. Both considered themselves scientists, but they were also religious men, if not in the formal sense, at least in spirit. What they did deplore was religious orthodoxy, which, in their view, substituted oppression for genuine religious experience and which cut off the search for truth by dogmatic assertion. For James, religious hypotheses, even if somewhat fantastic, remained options to be held if not exercised; science could not be sure it had any monopoly on ultimate truth.[11] For Whitehead, religion was "the longing of the spirit that the facts of existence should find their justification in the nature of existence." [12] Science was necessary to describe that nature. The *faiths* of James and Whitehead were that their worlds did ultimately support the values in which they believed. James presented one aspect of this when he said: "To anyone who has ever looked on the face of a dead child or parent the mere fact that matter *could* have taken for a time that precious form, ought to make matter sacred ever after . . . What practical difference can it make *now* that the world be run by matter or by spirit?" [13] Whitehead presented another aspect: "The great point to be kept in mind is that normally an advance in science will show that statements of various religious beliefs require some sort of modification. It may be that they have to be expanded or explained or indeed entirely restated. If the religion is a sound expression of truth, this modification will only exhibit more adequately the exact point which is of importance." [14] Whitehead and James had faith in the universe, if not, in James's case, confidence that their values would ultimately triumph. [15]

WHITEHEAD

Although they shared religious concerns and middle-class origins, James and Whitehead were otherwise markedly different in their backgrounds, temperaments, and interests. Whitehead was more of a piece with a tradition, area, and class than was James, and so emerges with perhaps less individual clarity. Whitehead was born in an ancient section of England; in his boyhood he was surrounded by symbols of the past, Canterbury Cathedral, Richborough Castle, built by the Romans, Flemish houses of the sixteenth and seventeenth centuries. His education was the traditional one, with its Greek Bible, the classics, and the romantic poets: his school claimed Alfred the Great as its pupil. Traditional, but not insular, or provincial, the outlook was imperial, based on the Roman model, and grandly historical, weighing current events on the scale of millennial precedent. Whitehead was good in sports, a school leader, and most decisively a fine mathematician. This was to be his career: he went up to Cambridge to take a course completely concentrated on mathematics, and stayed on as a teacher. But beyond the limits of his profession, Whitehead was broadened by the extraordinary discourse of students and dons which flourished at Trinity College in those years; and with his marriage, in 1890, he was led to a greater awareness of the aesthetic and moral aspects of life. (Certainly the tone of conversation throughout his *Dialogues* is that of a Cambridge student turned don; it is erudite, wide-ranging, one-upish, genial, and impersonal. Although Whitehead could strike other tones, more impassioned and personal, this one seemed to serve him in many affairs of life.) Publications in mathematics followed, including *A Treatise on Universal Algebra* (1898), which led to his election to the Royal Society, and his ten-year undertaking with Bertrand Russell, *Principia Mathematica* (1910), a work which provides a foundation in symbolic logic for all mathematics.[16] In 1910, he transferred his teaching from Cambridge to London, where he also gave considerable time to municipal education.

The loss of his son in World War I put a note of tragedy into his subsequent writing. Like the earthquake in Portugal for the eighteenth-century philosophers, his son's death was the undeserved evil in the world which must somehow be dealt with. Its memory perhaps kept him from an easy Victorian meliorism to which he might well have been prone. Russell attributed to the loss Whitehead's turn from mathematics to philosophy.[17]

It was, in any case, in the immediate post-war period that Whitehead published his trilogy of books on the philosophy of nature,[18] which in their psychological aspects seem to be reaching toward the more clearly realized ideas of his subsequent "metaphysical" period. At the age of sixty-three (1924), he accepted an invitation to teach philosophy at

Harvard. He became an emeritus professor in 1937 and died in 1947.

Those who met Whitehead never completely lost the sense of awe which hung about his person. Here was a cosmic figure, a living philosopher who was more than a technician or even a thoughtful man, but was rather someone who had gazed into the abstract and abstruse, and yet somehow the most essential, aspects of existence. He had a genial side, a pedestrian social nature, as those students learned who attended his famous open houses in Cambridge. But genius was his. It was not simply his driving intellectuality, which could bring out a nervous impatience with stupidity, but an all-humbling submission at the highest level of intelligence before the mysteries of the universe.

It was at Harvard, when in his sixties and seventies, that Whitehead wrote the books on metaphysics with which this study is primarily concerned. Chief among these are *Process and Reality, Science and the Modern World,* and *Adventures of Ideas,* which together develop a full-fledged metaphysics. These books are, like the works of James, essays in popular philosophy, despite some technical aspects, particularly in *Process and Reality.* Whitehead remarked, "I write for the layman, and in so doing I avoid the technical language usual among philosophers." Unfortunately, Whitehead was not a natural writer. He said himself, "I do not think in words. I begin with concepts, then try to put them into words, which is often very difficult." [19] His language, which can be unrelievedly abstract, sometimes resembles algebra or symbolic logic in which the symbols seem to structure and pattern themselves, so that manipulation of ideas creates hitherto unrealized truth. His emotional style is most likely modeled on Wordsworth. At its best, as in the closing chapters of *Adventures of Ideas,* it is very fine, indeed memorable.

What at once impresses the reader of Whitehead is the scope of his thought. In *Process and Reality,* Whitehead defines speculative philosophy as the "endeavor to frame a coherent, logical, necessary system of general ideas in terms of which every element of our experience can be interpreted." [20] A scheme of such audacity requires the service of the broadest generalization.

Elsewhere, Whitehead writes: "I hold that philosophy is the critic of abstractions. Its function is the double one, first of harmonizing them by assigning to them their right relative status as abstractions, and secondly of completing them by direct comparison with more concrete intuitions of the universe, and thereby promoting the formation of more complete schemes of thought." [21] What frequently happens in his later writings, however, is that Whitehead fails to show by exemplification what his generalizations might mean in a specific field or what correction of abstractions they might effect. For example, although a generalization might hold for *all* organisms, it may be essential to know what its specific application might be to such highly different "organisms" as subatomic particles, cells, or mammals. Moreover, with the partial exception of physics and mathematics, he seldom refers to the special areas of knowledge or particular works which have provided the background for his "working hypotheses," and almost never does he refer to works in biology or psychology. Whitehead's philosophy is one of "organism," but he apparently based his thinking frequently on models from mathematics and symbolic logic.[22] The result is a novel view of the biological sciences, although, at times, one that is overly formalistic.

JAMES

To this short sketch of Whitehead, James presents a number of sharp contrasts. Whitehead was a product of his country and locale; James was an early internationalist, with minimal ties to any one place. His father, Henry, Sr., was continually carting his wife and five children back and forth to Europe; never firmly planted, ducking in and out of cultures, the children in one school after another, the Jameses lived through the insecurities and problems of identity which are the lot of diplomats.

In comparison with the sedate Whiteheads, the house of James, wherever it might be, was alive with spirit and stimulating talk. To the house came the most brilliant minds of the day, for Henry, Sr., knew everyone—Emerson, Carlyle, Tennyson, J. S. Mill—and was widely sought for his society.

Where Whitehead's father was apparently a fairly dull man, Henry, Sr., was an eccentric of the first order. A pegleg, charming, brilliant, funny, gruff, and irascible by turns, he was also an unfathomable mystic. After his conversion to Swedenborgianism following a psychotic seizure in his early thirties, he devoted the rest of his life to writing and lecturing about his mystical faith. His books, though stylistically beautiful, were virtually unintelligible. Here was a man at the very center of intellectual society, without a profession and without any recognition whatsoever.

Where Whitehead seems to have passed in silence out of his father's home, impressed by his father's character but not by his mind, the young James was utterly absorbed in mind and spirit by his father and family. The father, independently wealthy and lacking other involvements, clung to his family with a ferocious love, teaching, exhorting, and amusing his talented children. And there were two other children of William's intellectual stature, Henry, the future novelist, and his sister Alice. Their influence is difficult to calculate— Henry, with his haunting eyes, his quality of never forgetting anything, of quietly mulling it over and over, and finally of turning it to the highest art; and Alice, with her quick Irish wit and sense for style, who although crippled by illness transcended it with a heroic, fighting irony. For William, the eldest son, and for all the children, family was class, country, and even profession.

Whitehead seems to have moved without too much distraction into his field of mathematics. But James went through years of anxiety before he finally, almost inadvertently, settled on his professional career. He studied art with William Morris Hunt; he studied science at Harvard and went up the Amazon with Agassiz; he took a Harvard degree in medicine but showed no interest in practicing. What profession after all could compete with the humane ideals of his father? (There are indications that his father subtly thwarted William's making up his mind.) Along with the indecision, James became increasingly the victim of what were undoubtedly psychosomatic illnesses, eye strain and crippling back pains, and sank deeply into what Erik Erikson has called a prolonged identity crisis.[23] In the midst of that, at the age of twenty-eight, when he had "touched bottom," as he put it, and was close to suicide, he suffered a psychotic seizure almost identical to that of his father.[24] Finally he began to pull himself together, although all his life he would be plagued by his psychosomatic illnesses.

James achieved psychic control by an act of free will. The will had been furnished with an ideology, the philosophy of the contemporary French scholastic Charles Renouvier, whom James had been reading at the time. Renouvier defined free will as "the sustaining of a thought *because I choose to* when I might have other thoughts." [25] The doctrine gave James the confidence that mental conditions did not have to have a physical base, that therefore insanity, which he seemed to fear, was not inevitable; alternatively, it supported the view that the mind could affect physiological conditions. James now asserted, "My first act of free will shall be to believe in free will." James had said similar things before, but this particular statement served him as a useful manifesto when he deeply needed one.[26]

Two years later, he accepted the offer of President Eliot of Harvard to give a course in anatomy; and in 1873, at the age of thirty, through this chance, he embarked upon the relatively calm waters of an academic career. He taught at Harvard until his retirement in 1907; he died three years later.

In a highly provincial age, James was totally cosmopolitan,

connected through his father with the leading minds of
Europe and America, and more than genial and witty enough
to nurture associations in his own right with the most brilliant
men of his own generation. He was, with his gift for friend-
ships, his perfect French and German, and his wide reading,
ideally suited to write the comprehensive text in psychology,
a field which prior to James lacked almost any integration.

National rivalries—Europe was beginning the long build-
up to World War I—prevented any European from playing
the same role as did James, the American. Throughout his
professional life, James sought, often in vain, to mediate between his hostile colleagues or set up direct lines of communication. His cosmopolitanism is comparable only to that of the
scholars of the sixteenth century, such as More and Erasmus,
with their common church and Latin tongue. It is difficult
to think of an American, or a European for that matter, who
has played a similar role *since* James. Where Whitehead
achieved universality through the time scale of his classical
background and the scope of his abstractions, James did so in
part through the variety of his associations.

A primary source for James's understanding of psychology was his own suffering. He was, in his own phrase, a "sick
soul," barely keeping going, whose sister and three brothers
struggled, usually with less success, against mental illness.
The evil he knew was closer than Whitehead's loss of his son,
for it was in himself. It kept him, like Whitehead, from a
naive Darwinian view of progress. Rollo Walter Brown, one
of James's students, wrote that "he seemed to be a man who
had passed through some great fire of suffering and purifying
that made him alert to the world about him and responsive to
almost every kind of people in it, so that he moved energetically along a sensitive, universal awareness." [27]

However, coping with his own problems may in other ways
have inhibited his understanding. One feels in the whole of
the James literature a creeping fear of the unconscious (perhaps stemming from a fear of the renewal of the psychosis

indicated in his seizure) and a corresponding effort to claim for consciousness the whole of psychic life. His reactions to Freud testify to this. Although he always encouraged work in "depth psychology," James never integrated its findings into his own thought, despite their enormous implications for his theories of consciousness, attention, self, and the will. (It is true that after 1890 James left psychology for general philosophy, but this cannot fully explain why James ignored the new evidence.) Indeed, as late as 1909, when James heard Freud at Clark University, he could "make nothing" of Freud's dream theories and he found symbolism "a most dangerous method." As a consequence of his rejection of the unconscious, James never achieved much understanding of insanity, and in the *Psychology* (1890) he attributed it to mere weaknesses in the mental machinery controlling bodily effects and could find no motivation behind it.[28]

Despite this inhibition, James's sympathies were vast and his range of understanding impressive. Like Whitehead, he moved into philosophy relatively late after a lifetime of wide reading and a thorough grounding in another discipline. His work in psychology gave his philosophy, until almost the end, an immediate contact with an empirical field. The *Psychology* reflected this relation between philosophy and other fields which, at the outset of his career, James took as ideal. Although philosophy had always been his main interest, he found pure philosophy too disturbing, for a philosopher had to doubt everything; an empirical field gave James a "stable reality to lean upon," "a fixed basis from which to aspire . . . to the mastery of the universal questions when the gallant mood [was] on him." [29]

As a writer, James's only peer in psychology is Freud, with whom he shares the distinction of communicating equally well with laymen and specialists. James's writings remind one of the campaign stops of a politician, however honest. They are clearly fitted to the preconceptions and style of his audience. When he is speaking to psychologists, he talks like one; to ministers, he admits the possibility, nay the wish, that the Divine might exist; to the general public, he declares the value of good common sense, the practical workaday aspects of philosophy. James's adaptation of style and even content to his respective audiences reflects the deep strain of pragmatism running through his thought. Truth by itself was not enough; he had to ask, truth for whom?

Although both Freud and James were adept communicators, their fundamental styles are different. Where Freud in dialectical fashion anticipates our psychological questions, James seems to be pointing out things on the surface like a masterful guide who enhances our pleasure in the trip by his acuity and wit and especially by an almost unsuspected ability to probe matters to their depths.

Whitehead wrote that "the true rationalism must always transcend itself by recurrence to the concrete in search of inspiration." [30] This was the rule for James, not only in substance but in style. The vivid colors of his language, the metaphors and phrases, rivet the mind on facts as decisively as the empirical detail. James abjured the "objectivity" of professional language, the agreement on which by the learned was doubtful in any case. In *Pragmatism* and *The Meaning of Truth*, he questioned whether objective truth existed at all. Truth, he felt, dissolved into the experience of its verification; it could not be torn away from its peculiar experiential environment. Accordingly, it always bore a somewhat private character. Standard methods of experience—"experimentation" in the scientific sense—could standardize truth, but then James was never much of an experimentalist; he found laboratory work too boring and gave it up fairly early in his career. [31] Much of the original writing in the *Psychology* is derived from James's private experience, and although he was conscious of the needs of his profession to be standard, objective, and universal, his truths were usually somewhat intimate; his style, the bearer of those truths, was even more so.

When James turned to philosophy, he found the post-

Kantians or absolutists in possession of most of the academic chairs. He wrote of them, "The more absolutist philosophers dwell on so high a level of abstraction that they never even try to come down." [32] Distrustful of direct experience, extravagant in their claims for an intellectual order, intolerant of anyone who would profane their truth by questioning its perfection, they were for James an antipathetic crowd. [33] James's fight with the absolutists was an almost daily affair (by the time Whitehead was writing metaphysics, they were passing from the scene). James's direct style can be seen in part as a reaction to the obscurantism which he found around him. [34] To the absolutists, James was not a little obscene; and in speaking of him, the philosophic priests were often intemperate. Time and time again, James, who fundamentally liked to be liked, would wring his hands with exasperation. Why were they so obscure, why didn't they at least make an effort to meet him halfway, at least try to understand him as he was trying to understand them, why were they so hostile? In *Three Lives,* Gertrude Stein, James's pupil, wrote of fat people being anxious because they have so much area to protect. [35] The rationalists were in a way philosophically, as well as vocationally, fat, for were they to admit any fact outside their deterministic explanations, any glimmering of pluralism, their structure would collapse. A man like James was more than an opponent; his style and thought swung freely like an ax.

A PHILOSOPHY OPEN TO ALL EXPERIENCE

James's receptivity to experience, the open-ended nature of his thought, led him to admit into philosophy data not generally accepted in his field. Whitehead wrote of James, "His intellectual life was one protest against the dismissal of experience in the interest of system." [36] Although Whitehead *was* a systematic thinker, he was like James in his openness to varied data. For example, in opposing nineteenth-century materialism, Whitehead used the romantic poets to illustrate

important factors in nature which science had ignored.[37]
James conducted psychical research, following up mediums
and reports of clairvoyance, and so forth, because he thought
that the learned might have overlooked essential evidence.
James wrote, apropos of psychical research, that "when our
science once becomes old-fashioned, it will be more for its
omissions of fact, for its ignorance of whole ranges and orders
of complexity in the phenomena to be explained, than for
any fatal lack of its spirit and principles." [38]

Both James and Whitehead credited religious feelings as
such, James particularly in *The Varieties of Religious Experience,* Whitehead in *Religion in the Making.* For example,
Whitehead wrote: "It is characteristic of the learned mind
to exalt words. Yet mothers can ponder many things in their
hearts which their lips cannot express. These many things,
which are thus known, constitute the ultimate religious
evidence, beyond which there is no appeal." [39] This passage,
which poignantly echoes the annunciation to Mary in the
Gospels, is at bottom a statement about evidence. It says that
what is strongly felt must be accounted for as such, that it
must not be explained away as mental aberration or illusion.
James took essentially the same view, though he expressed it
in more existential terms, when he said, "The plain truth is
that to interpret religion one must in the end look at the
immediate content of the religious consciousness." [40]

Along the same lines, both entered as direct evidence various feelings, such as those of causality, and, in Whitehead's
case, the direct intuition of the divine purpose, whose existence had been doubted altogether by other philosophers.
One of James's major contributions to psychology is his
reckoning with transitional states of mind which others had
ignored or considered insignificant.

However, James sometimes only collected data; this is partially reflected in his *Varieties of Religious Experience,* his
psychical research, and his reading in psychopathology. One
explanation might be that here James was delving into what

were for him areas of anxiety and that collecting was less threatening than integrating the data into a scheme of thought, since for James all thought was personal. "Scientific" investigation and collecting—the white coats, the scientific parlance—were forms of resistance, as Freud was relentlessly to point out. James managed better than practically anyone else in the century to avoid scientism, particularly its cant and professional mysticism, but he was not altogether successful in avoiding its collective defenses.[41]

Whitehead attempted to integrate all experience into his system, although he was by temperament somewhat unsympathetic to experiences which seemed to him overemotional or psychotic. Only in dealing with historical material, however, does he seem somewhat the Victorian collector, more concerned at times with exhibiting his specimens than in constructing a coherent theory about them.[42]

EVOLUTION AND HISTORICISM

Both James and Whitehead gave allegiance to the twin movements of evolution and historicism dominating the nineteenth century. This allegiance is implicit in James's notion of an unfinished creation and in Whitehead's "creative advance." And it underlies their basic conviction that any actually entertained idea must be seen as a phase of biological or cultural development or as an act of construction by an individual. Both thinkers shared a suspicion of the "givenness" of such ideas (or things), or, in other words, their so-called atemporality. Thus, in the *Psychology,* James showed how Newtonian space is constructed from the earliest simple experiences; and Whitehead, in *Religion in the Making,* wrote a modal anthropological history leading up to conventional ideas of God. Finally, Whitehead took the approach to the absolute limit by making each individual at each moment a constructive act.

It is important, however, to distinguish the attitude of historicism[43] from history as such. James seldom referred to history; for him it seemed little more than adventitious events. Here and there, a Napoleon, a constitution, a social institution might point up a lesson, but always as a detached insight. To James, history seemed neither unified, purposeful, nor particularly useful. Whitehead, on the other hand, at times seemed to view the entire history of the West as a single complex fact; indeed, the idea of an evolving civilization was a significant part of his metaphysics.

AN ESSENTIAL PERSONAL FLAVOR

In a private letter, Bertrand Russell wrote: "Abstract work, if one wishes to do it well, must be allowed to destroy one's humanity; one raises a monument which is at the same time a tomb, in which, voluntarily, one slowly inters oneself." [44]

James and Whitehead met this danger in philosophy with the vitality of their individual passions. Whitehead's was cosmic; he was, for example, genuinely concerned about whether the electromagnetic laws pertain only to our "cosmic epoch." Freud might say that such concern is a sublimation of a libidinal passion more mundane. But perhaps the glory of human life lies in such transformation. Lucien Price wrote of Whitehead:

"Suddenly he stood and spoke with passionate intensity. *'Here we are with our finite being and physical senses in the presence of a universe whose possibilities are infinite, and even though we may not apprehend them, those infinite possibilities are actualities.'* " [45]

James, the passionate introspectionist, is perhaps seen most characteristically recording his own reactions. During the San Francisco earthquake of 1906, he was staying in a little house nearby at Stanford University. Later, he wrote:

"The emotion consisted wholly of glee and admiration; glee at the vividness which such an abstract idea or verbal term as 'earthquake' could put on when translated into sensible reality and verified concretely; and admiration at the way in which the frail little wooden house could hold itself together in spite of such a shaking. I felt no trace whatever of fear; it was pure delight and welcome.

'Go it,' I almost cried aloud, 'and go it stronger!' " [46]

THE TRADITION OF THOUGHT

James once remarked to a friend that the "barbarians are in the line of mental growth, and those who do insist that the ideal and the real are dynamically continuous are those by whom the world is to be saved." [47] But James and Whitehead did not themselves appear to be barbarians. Indeed, they seemed quintessentially Western thinkers, in the very mainstream of Western thought. How well their innovations were disguised! James, now and then, enjoyed creating a shock, but his good breeding always ensured that it would be accepted as, at worst, an eccentricity;[48] Whitehead seemed above reproach, an innocuous professor, careful to justify himself at every point by reference to some major Western thinker.[49]

But with the barbarians, James and Whitehead hold that "the ideal and the real are dynamically continuous," and in so doing, they oppose much of modern Western thought.

DESCARTES: DUALISM OF SOUL AND BODY

The thinker on whom consciously or unconsciously they center their attack is Descartes. As the heir to the medieval tradition, Descartes brings into modern thought the dualism of soul and body. This dualism is necessary to work out the drama of Christian theology. Salvation after death has to have an object, and this object, the soul, has to be tested during its earthly sojourn by the situations which its union with the body provides. But as the object of salvation, it must be separable from the body, and thus it must be of different metaphysical stuff.

Although Descartes tries manfully to mediate the dualism, he never succeeds in shaking off the idea that soul and body are separate metaphysical categories. In *The Meditations* and particularly in *The Passions of the Soul*,[50] Descartes traces the interactions of the body and soul. The soul, he says, can cause actions in the body, as by willing the body to move, and it receives the forms of perception from the world by way of the body. But Descartes also maintains that the soul *independently* doubts, understands, affirms, denies, and wills, and so is separate from the body. In other words, its existence is in no way dependent on its experiences of the external world, even when that includes its own body. Localizing the interaction between the soul and body at the pineal gland, as Descartes does, pinpoints the problem, but does not remove it. That is: how do things which are metaphysically different exert causal influence on one another, or contribute to one another's existence?

Another related problem is Descartes' acceptance of the substance-quality mode of thinking. For Descartes, souls and bodies are substances; thoughts and colors are qualities or accidents. But the jump from the qualitative or accidental to the substantive is fraught with risks. In this sense, his "I think, therefore I am" is a leap of the imagination, as Hume would point out.[51] Descartes maintains that "when we perceive any attribute, we therefore conclude that some existing thing or substance to which it may be attributed, is necessarily present,"[52] that is, *something* is thinking, if thinking is going on. But this something does not need to be the soul, as Descartes insists it is.

Descartes hints at another interpretation when he states: "For we experience some difficulty in abstracting the notions that we have of substance from those of thought or extension, for they in truth do not differ but in thought."[53] According to this language, the soul's present existence could be its present thoughts. This would suspend the question of agency. But Descartes' dominant thought is that the soul as a substance stands over and above its present activity. Some of James's most brilliant writings are efforts to work back to Descartes' hint that perhaps the soul is constituted by its present thoughts, and to construct out of these present thoughts a concept of identity which corresponds to Descartes' substantive soul.

Descartes also has trouble establishing bodily substances and, more generally, our experience of the external world. Descartes maintains that our direct experience of external things comes by way of sensations. The sensation of green, for example, represents the terminus of an agitation from an object, say, a tree, transmitted through the air, thence to our nerves, to the brain, and finally to the soul. For Descartes, sensations are the "various dispositions of these objects which have the power of moving our nerves in various ways." [54] But he gives no reason why sensations need be anything more than private entertainments of the mind except his faith that God would not so deceive us.

He maintains that the nature or essence of corporeal substance is extension in length, breadth, and depth. But this essence is not grasped through sensation. In a passage which anticipates Kant, he writes that "it is now manifest to me that even bodies are not properly speaking known by the senses or by the faculty of imagination, but by the understanding only, and . . . they are not known from the fact that they are seen or touched, but only because they are understood." [55] The nature of this understanding (*inspectio*) is never adequately defined, and the foundations of the sciences are therefore left in doubt.

CARTESIAN ASSUMPTIONS OF MODERN SCIENCE

The assumptions of Descartes are for the most part also the assumptions of modern science in the period preceding Maxwell, Planck, and Einstein. First of all, modern science concerned itself with the movements and positional inter-relations of lumps of matter, which had the same characteristics as Descartes' bodies. Like Descartes' bodies, they are ultimately unknowable and devoid of mentality, and follow fixed routines which seem imposed on them rather than being, in some way, a product of their natures. This assumption Whitehead calls "scientific materialism." [56]

Scientific materialism is concerned with the transmission of effects between bodies. Along these lines, Descartes traces the transmission of effects from a perceptual object through its intermediaries to the brain. But in the final analysis, he believes that all objects can be completely defined by what they are within limited coordinates of time and space, because for him they are substances and substances are self-sufficient entities: "By substance, we can understand nothing else than a thing which so exists that it needs no other thing in order to exist." [57] If this is true, then all relations between substances or lumps of matter must be defined by scientific materialism, that is, they must be external relations.

The assumption that lumps of matter are self-sufficient substances within limited coordinates is what Whitehead calls the assumption of "simple location." The classical example is Newtonian particles, with their four coordinates, three space and one time. This concept is opposed by modern field theory. Whitehead's explanation is worth considering in detail:

"The physical things which we term stars, planets, lumps of matter, molecules, electrons, protons, quanta of energy, are each to be conceived as modifications of conditions within space-time, extending throughout its whole range. There is a focal region, which in common speech is where the thing is. But its influence streams away from it with finite velocity throughout the utmost recesses of space and time . . . [A]t every instantaneous point-event, within or without the focal region, the modification to be ascribed to this thing is antecedent to, or successive to, the corresponding modification introduced by that thing at another point-event. Thus if we endeavor to conceive a complete instance of the existence of the physical thing in question, we cannot confine ourselves to one part of space or to one moment of time." [58]

This means that *things* enjoying simple location in the Newtonian scheme are really abstractions. Examples are an electron and a molecule. And because these are the constituents of all larger entities, such as chairs and dogs, what is true of the constituents is true of the larger entities.

But Whitehead is quick to point out that an abstraction is still a definite factor in the structure of events. An electron or a molecule is such an abstraction. But this simply means that one cannot wipe out the entire structure of events *of which* the electron or molecule is an abstraction and yet keep it in existence: "In the same way the grin on the cat is abstract; and the molecule is really in the event in the same sense as the grin is really on the cat's face." [59]

The rejection of simple location in physics means in philosophy the rejection of Cartesian substances. The substitution of the field for Cartesian substances is one of the major aspects of Whitehead's work. An analogous notion, the conscious field, is the basic operating concept for James's theory of mentality.

Descartes maintains that perceptions are ultimately accidents inflicted upon the soul by external things and that these things are unessential to the soul's existence. In this sense, the soul is a substance that "needs no other thing in order to exist." But for Whitehead, and for James implicitly, external things actually contribute to the thoughts or mental activity which constitute the soul. The soul then does not enjoy simple location, but rather is the mental focus of a world of convergent causal inputs, that is, it is the focus of a field.

James and Whitehead would agree with Descartes that something must think. But that something is the organism, or, in Whitehead's phrase, the "actual occasion," rather than the soul. Thus perception is the experience of the organism, or actual occasion, rather than, as for Descartes, the soul's experience of the body. Accordingly, it is the organism which unites and experiences its world, of which the perceived is a part. The advantage of this doctrine, explicitly formulated by Whitehead, is that all mental functions are referable to one agency, the organism. This eliminates Descartes' awkwardness in explaining which mental functions are dependent on the body and which on the soul.[60]

HUME AND LOCKE

An attempt to avoid the difficulties inherent in an explanation of the world based on substances can be found in David Hume's *Treatise of Human Nature*. According to Hume, all perceptions of the human mind are based upon "impressions" and "ideas." Impressions consist of "all our sensations, passions and emotions, as they make their first appearance in the soul." "Ideas" are "the faint images of these in thinking and reasoning." [61] Substances are then sensations associated together. For example, "round," "red," and "heavy" are experienced together and are attributed by the mind to a substance, a ball. But Hume maintains that we know no more than the sensations so associated and that the attribution to a substance is gratuitous.

In Hume's system there is nothing in the experience of sensations which gives a warranty for an external world, because sensations arise "in the soul originally, from unknown causes." Indeed, Hume explains that "it will always be impossible to decide with certainty, whether they arise immediately from the object, or are produced by the creative power of the mind, or are derived from the Author of our being." [62] This is the Cartesian scheme denuded of its substantial metaphysics. Hume's soul is very much like Descartes', except that Hume maintains that we can know nothing about any substantive agency which experiences sensations and which thinks, however familiar we may be with the functions themselves. Nor can we know anything about an external substantive agency or "power" to which we may attribute our sensory experiences.

The end result is to deny any direct experience of causality altogether and to make causality a product of inference. Accordingly, Hume maintains that "every effect is a distinct event from its cause" and cannot be discovered in the cause. The idea of a cause is for him a priori and entirely arbitrary; and even when we have the idea, it is impossible to discover it in a single event. The only recourse for Hume is "observation and experience," by which we establish in a variety of contexts which "effect" invariably follows which "cause." [63]

This, in barest outline, is the system of sensationalism which Hume extracted from the writings of John Locke. To be sure, the system is there in Locke, principally in the second book of his *Essay Concerning Human Understanding*,[64] published in 1690, fifty years before Hume's *Treatise*. But in attempting to confine Locke to a sensationalist system, Hume severely limits him. Sometimes these limitations occur because Hume flatly refuses to concede that Locke has any foundation for his assertions; at other times they occur because Hume chooses to ignore the evidence which Locke brings forward. At still others, Hume consistently takes one of Locke's many conflicting positions on a particular question. What is striking in the case of James and Whitehead is how much of their writing can be pieced together from fragments of Locke; it is almost as if they had rallied Locke's scattered army of ideas to defend their master against the absurdities to which Hume had pushed him.

Locke would seem to anticipate Hume's skepticism when he says that we have "but some few superficial ideas of things, discovered to us only by the senses from without, or by the mind, reflecting on what it experiments in itself within," and when he despairs that we can attain any "knowledge beyond that, much less of the internal constitution, and true nature of things, being destitute of faculties to attain it." [65] But unlike Hume, Locke believes that we can attain some knowledge of the external world and some direct sense of agency from our experience. He explicitly believes in the idea of power, whereas Hume denies that we have any real foundation for it. For Locke, power is a "simple" idea which we receive from sensation and reflection. We thus observe the power in ourselves to think and to move our bodies, and the power that external bodies have to produce effects in one another, as, for example, the sun's power to melt wax. We also observe the power of an object to produce ideas in us, the power of a snowball, for example, to produce in us the ideas of white, cold, and round. At one point Locke speaks of "that perception and consciousness we have of the actual entrance of ideas from [external objects]," and again, of the *"actual receiving* of ideas from without that gives us notice of the existence of other things." [66] Here is the germ of Whitehead's theory of the reenaction of the ideas of the perceived in the perceiver; it is also the basis of his belief that we are not entirely cut off from the nature of things as they are in themselves.

Finally, for Locke, causality is plainly felt. Anyone, Locke says, who puts his finger in a candle flame "will little doubt that there is something existing without him, which does him harm, and puts him to great pain." [67] Here causality is not inferred but directly experienced, a possibility which Hume flatly denies. This is the principal argument that Whitehead employs against Hume's notion of causality.

As a doctor, Locke had a highly developed sense for organic existence and for the preservation and transmission of life; thus it is not illogical that he should have anticipated Whitehead's philosophy of organism. With Whitehead, he maintains that the life of an organism results from the "continued organization" of its parts; that, reciprocally, life changes all the parts into constituents of the organism; and finally that the organism's identity is the transmission of

its common character from occasion to occasion of its existence.[68] The notion of a Cartesian substance dissolves into the
idea of a momentary organization transmitting its character
from occasion to occasion. With intuitive genius, Locke
completes the argument against substances with a full-scale
attack on simple location several hundred years before the
appearance of the physics needed to support him:

"For we are wont to consider the substances we meet with,
each of them, as an entire thing by itself, having all its
qualities in itself, and independent of other things; over-
looking, for the most part, the operations of those individual
fluids they are encompassed with, and upon whose motions
and operations depend the greatest part of those qualities
which are taken notice of in them . . . Put a piece of gold
anywhere by itself, separate from the reach and influence of
all other bodies, it will immediately lose all its colour and
weight, and perhaps malleableness too; which, for aught I
know, would be changed into a perfect friability." [69]

When Locke turns to human life, he looks not to continuity of substance but to consciousness in order to establish
personal identity. We are the same self as the one who
performed a past action because in recollection we connect
the action to our present conscious moment. It is equally so
with the body: we are made of different substances now than
we were ten years ago but we *identify* the past body with our
present one. For Hume as well, the "frequent placing of
these resembling perceptions in the chain of thought" is the
basis for personal identity. But in order to affirm this, Hume
must abandon his argument that we do not directly experience causal inputs. This is precisely what he does in one of
the most spectacular turnabouts in philosophy: "We only
feel a connection or determination of the thought to pass
from one object to another. It follows, therefore, that the
thought alone feels personal identity, when reflecting on the
train of past perceptions that compose a mind, the ideas of

them are felt to be connected together, and naturally introduce each other." [70] In this way, Hume joins Locke in anticipating James's theory of the transmission of the self.

Of the modern philosophers, Descartes, Locke, and Hume are the ones to whom James and Whitehead habitually return. The major problems were raised by Descartes, and, indeed, there are sections of James which seem so close to those of Descartes as to suggest that James's contributions are conscious reworkings.

However, it was Locke, not Descartes, who was James's chief mentor. It is instructive to compare James's *Psychology* with Locke's *Essay,* published exactly two hundred years earlier. How similar their discursive modes, their lack of dogmatism, and their receptivity to new evidence; how close their range of topics. What is new is James's appeal to physiology, however tentative, and the experimental evidence which he introduced from the German laboratories. Although there are differences, it is the similarities which are striking.[71]

At bottom, both James and Whitehead belong to the same school of thought as does Locke, English empiricism. As for James, Perry is unequivocal: "He belongs unquestionably to the British school founded by Locke, and from an early age his mind was nourished by a direct and thorough study of the leading representatives." [72] Whitehead relies heavily on Plato and Kant in his later writing, but there is still a strong empiricist current; his earlier work, such as *The Organization of Thought,* is unambiguously empiricist.

Whitehead remarks that it was Locke who "discovered that the philosophical situation bequeathed by Descartes involved the problems of epistemology and psychology." He adds:

"The germ of an organic theory of nature is to be found in Locke . . . But it is to be noticed that in the first place Locke wavers in his grasp of this position; and in the second place, what is more important still, he only applies his idea to self-consciousness. The physiological attitude has not yet established itself. The effect of physiology was to put mind back into nature." [73]

And, indeed, this was James's path. The difficulties inherent in the Cartesian scheme drove James from medicine to physiology, from physiology to psychology, and finally to philosophy. In a way, James's philosophy, and Whitehead's as well, can be seen as an attempt to take up the Lockean attack on Descartes where Locke, owing to lack of knowledge, was forced to leave it; it is also, as has been said, an attempt to rally Locke against Hume.

THOUGHTS AND THINGS

Ironically, in his preface to the *Psychology,* James reaffirms the Cartesian dualism: "This book . . . contends that psychology when she has ascertained the empirical correlation of the various sorts of thought or feeling with definite conditions of the brains, can go no farther—can go no farther, that is, as a natural science." [74] Although the *Psychology* often repudiates its preface, it is significant that James considers himself thus restricted by the limitations of the prevailing scheme of scientific thought.

Scientific materialism did not trouble with mentality, but confined itself to bodies, and achieved enormous success. But when, in the nineteenth century, psychology began to emerge as a science, Cartesian dualism suggested a way in which mental phenomena could be handled, that is, by correlation. The method seemed perfectly sound in the case of perception: to the agitation of the neurons would correspond certain pictures or sounds. Why couldn't the same apply to what Descartes considered the independent actions of the soul, willing, doubting, and understanding?

Descartes wrote at the beginning of the scientific era and, with his interest in the soul, was willing to grant mental and bodily phenomena equal status. Many scientists at the end of the nineteenth century were not. The result was a characterization of mental phenomena as epiphenomenal and a denial that they had any causal effects on the body, thus a denial of precisely what Descartes had affirmed. For example, T. H. Huxley declared that "our mental conditions are simply the symbols in consciousness of the changes which take place automatically in the organism; and that, to take an extreme illustration, the feeling we call volition is not the cause of a voluntary act, but the symbol of that state of the brain which is the immediate cause of that act. We are conscious automata." [75]

The task of science was to describe what physical experiences, as discerned by scientific observers, were mental experiences for living or any other subjects. It might also be to show how such mental experiences effected physical changes, although Huxley denied the latter possibility in theory.

There are two difficulties in such a task, one scientific, the other philosophic. In 1690, Locke had declared, "How any thought should produce a motion in the body is as remote from the nature of our ideas, as how any body should produce any thought in the mind." [76] Both Locke and Descartes believed that our perception of secondary qualities, such as warm and red, depended on the agitations of the neurons by the size, figure, and motion of the perceived object, but *how* this worked was past knowing.

The case was the same in James's day. James himself remarked, "Let us therefore relegate the subject of the *intimate* working of the brain to the physiology of the future." [77] (Freud's seminal but ultimately unsuccessful *Project for a Scientific Psychology* (1895) [78]—it had to be abandoned—further underscored the difficulties.) But the crucial *difference* was that by the late nineteenth century the scientific method had established itself in psychology, and the possibility of the kind of knowledge Locke sought was conceivable. By the time Whitehead wrote, field theory, relativity, vector analysis, and the beginning of quantum mechanics were spurring philosophic inquiry to rise to the new modes of thought.

The other difficulty in accounting for the role of ideas in the physical world was philosophic. In limiting Locke to the theory of sensationalism, Hume had brought philosophy to what appeared to be a dead end. James remarked: "I for one must confess that if by an effort of abstraction I am able for a moment to conceive the world in Humean terms—of representation sprouting upon representation by absolute happening, of everything being only once, of evolution with nothing involved, of our mental life, for example, as having come to be with no ideal pre-existing determinant of it—I feel as if the breath was leaving my body." [79] In opposing the sensationalism of Hume, James and Whitehead reverted to suggestions of Locke, and, in the case of Whitehead, to Kant and Plato.

ASSOCIATIONISM

The more immediate opposition for James and Whitehead was two lines of philosophy which stemmed from Hume, one directly, that of the associationism of the Mills,[80] and one in partial reaction, that of Kant and his followers. To the extent that scientific positivism could be explained psychologically, associationism did it. In James's day, associationism was the major theory to be reckoned with in psychology, and, in modified form, it is still with us today. The basic rationale for associationism was stated clearly by Hume:

"Were ideas entirely loose and unconnected, chance alone would join them; and it is impossible the same simple ideas should fall regularly into complex ones (as they commonly do), without some bond of union among them, some associating quality, by which one idea naturally introduces another . . . The qualities, from which this association arises, and by which the mind is, after this manner, conveyed from one idea to another, are three, viz. *resemblance, contiguity,* in time or place, and *cause* and *effect*." [81]

The laws of thought, as disclosed by associationism, operated in an autonomous fashion, and, as with the laws of nature, their discovery provided a goal for scientific research. Resemblance, contiguity in time and place, and, by inference, cause and effect could be easily worked into scientific experiments, as well as into introspective analysis. By focusing on mental *behavior*, associationism avoided the metaphysics of substances, and although it lacked much of a theory of agency, it made up for the loss by its sense of progress in discovering "hard facts." Moreover, it was most adroit in using the associationist mechanisms to explain such phenomena as memory, emotion, will, perception, and cognition. Finally, associationism attempted to construct the self or ego out of what it considered the atomic materials of mental life. James called it a *"psychology without a soul."* [82]

But useful as it was, associationism couldn't explain for James a host of facts. Why, he asked, if memory proceeded from the "laws" of associations, was it affected by fever, exhaustion, old age, and hypnotism? What determined the "laws"? Why did ideas act not as discrete entities but as elements in a conscious field? James's objections to associationism were serious, and much of the *Psychology* is taken up with them. [83] As opposed to James, Whitehead refused to restrict his attention to human mentality, but rather was concerned with organisms in general. This obviated the need for him to deal directly with associationism; a broader attack on sensationalism of the Humean sort sufficed.

KANT

As for Kant, despite his commanding position in modern thought, James and Whitehead claim that his influence on them is slight. Whitehead refers to his own work as "a recurrence to pre-Kantian modes of thought," [84] and James states

that the "true line of philosophic progress lies . . . not
so much *through* Kant as *round* him." [85]

To begin with, Kant assumes Hume's analysis of sensations, that is, that the *basic* materials of mental life are bare
fragments of sound, color, smell, and so forth. Kant then
maintains that in order to be knowledge, these sensations
must be put together by the understanding: "experience, as
a kind of knowledge, requires understanding, and I must
therefore, even before objects are given to me, presuppose
the rules of the understanding as existing within me *a priori,*
these rules being expressed in concepts *a priori,* to which all
objects of experience must necessarily conform, and with
which they must agree." [86] What the understanding effects
is the "synthesis" of the sensations, as mediated by a complex
hierarchy of a priori forms, schemes, and categories. These
include time and space, various schemes of the imagination,
and the final categories of the understanding, such as
substance and causality. The result is the unification of the
intellectual world of the knower.

Both James and Whitehead exhibit a deep suspicion of this
view, which seems to imply that the mentality of the subject
structures his experience, and yet is not *of* experience. With
Descartes and Kant, James and Whitehead accept the
subjective nature of our experience. But for them, mentality
is not something *extrinsic* to the data transforming them to
their final character; rather mentality is *intrinsic* to the data
themselves. It is essential for both James and Whitehead to
find in the dative experience itself the constructive agencies
whereby it achieves the character of mentality which we
enjoy. The result of Kant's theory is that we can have no
knowledge of things as they are in themselves (the
noumena); we can only have knowledge of appearances
(the phenomena). James and Whitehead frame a theory of
knowledge which, attempting to refute Hume and Kant,
claims some intimacy with the real world of things-in-
themselves.

It should be pointed out, however, that Kant's "synthesis" does show striking similarities to Whitehead's concept of the unification of the organism, or, in his phrase, its "concresence." To be sure, there is in Kant the stress on sensations rather than mere data, there is the emphasis on mentality rather than total organic construction, and finally there is the separation of the forms by which the data are transformed from the data themselves; but if all these are discounted, Kant's analysis is comparable to Whitehead's. That our experience is an act of construction, however performed, is, according to Whitehead, Kant's great philosophic insight.[87]

James and Whitehead also owe to Kant several other major insights. Kant posits transcendental schemata mediating between sensations and the understanding; these are schemata of cause and effect, relation, necessity, number, and so forth, which structure experience.[88] James also develops schemes which control lower-level sensory experience, although his explanation of how these schemes are formed differs radically from Kant's.

In addition, Kant gave to James and Whitehead the insight that aesthetics lies at the heart of the process by which the subject constitutes itself. In his *Critique of Judgement,* Kant analyzes the feeling of beauty as a feeling of self-unification or harmony of the faculties under the stimulus of the noumenon; and throughout the *Critique of Pure Reason,* Kant views the process of synthesis in aesthetic terms. Along Kantian lines, Whitehead sees aesthetics and logic as the analytical bases of the "concrescence," or unification, of the organism. (Unlike Kant in the *Critique of Pure Reason,* Whitehead includes taste, preference, and value in his concept of aesthetics.) Moreover, Kant's treatment of organisms and organic ends or final causes is generally parallel to Whitehead's.[89]

If James's *Psychology* seems a rewriting of Locke's *Essay,* Whitehead's *Process and Reality* may be considered a reworking, however fundamental, of Kant's major *Critiques.*

The affinity of Whitehead for Kant is clear throughout the work. And yet, how is one to explain the fact that Whitehead explicitly rejects Kant, refers to himself as "pre-Kantian," and so on? Perhaps it is because the rejection is merely on the surface, that Kant, in a way Whitehead might be loath to admit, forms his philosophic unconscious. Whitehead remarked, "By the time that I gained my fellowship in 1885 I nearly knew by heart parts of Kant's *Critique of Pure Reason*. Now [1941] I have forgotten it, because I was early disenchanted." [90] From this first love, perhaps Whitehead never fully recovered.

Kantian thought, and the reaction against it, were behind the division in psychology in James's day between the nativists and the empiricists.[91] The nativists, who maintained that certain psychological mechanisms were built into the organism, seemed to take their cue from Kant; the anti-Kantian empiricists held that the mechanisms were developed through experience. Ideally, further research should have been able to settle the question. (The theory of evolution allowed the mechanisms to be developed in the species, rather than in the organism.) But Kant's a priori mechanisms seemed mystically to condition phenomenal experience while lying beyond it; to this extent the mechanisms also seemed to lie beyond the reach of research.

For James and Whitehead, the problem with Kant is not fundamentally different from that with Descartes, for if the a priori mechanisms are substituted for the "soul," they might well ask: How do things which are metaphysically different exert causal influence on one another? If *experiential* fact covers all existence, the Kantian mechanisms lose their mystique, and become simply operations of experiential fact with itself, and so open to free inspection. This is the general solution of James and Whitehead.

Even more basically, Whitehead believes that what he calls "occasions" are the real facts of the world. Each one, whether an electron or a man, is both physical and mental. Its mentality emerges in the process of its self-creation and guides it; the synthesizing forms of this mentality do not *antedate* the process, as Kant seems to assume. But the philosophic question which must be asked is to what extent Whitehead's distinction between the physical and mental sides, or "poles," of experience avoids the problems of incompatibility posed by Kant and Descartes.

BETWEEN FACT AND IDEA

In the end, a philosophy stands or falls by its ability to deal with human experience as we know it. To effect an explanation, James and Whitehead attempt to walk between the fires of empiricism and rationalism, between a philosophy starting from facts and one starting from ideas.

James aligns himself with empiricism, but it is an uneasy alignment. His insight that living organisms not only sense but feel, not only receive experience but select it, not only conjoin it in consciousness but synthesize it, not only take it in but, in short, *create* it, puts him at some odds with the entire school. As for the influences on James, they were many and complex; the reader is referred to Perry's superbly scholarly work, which spells them out.

Whitehead is more difficult to associate with any one school. In addition to James, he acknowledges indebtedness to Henri Bergson, F. H. Bradley, John Dewey, and Samuel Alexander. Similarities to Russell in syle and approach during Whitehead's second period indicate that their long association was not, for Whitehead at least, barren, although Russell indicates that as philosophers the two had little to say to one another in later years.[92]

It is to Plato that Whitehead felt closest, despite his freely confessed empirical origins and his unadmitted indebtedness to Kant. Indeed, there is evidence to show that in Whitehead's later years Plato became for him something of a secular saint.[93] But Plato's dialogues are not a system but a series of suggestions, sometimes on all sides of a question. It was necessary for Whitehead to exercise his choices and go as far as he could—farther certainly than Plato—in constructing a consistent cosmology.

The cosmology that resulted was closer to James's than might have been expected.

I The Knowing of Things Together

[James] had a painter's eye. He had a capacity, perhaps never
equaled, of seizing and exposing the evanescent moments and
fugitive sequences of conscious life.[1]—Ralph Barton Perry

THE SUBJECTIVE FIELD

The task of philosophy is to construct a world from our
present experience; in the final analysis, this experience is all
we have. With James's analysis of the "sequences of conscious
life," Whitehead is in almost complete agreement.

LIMITS OF SENSATIONALISM

Both Hume and Kant assume that sensations are the
primary material of conscious life.[2] This is not to say that for
them the sensation is a direct reception from the "external
body," say, red from a red ball. Indeed, Locke earlier pointed
out that the sensation of red is the result of the action of the
ball on us, that is, the reaction of our own bodies to the ball.[3]
But if neither the ball out there nor our own bodies can be
directly known, as Hume and Kant say they cannot be, the
sensation achieves the status of primary phenomenal fact.
When Hume says sensations "strike upon the mind," the
mind, whatever *that* is, is clearly conceived as passive as far
as the experience of pure sensation is concerned. (It should
be noted that Hume assumes a mind upon which the sensations strike.) Kant's view is similar: sensations are the primary
mental materials which are transformed by his intuitional
forms, schemes, and categories into the final synthesis of
consciousness.

Both Hume and Kant also maintain that the sensations, such as red, hot, and round, are, in Kant's phrase, "found in the mind singly and scattered." Out of the agglutination of these discrete sensations are created mental states, objects, and the world.

To this doctrine of discrete sensations as primary mental material both James and Whitehead strenuously object. James says, "No one ever had a simple sensation by itself." [4] Accordingly, in Whitehead's language, "the conscious recognition of impressions of sensation is the work of sophisticated elaboration." [5] For example, we can identify the individual sensation 'red' for the first time only by making a series of differential discriminations between several objects in which it is contained, such as a red ball and a red box, and in which it is absent, such as a black hat. To be distinguished in a larger experience without such discriminations, a sensation must already have been previously identified.

Rather than sensations, James maintains that objects are what we directly perceive. James writes, "Experience, from the very first, presents us with concrete objects, vaguely continuous with the rest of the world which envelops them in space and time." [6] Such concreted objects, such as a dog, are gestalts. James maintains that *"all brain-processes are such as give rise to what we may call* FIGURED *consciousness. If paths are irradiated at all, they are irradiated in consistent systems, and occasion thoughts of definite objects, not mere hodge-podges of elements." [7] This is a function of a principle of James that *"any number of impressions, from any number of sensory sources, falling simultaneously on a mind* WHICH HAS NOT YET EXPERIENCED THEM SEPARATELY, *will fuse into a single undivided object for that mind." [8]

Classical psychological theory, which was based philosophically on the sensationalists and on Kant, made a sharp distinction between simple, discrete sensations and complex, organized perceptions. "The classical doctrine," wrote Hans-

Lukas Teuber in 1965, "assumes that perception occurs in two successive stages, first a primary, sensory level, and thereafter on a higher cognitive level in which the raw data of sensation are elaborated into meaningful perceptual objects." Dr. Teuber maintains, however, that recent research makes clear that this notion "cannot be the entire truth and important parts of it may well be false." He points out that there seems to be no place in the neocortex for elementary sense-data in the classical sense to converge. The primary projection areas already interpret and categorize their input, for example, by distinguishing the direction of lines. Such interpretation and categorization go far beyond the level of simple registration assumed by the classical theory.[9]

In holding that objects are directly perceived as gestalts, James dismisses sensations as primary mental facts and relegates them to the status of analytic components of objects. Moreover, he denies that perception occurs in a two-stage operation involving first sensations and then complex objects. (He does allow for a certain amount of secondary associational activity in the construction of unified objects, as, for example, the connection of a dog's bark with the image of his body or of a smokestack with the rest of a factory.[10]) Kant himself did not assume that the two stages of sensations and complex objects were successive in time; for him they were purely analytic. Thus James offers not so much an argument against Kant as a refutation of sensationalism and of classical psychological theory.

James and Whitehead anticipate modern psychological research perhaps more clearly by their dispute with the sensationalists over the status of relations. The sensationalists, they charge, denied that relations, unlike sensations, are directly experienced.[11] James disagrees: "There is not a conjunction or a preposition, and hardly an adverbial phrase, syntactic form, or inflection of voice, in human speech, that does not express some shading or other of relation which we at some moment actually feel to exist between the larger

objects of our thought." Accordingly, there are feelings of
" 'is,' 'isn't,' 'then,' 'before,' 'in,' 'on,' 'beside,' 'between,'
'next,' 'like,' 'unlike,' 'as,' and 'but,' " [12] as well as 'green'
and 'tree'. Where thought rests, there we have the nouns and
adjectives; where it hurries on, there are the verbs, adverbs,
exclamations, and conjunctions. Whitehead puts the same
thing epistemologically when he says, "The relationship is
not a universal. It is a concrete fact with the same concreteness as the relata." [13]

In maintaining a perceptual world of sensations and
objects, the sensationalists neglected aspects of experience
which do not achieve sufficient clarity or permanence. These
thoughts were first expressed by James in 1884, in his seminal
article "On Some Omissions of Introspective Psychology":

"Once admit that the passing and evanescent are as real parts
of the stream as the distinct and comparatively abiding;
once allow that fringes and halos, inarticulate perceptions,
whereof the objects are as yet unnamed, mere nascencies of
cognition, premonitions, awarenesses of direction, are thoughts
sui generis, as much as articulate imaginings and propositions
are; once restore, I say, the *vague* to its psychological rights,
and the matter presents no further difficulty." [14]

Whitehead also seeks a wider field of evidence than is
generally given philosophic consideration: "experience drunk
and experience sober, experience sleeping and experience
waking . . . experience self-conscious and experience self-
forgetful . . . experience normal and experience abnormal."
Philosophy, he says, cannot restrict itself to the clear-cut
experience of introspection while neglecting "the vague
compulsions and derivations which form the main stuff of
experience." [15]

Nor can it neglect, as did generally the sensationalists and
many other philosophers, the salient fact that experience is
not a series of static "takes" of reality; it is itself a continuous
stream. This is the subject of the great chapter "The Stream

of Thought" in James's *Psychology* and a vital component of Whitehead's analysis of "process." Thus, not only do James and Whitehead maintain that sensationalist doctrine is wrong; they also hold that it is inadequate, that it fails to deal with important aspects of experience.

SUBJECTIVISM: THE TOTAL OBJECT OF THOUGHT

Sensationalism is essentially a technique for constructing an "objective" world: the sensations are the "facts" with which we put things together. But it is one of the paradoxes of modern thought that sensationalism should generally assume as its basis the doctrine of subjectivism. The subjectivist principle, according to Whitehead, is "that the datum in the act of experience can be adequately analyzed purely in terms of universals." [16] In sensationalism, the universals would be the impression or sensation, for example, 'green'. The paradox is that the universals are those qualifying the *subject* or perceiver and that solipsism thus seems almost inescapable.

Whitehead and, in part, James attempt to reform subjectivism by avoiding this implication. They do this by attacking the substance-quality description of experience which underlies it (see below). But the basic insight of subjectivism they accept: that the primary fact in the universe is the subjective experiential world of the individual. Such a world of feeling and thought, based on the *cogito,* must be the starting point of philosophy, as Descartes and present-day phenomenologists make clear. Moreover, the enjoyment of the world, that is, experience itself, is private at the moment of enjoyment. James writes: "Every thought tends to be part of a personal consciousness . . . no one of them is separate, but each belongs with certain others and with none beside . . . No thought even comes into direct *sight* of a thought in another personal consciousness than its own. Absolute insulation, irreducible pluralism, is the law." [17]

James reforms Descartes by doing away with the soul and

allowing the thoughts themselves to achieve subjective unity in the conscious field. His subjective unity is the enjoyment of a unified world, the conscious field. His analysis is limited to consciousness; Whitehead's extends to the entire organism. But for both James and Whitehead, subjectivism means the *unification* of the world as a private experience.

The connection between the attack on discrete sensations and the endorsement of subjectivism is now clear: discrete sensations are meaningless because they are part of a unifying subjective whole. The final product of togetherness in the mind is not just so many bits of information, sensations, or even objects, but a single fact, however loosely structured, which James calls the "total object of thought." This is the plenary load of experience as one integrated moment. As such a unit, it is not just a symbol for collectivity, but a qualitatively different fact. This concept might logically suggest an agent, such as the soul, holding the constituent feelings together. James, however, has an important disclaimer: "We say . . . a higher state *is* not a lot of lower states; it is itself. When, however, a lot of lower states have come together, or when certain brain-conditions occur together which, *if they occurred separately, would produce* a lot of lower states, we have not for a moment pretended that a higher state may not emerge. In fact it does emerge under those conditions." [18] The unity which is achieved is thus not conjunction but synthesis; moreover, the product of synthesis is on a higher level than its components. This concept, which recalls Kant, is also the basis of Whitehead's central doctrine of concrescence (see Chapter III). What is at issue here, however, is the unity of experience as feeling.

EXPERIENCE AS ONE STUFF

This unity requires that all the stuff of experience be of one metaphysical type; otherwise we have the problem noted in Descartes and Kant of reconciling their differences. In considering all experience as feeling, James and Whitehead break down the division of experience which is usually made between feelings on the one hand and thoughts and ideas on the other. James takes the line that whatever value or qualification is attached to a mental fact, for instance, being considered a universal, it is still a feeling: "Why may we not side with the conceptualists in saying that the universal sense of a word does correspond to a mental fact of *some* kind, but at the same time, agreeing with the nominalists that all mental facts are modifications of subjective sensibility, why may we not call that fact a 'feeling'?" [19] And Whitehead maintains not only that the primitive form of physical experience is emotional, but that even a traditional sensation, such as 'green', is the "qualifying character of an emotion." [20] Here is a doctrine of homogeneity, from which unification can proceed.

An outline of the position of James and Whitehead is beginning to emerge. It is basically this: "Sensations" and "Ideas" lose their independence in a thought or experience which has integrated the subject's world. Corollaries are that objects are experienced as integral *within* the larger context of the unified field and that the object of thought must be defined as the *total* deliverance of the unified moment. Thus James maintains that the psychological values of a color for a perceiver depend on its contrasts with other colors, and the values of a bear depend on whether or not the perceiver possesses a gun.

AESTHETICS: DREAMS AND CONSCIOUSNESS

James's example of the contrast of colors suggests that analogues from aesthetics might be useful in analyzing the perceptual field. Unfortunately, aesthetics is a subject James devotes little attention to. But Whitehead uses aesthetics as a paradigm for the living process of conscious and, indeed, organic life. In his analysis, he finds that elements, such as daubs of paint, together establish a "multiple contrast." It is only *within* this multiple contrast that such individual

elements achieve the particular value they have in that set-
ting. This is not to say that the daubs of paint are themselves
without effect: in relation they determine the total composition or "multiple contrast." [21]

The analogy between art and consciousness is closest when
art is regarded as a *process* of creation rather than as a finished
product. Whitehead makes the similarity clear: "That portion of experience irradiated by consciousness is only a selection. Thus consciousness is a mode of attention. It provides
the extreme of selective emphasis . . . Consciousness itself
is the product of art in its lowliest form." [22] One is reminded
of Freud's saying that every man is an artist when he dreams.
Indeed *The Interpretation of Dreams* is essentially a study of
the associative assembly and of the distortions and adjustments needed to create "artistic" dreams. [23] Dreams, then, can
be taken as a model for the same processes which Whitehead
and James attribute to consciousness and art.

THE COMPLEXITY OF CONSCIOUSNESS

There is an obvious analogy between consciousness and
art, such as might be suggested by the sensationalists: the
artist has his paints and these are composed into his painting,
just as sensations are composed into consciousness. But in the
formation of consciousness, there are at the outset no simple
materials corresponding to the paints; there are only energetic
particles, waves or impulses, some flowing into the organism
from "outside," and others already integrated into the organism. These are the basic materials out of which the conscious
field, with its objects, emerges, and from which sensations
may be abstracted. Thus "perception" loses all its simplicity
when examined closely.

The complexity of the process is ever in James's mind. In
a basic passage he writes:

"The highest and most elaborated mental products are filtered
from the data chosen by the faculty next beneath, out of the

mass offered by the faculty below that, which mass in turn was sifted from a still larger amount of yet simpler material, and so on . . . We may, if we like, by our reasonings unwind things back to that black and jointless continuity of space and moving clouds of swarming atoms which science calls the only real world. But all the while the world *we* feel and live in will be that which our ancestors and we, by slowly cumulative strokes of choice, have extricated out of this." [24]

The physiology of the creation of consciousness was beyond James's reach; but James was willing to face up to his own ignorance rather than allow his philosophy to fabricate a simplicity where none existed. Sensationalism, by making basic units out sensations, fell between stools. It neither suggested the complexity involved in the transformation of incoming data into consciousness nor allowed that at levels even below consciousness objects might be more basic units than the sensations out of which they were supposed to be composed.

In rejecting the sensationalists, James and Whitehead do not replace the division of the conscious field into sensations by its division into objects, although at times James seems to speak this way. For them, objects are what happen to *interest* us. For example, we notice a dog, rather than individual bushes behind him, because the dog interests us. Following Helmholtz, James says this interest is of two kinds, practical or aesthetic. [25] By practical, James means our "substantive" interest in the dog as a dog; by aesthetic, he means our interest in the dog as a figured shape or gestalt. In any case, interest is what creates objects *out of* the sensory field. But the object emerges from a *field* in which interest plays its part *throughout,* so that at this level the field and not the object is the basic unit of analysis.

For James, the unity of the conscious field is the field unified by interest: "Millions of items of the outward order are present to my senses which never properly enter into my experience. Why? Because they have no *interest* for me. *My experience is what I agree to attend to.* Only those items which I *notice* shape my mind—without selective interest, experience is an utter chaos. Interest alone gives accent and emphasis, light and shade, background and foreground— intelligible perspective, in a word." [26] For Whitehead, too, experience is created as a unified practical field *out of* its givens, or data. Conscious unity is not mere togetherness in consciousness; it is an active process with an inner dynamic. [27]

SUBJECTIVE INTEGRATION

James disposes of the soul (or the synthesizing ego of Kant) by assuming that what takes place is a product of the thoughts themselves in their interrelations. [28] James and, more extensively, Whitehead elaborate theories to account for this interrelation and its results.

They both hold that ultimately all unification is unification of feeling. However, this does not mean that unified thoughts need not proceed from a physical unification which supports them. Indeed, for James, mental pathology lends support to such a theory of unification: the "facts of mental deafness and blindness, of auditory and optical aphasia, show us that the whole brain must act together if certain thoughts are to occur. The consciousness, which is itself an integral thing not made of parts, 'corresponds' to the entire activity of the brain, whatever that may be, at the moment." [29]

Though actual physical integration is beyond the pale of scientific demonstration, James attempts to frame a hypothesis of what actually occurs. He speculates that inputs from external objects bring together elements in the brain and that this collocation sets "new internal forces free to exert their effects in turn." [30] For example, inputs from a chair bring elements together in the brain which create a chair image. Next, the "new internal forces," such as a desire to sit down, are set free under the stimulus of the collocation, that is, the chair image. This new force has a teleology, purpose or interest, which in turn creates a practical unity in the conscious field. In a late book, James suggests that in the creation of the "activity-train" the components of the teleological field really work on each other, that "they check, sustain, and introduce"; that these elements are really thoughts; and that all the other thoughts acquire tone from the one dominant desire or thought of purpose.[31]

Except that this theory operates on the plane of high-level mentality, it is similar to Whitehead's description of the central process of all creation, what he calls "concrescence": "Although in any incomplete phase [of the concrescence] there are many unsynthesized feelings, yet each of these feelings is conditioned by the other feelings. The process of each feeling is such as to render that feeling integrable with the other feelings." The reason this is so is that "the one subject is the final end which conditions each component feeling." [32] This "final end" is James's "intelligible perspective," or "practical unity of the field."

TEMPORAL EXPERIENCE

In radicalizing Locke, Hume states that the primary materials for thought are sensations, for example, colored points. Time and space, then, must somehow be constructed out of these; and yet time and space themselves are not sensations. Hume says that we get the idea of space or extension from the fact that the points are "disposed in a certain manner." This begs the question of the origin of the idea, for we do not know why we perceive the points as disposed. Hume also says, "As it is from the disposition of visible and tangible objects we receive the idea of space, so, from the succession of ideas and impressions we form the idea of time." [33] Again the origin of the perception of time or succession is unexplained. Faced with these difficulties, and accepting Hume's theory of atomic sensations, Kant posited that space and time were a priori forms in the mind and that the origin of space and time must therefore be sought in the given constitutions of cognitive beings.[34] In their theories of time and space, James and Whitehead attempt to explain phenomena observed by Hume (and earlier by Locke [35]) without resorting to the a priori solutions of Kant.

THE SPECIOUS PRESENT

As for temporal relations, James and Whitehead begin with the observation of Locke and Hume that a *stream* of mental facts constitutes consciousness. They find that materials which are clearly separable in clock time are nevertheless related in consciousness. James gives the following example: "Into the awareness of the thunder itself the awareness of the previous silence creeps and continues; for what we hear when the thunder crashes is not thunder *pure,* but thunder-breaking-upon-silence-and-contrasting-with-it." [36] What are related here are elements in the "past" (the silence) with elements in the "present" (the thunder). But for a complete relation to be felt, its relata, the experience of the "past" and the "present" objects, must be co-present psychic experiences. Otherwise the relation is the span of a bridge, one end rooted in the present, the other hanging into the nonexistent void of the past. James says, "Awareness of *change* is thus the condition on which our perception of time's flow depends." [37] Again, how can we become aware of change if what is changed is not co-present with what it is changed from?

The answer of James and Whitehead is the "specious present." [38] The theory of the specious present is founded upon this type of fact, as presented by James:

"Objects fade out of consciousness slowly. If the present thought is of A B C D E F G, the next one will be of B C D E F G H, and the one after that of C D E F G H I— the lingerings of the past dropping successively away, and the incomings of the future making up the loss. These lingerings of old objects, these incomings of new, are the germs of memory and expectation, the retrospective and the prospective sense of time. They give that continuity to consciousness without which it could not be called a stream." [39]

In the example above, A is not merely experienced and then not experienced, it is experienced as dying or falling away; and equally H is not experienced and then experienced, but is experienced as growing in vividness. There is thus a feeling of sequential movement. Moreover, our memory of earlier such feelings in our experience of a sequence will reenforce our sense of the sequence's direction. The specious present in the same way interprets the perception of "thunder-breaking-upon-silence-and-contrasting-with-it."

The specious present also accounts for the feeling of temporal relation, or connection, between past events. The direct perception of succession in the specious present will, as time moves on, produce a *memory* of succession in the present. Thus, the experience of A will be thought of *in memory* as preceding B. [40]

The specious present seems to make clear why we feel that the present is the present: the present is the peak of the curve of our strength of perceptual awareness. At one end is the dawning of experiences and at the other their dying, and this moment is felt. Only when vivid memories crowd into the present moment are we confused.

Although James and Whitehead disagree on their estimates of the length of the specious present—James's is a few seconds with up to forty discernible subdivisions; Whitehead's is between a tenth and a half of a second [41]—they agree on the basic phenomenon. James also holds that the length of the specious present and the number of discernible gradations within it must be arbitrary features of the species, and that they must vary greatly throughout the animal kingdom. He also maintains that they can be altered in man by such factors as fatigue and drugs. [42]

In any case, the fact that consciousness has temporal duration adds a temporal dimension to the concept of the total object of thought. It is thus not only the total conscious field, but it is the total conscious field through a space of time.

The theory of the specious present also accounts for the persistence of immediate experience that allows it to be remembered. James says that *"for a state of mind to survive in memory it must have endured for a certain length of time."* How does that occur? The mechanism James invokes is the "primary memory." This turns out to be merely another term for the specious present, and is the result, in his view, of the plasticity of neural matter in retaining impressions. The overlap between dying impressions and fresh ones is the span of the specious present. James calls this feeling of the just past the primary memory.[43] This mechanism would seem to resolve the difficulties of the past being in the present.

But there remains the question of why earlier states of the neural matter are felt as contributing to the present, or, in other words, why they are included in the present. A related question is why massive bodily experience gives rise to feelings of derivation from the just past, feelings which also imply a sense of duration. James talks about the "plain conjunctive experience" or "felt transition" between the just past and the present.[44] What is required is a theory of how the just past is immanent in the present and is felt as issuing into the present. The problem will be discussed in Chapter II, in connection with Whitehead's theory of prehensions and causality and James's theory of personal transition.

The Newtonian concept of the present can be expressed as a knife-edge moving into the future, or mathematically as the limit to zero, or still again as the interface between a continuously juxtaposed past and future. This concept is discarded by James and Whitehead as not being a deliverance of immediate experience, and replaced with an experienced present which has definite duration. The length of the specious present is, as James suggests, an arbitrary feature. But going beyond the problem of perception, some duration is necessary beyond zero length, else the present and with it all existence disappears. Clearly some temporal space is required in the present, else there is no room for existence at all.

THE DISTANT PAST

The other matter to be accounted for in this preliminary discussion of time is the distant past, those experiences which are not part of the primary memory. The discussion of the specious present has been a prerequisite, for *"the original paragon and prototype of all conceived times is the specious present, the short duration of which we are immediately and incessantly sensible."* [45]

According to James, the specious present is the basis for memory. Thus, when an event is reproduced in memory, it is reproduced with the neighbors it originally had in the linked succession of the specious present. James also argues, perhaps less convincingly, that it is reproduced with its original duration. In any case, it is a "dated fact," dated as being before and after other things. It is also an entirely different kind of fact from something experienced in the primary memory or specious present: "A creature might be entirely devoid of *reproductive* memory, and yet have the time-sense; but the latter would be limited, in his case, to the few seconds immediately passing by." [46]

Nevertheless, there are analogies between the specious present and the distant past. Recognition of the passage of time in the distant past, as in the specious present, depends on content: *"In general, a time filled with varied and interesting experiences seems short in passing, but long as we look back."* Equally, "the foreshortening of the years as we grow older is due to the monotony of memory's content, and the consequent simplification of the backward-glancing view." [47]

Memory itself, according to James, involves the "revival in the mind of an image or copy of the original event." But from the outset, he makes clear that "image or copy" is only a figure of speech. It is true that the same external object may be recollected, but never in the same way as it was initially experienced: the light is different, the context has changed; the rememberer is older, he is sick or well, he has acquired more experience. (Whitehead would put it that the earlier organism has "perished" while maintaining a personal line of inheritance with its successor.) James writes: "Experience is remoulding us every moment, and our mental reaction on every given thing is really a resultant of our experience of the whole world up to that date." [48]

There are two conclusions for James: (1) there are no individual self-sufficient memories; and (2) remembered ideas are qualitatively different because they are thought of in a different mind. This is a direct application of the thesis of James and Whitehead of the unity of the subjective experience, as opposed to the building block views of the associationists. Thus, at the moment of remembrance, remembered ideas, like sensations, are integral parts of the "total object of thought."

This means that "no two 'ideas' are ever exactly the same." It is a point that Whitehead, with his Platonism, sometimes loses sight of, as does James when he slips into unqualified associationist ways of thought. But by and large, for both, memory is only of *similar* thoughts, not of identical copies.[49]

Yet mere recall does not place the idea in the past, because by itself the recalled idea might be considered merely a present thought. Association with dated things, most obviously a particular day or hour, will do the trick. Although James thus employs the associationist argument, he avoids the naiveté of thinking the experience lies ready made in the mind waiting for recall: "The retention of an experience is, in short, but another name for the *possibility* of thinking it again, or the *tendency* to think it again, with its past surroundings." [50] James thus reduces the possibility of memory to a morphological feature of the "neural paths."

ASSOCIATIONISM AND THE RELATION TO FREUD

James relies mainly on associationism for the reconstruction of the past. One particular recalls another which recalls another until a context is established. Despite his problems with the discrete self-identified ideas of Hume and Mill, James finds that the mechanisms of associationism seem to work. He credits a physiological explanation, found in Locke, that "objects thought of through their previous contiguity in thought or experience *would thus be an effect, within the mind, of the physical fact that nerve-currents propagate themselves easiest through those tracts of conduction which have been already most in use.*" [51]

James labors to explain why, given the same frequency of experience or contiguity in time or space, some ideas are remembered more easily than others. The reason he fixes on, borrowing from S. H. Hodgson,[52] is interest. James's tracing of interest in a line of association ("the jeweller's shop suggested the studs, because they alone of all its contents were tinged with the egoistic interest of possession") recalls Freud. But with James, the interest at the time of the experience is conscious, and the things remembered salient; with Freud, the interest may be unconscious, and so the things remembered are often those which at the time seemed insignificant or were seemingly ignored.

James advances with Freud, however, a theory asserting that what is remembered may be a mere aspect of an object which happens to interest us and that this aspect, rather than the whole object, can form the basis for association:

"let us suppose that that selective agency of interested attention . . . accentuates a portion of the passing thought, so small as to be no longer the image of a concrete thing, but only of an abstract quality or property. Let us moreover suppose that the part thus accentuated persists in consciousness (or, in cerebral terms, has its brain-process continue) after the other portions of the thought have faded. *This small surviving portion will then surround itself with its own associates.*" [53]

What is striking in James's explanation is the seeming autonomy of the interested thought in picking up associative material, the same autonomy which Freud's repressed material seems to enjoy in creating dreams. The associated material, according to Freud, is connected by similarity to an aspect of a repressed object of thought and can represent it in the dream, as, for example, a jar may represent the womb. Although James shies away from the unconscious motives which might thus be symbolized, he does suggest that "emotional congruity" might be an element. But James never applies his ideas to repressed material, and although he is inventive in suggesting why things should be remembered, he says nothing about why they should be forgotten. An attempt will be made to bridge James's and Freud's theories of the unconscious when James's theory of the self is discussed in Chapters II and III.

TEMPORAL SCHEMES

Association does not entirely account for the reconstruction of the past. Time has structures, the structures of calendars and Newtonian time, for example, around which the mind fixes events and things. Such structures seem to be features of the mind passed on from moment to moment, and yet they also seem to involve a different process than what is involved in the specious present.

An example of such a structure, which James provides, is the sentence "Columbus discovered America in 1492." James makes clear that the object of thought is "neither Columbus, nor America, nor its discovery. It is nothing short of the entire sentence." But the *thinking* of the sentence, as one says it, is a process, and changes at each point in the

sentence. "The same object is known everywhere, now from
the point of view, if we may so call it, of this word, now from
the point of view of that. And in our feeling of each word
there chimes an echo or foretaste of every other." Thus, not
only is the thought unified, but it is unified in every moment, and every moment flows into the next. James says that
as we say the sentence, we cannot take a durational part of it
"so short that it will not after some fashion or other be a
thought of the whole object . . . They melt into each other
like dissolving views, and no two of them feel the object just
alike, but each feels the total object in a unitary undivided
way." [54]

One such view, which both James and Whitehead instance,
would be at the outset of the sentence having the intention to
say it. James asks: "how much of it [the intention] consists
of definite sensorial images, either of words or of things?
Hardly anything! Linger, and the words and things come
into the mind; the anticipatory intention, the divination is
there no more. But as the words that replace it arrive, it welcomes them successively and calls them right if they agree
with it, it rejects them and calls them wrong if they do
not." [55] The intention is "of the whole object," but this
intention does not contain words; it also seems to "control"
the enunciation of the sentence by "testing" whether it is
right or wrong. In short, it seems to be a scheme in the sense
used by F. C. Bartlett, Jean Piaget, G. A. Miller, J. S.
Bruner, and Ulric Neisser.[56] James describes a similar scheme,
such as a "sense of at least the form of the sentence yet to
come," which somehow, even without knowledge of the
meaning, controls the "proper accent." Here he anticipates
the work of Noam Chomsky.[57] Looking toward the past,
James talks of "that shadowy scheme of the 'form' of an
opera, play, or book, which remains in our mind and on which
we pass judgment when the actual thing is done"; and
looking toward the future, he speaks of "this permanent
consciousness of whither our thought is going." [58]

It is important to recall James's words that we cannot take any one durational part "so short that it will not after some fashion or other be a thought of the whole object." It implies that as far as we wish to go toward the limit of zero duration the scheme will be there. Whitehead also seems to deal with intentionality without reference to durational time.

Nevertheless, these schemes of intention and of memory seem very much related to the idea of time. In fact, it seems clear in the thought of James and Whitehead that there are several levels of the mind involved in time perception: (1) a lower-level durational sense involving sensations, objects, and words, such as thunder following lightning; and (2) higher-level schemes involving intention, anticipation, and memory.

For example, there is a schematic sense of saying the alphabet. Most people say it in groups, such as ABC D EFG HIJ K LMNOP QRS TUV WX Y Z. Now this lower level could be *triggered* by a higher level in the form A.. D E.., and so forth. (James's example of a single letter coming in at one end and a single letter dropping out at the other end of an advancing seven letter group would not take into account such a schematic operation.) Further, the intention to say the alphabet as a *whole* would rely on a still higher level, which has even less durational sense than the lower two.

Such a higher-level scheme would be Newtonian time, as it is passed on from occasion to occasion of a man's life. As has been seen, James talks of other such structures with which we order past experience, which "aid" memory, such as "the form of an opera, play, or book." James speaks only of schemes around which we organize memories, although he points the way for more recent psychologists, such as Ulric Neisser, who have conjectured that memories themselves are such schemes.

SPATIAL EXPERIENCE

Both James and Whitehead maintain that the datum for our conceptions of space and time is immediate experience. They disagree both with Hume's description of atomic sensations and with Kant's position that space and time are a priori forms of the mind. James says:

"That one Time which we all believe in and in which each event has its definite date, that one Space in which each thing has its position, these abstract notions unify the world incomparably; but in their finished shape as concepts how different they are from the loose unordered time-and-space experiences of natural men! . . . Cosmic space and cosmic time, so far from being the intuitions that Kant said they were, are constructions as patently artificial as any that science can show." [59]

In an early work, Whitehead makes the same point, and describes how our final conceptions of such things as space and time are created out of our immediate experiences. He explains that as concept is built upon concept, we finally arrive at conceptions which both cover the immediate experiences and have smooth logical relations among themselves. [60]

As for space, James holds, with Locke, that our immediate experiences are themselves spatial and declares that he is "wholly at a loss to understand" the Kantian view that "our sensations are originally devoid of all spatial content." [61] But while maintaining that sensations are initially spatial, James also holds that our conception of space must be *constructed*. He explains two methods by which this construction is effected, although he never formally distinguishes them. The first method is based upon sensory experience attended to, or, what is the same thing, focused upon. The second is based upon global, preattentive sensory experience which is then attentively subdivided.

In both theories, James employs the concept of attention

in a distinctly modern sense, that is, in the words of Ulric Neisser, as "simply an allotment of analyzing mechanisms to a limited region of the field." [62] Attention as such does not distinguish, analyze, and relate, but it is, James says, "a condition of our doing so." [63]

SPACE FROM ATTENDED EXPERIENCE

This theory is based on the idea that a particular attended sensation is in the nature of the experience a *located* sensation:

"By his body, then, the child later means simply *that place where* the pain from the pin, and a lot of other sensations like it, were or are felt. It is no more true to say that he locates that pain in his body, than to say that he locates his body in that pain. Both are true: that pain is part of what he *means by the word body.* Just so by the outer world the child means nothing more than *that place where* the candle flame and a lot of other sensations like it are felt . . . [T]he candle is part of what he *means* by 'outer world.' "

James points out that initially for a child a sensation or object is not in spatial *relation* to anything in the world; it is a place, but it is not placed or located. While the places are initially objects, the objects change with the child's movements, so that the places become *possible* sensations or objects for the child rather than any particular ones. "The imagined aggregate of positions occupied by all the actual or possible, moving or stationary, things which we know, is our notion of 'real' space—a very incomplete and vague conception in all minds." Space follows by construction:

"Gradually the system of these possible sensations, takes more and more the place of the actual sensations. 'Up' and 'down' become 'subjective' notions; east and west grow more 'correct' than 'right' and 'left' etc.; and things get at last more 'truly' located by their relation to certain ideal fixed co-ordinates than by their relation either to our bodies or to those objects by which their place was originally defined." [64]

Such ideal coordinates represent a scheme in the sense discussed above.

SPACE FROM GLOBAL EXPERIENCE AND SPATIAL RELATIONS

Another primitive kind of feeling is that of a total extensity, vastness, or voluminousness, with no order or parts. This is the unanalyzed field, "a simple total vastness, in which, *primitively* at least, no *order of parts* or of *subdivisions* reigns." In order to construct the kind of space we actually believe in, James says, this primitive extensity must be subdivided and measured by consciousness.

At this point, James moves from global perception of extensity to attentive perception of particulars. But in establishing the order of space, James must posit *primitive spatial relations* among particulars which attention distinguishes in the preattentive field; these relations for James are *sensations,* as simple as the conventional 'hot' and 'round'. It can be pointed out, however, that if we do not attend to a *particular* object or objects, the preattentive field stretches out as a variety of vague sensations in vague relations, perhaps *more* primitive because not requiring conscious attention. In any case, the relations among particulars, such as rightness, upness, and so on, are sensations of particular lines, angles, forms of transition, and feelings of more or less, for instance, after two figures have been superimposed. From such relations, subdivisions of the "total vastness" are created, and such subdivisions constitute the structure of space. *"The bringing of subdivisions to consciousness constitutes, then, the entire process by which we pass from our first vague feeling of a total vastness to a cognition of the vastness in detail."* James insists he has a purely sensory theory, because "all the subdivisions are themselves sensations, and even the feeling of 'more' or 'less' is, where not itself a figure, at least a sensation of transition between two sensations of figure." [65]

Here then are the two theories: the first involves the *construction* of space from attentive sensations or objects; the second involves the *subdivision* of *preattentive* space.

JAMES AND THE KANTIANS ON SPACE

Kant spells out his theory of space:

"In a phenomenon I call that which corresponds to the sensation its *matter;* but that which causes the manifold matter of the phenomenon to be perceived as arranged in a certain order, I call its *form.*"

"Now it is clear that it cannot be sensation again through which sensations are arranged and placed in certain forms. The matter only of all phenomena is given us *a posteriori;* but their form must be ready for them in the mind (Gemüth) *a priori,* and must therefore be capable of being considered as separate from all sensations." [66]

In relating his ideas to Kantian theory, James must explain how mere sensations get transformed into spatial elements. Kant's answer is that they do so by the work of the a priori intuitional form of space.

James accepts part of this position when he dismisses the theory that with spatial feelings the "anatomical condition of the feeling *resembles* the feeling itself," that, for example, "the retinal path that produces a triangle in the mind is itself a triangle." James points out: "The immediate condition of the feeling is not the process in the retina, but the process in the brain; and the process in the brain may, for ought we know, be as unlike a triangle,—nay, it probably is so,—as it is unlike redness or rage." Thus, the idea of the triangle is the result of higher operations of the brain on incoming data.

More basically, while rejecting Kant's a priori form of space, James holds that sensations are the work of the mind and are spatial.[67] If the sensations of Kant or James lacked spatiality, it would be because sensations were products of abstraction and their spatiality had been abstracted out. (In Kant, such an abstraction would be the *analytic* separation of the matter of sensation, for example, blueness, from the form, that is, space.) James meets the Kantian claim of a full-blown space present a priori in the mind by describing how our notions of space are *constructed*.

LOCAL SIGNS AND PROJECTION

James's explanations of how space is constructed depend on his assumption of the "local sign" theory of R. H. Lotze. This theory posits a distinct feeling of origination from every point in the nervous system, without that feeling by itself indicating relative location, spatial order, or arrangement. Lotze writes:

"Since the spatial specification of a sensory element is independent of its qualitative content (so that at different moments very different sensations can fill the same places in our picture of space), each stimulation must have a characteristic peculiarity, given it by the point in the nervous system at which it occurs. We shall call this its *local sign*." [68]

This will be recognized as the basis for James's referring to *"that place where* the pain from the pin" came from. It is what Whitehead calls the "withness" of the body (see Chapter II).

A "local sign" corresponds to the stimulation of a point of the nervous system, but such signs may also originate from other causes, such as disturbances of the brain. James's caveat that the proximal stimuli are *not* the sensation, but only occasions for its production, is to this effect. Whitehead makes the same reservation.

In any case, local signs [69] establish the simultaneous manifold of sensations which constitute the perceptual field, the "extensity," or "vastness," which James takes as a sensational given, and they also seem to establish the basis for points of attention, such as the pain from the pin, which can be spatially related to other such points.

But to establish a 'there' for a spatial sensation is not sufficient; something else, according to James, is needed, although James himself does not integrate this factor into his discussion of local signs. Curiously enough this factor appears in a section of the *Psychology* devoted to "feelings in joints":

"But when we say 'projection' we generally have in our mind the notion of a *there* as contrasted with a *here*. What is the *here* when we say that the joint-feeling is *there?* The 'here' seems to be the spot which the mind has chosen for its own post of observation, usually some place within the head, but sometimes within the throat or breast—not a rigorously fixed spot, but a region from any portion of which it may send forth its various acts of attention. Extradition from either of *these* regions is the common law under which we perceive the whereabouts of the north star, of our own voice, of the contact of our teeth with each other, of the tip of our finger, or the point of our cane on the ground, or of a movement in our elbow-joint."

Thus we have a 'there,' which is the local sign feeling, and a 'here,' which is the mind's post of observation. Whitehead's theory of "strain loci," by which he explains spatial experiences, uses essentially the same elements (see Chapter II).

The relations between the 'here' and the 'there' provide the basis for the "projection" of the sensa. To know where a pain is one must feel its distance from the post of observation, the 'here' of the mind. James explains that *"for the distance between the 'here' and the 'there' to be felt, the entire intervening space must be itself an object of perception."* [70] When the 'there' is a point on the body, the distance can be observed by the eye or by exploratory movements, and also "by the resident sensations which fill its length." These resident sensations are the local signs which establish the feeling of extensity in that portion of the field.

James also deals with how we project sensations beyond our skin, that is, how we see objects as distant from us. The 'us' in this case is a portion of our skin already located by the process described above. James explains that "for extradition to occur beyond the skin, the portion of skin in question *and* the space beyond must form a common object for some other sensory surface." The eyes provide this sensory surface, or sometimes other parts of the skin, either in motion or not.[71]

Finally, James considers the felt relation between two 'theres'. To explain this feeling, he has recourse to a complicated argument based on associationism. When any point is stimulated, the argument goes, the area around it is also excited, because this area's stimulation is habitually associated with the point. James then explains that the overlap of the habitually excited areas of two points is an innervated area, or vague line, which provides the sensation of spatial relations between the points. (Such felt relations were the basis for dividing up the total vastness or extensity.) Fortunately, James has an even clearer explanation, that is, the experience of laying one bodily surface over another,[72] although both techniques are used.

All the elements are now at hand to explain James's two theories of spatial construction, as alternatives to Kant's a priori space. In the theory of *space from attended experience,* the pain from the pin is a local sign and is a located sensation in relation to the 'here' of the mind. Sensations or objects are where they are felt; objects beyond our skin are located by projection. When the sensations or objects change, either owing to our movements or to the movements of the objects, these changes give the idea of possible experience, or, in other words, the abstract idea of spatial position. (The coordination of changes with our movements enforces the idea of possible experience, because the changes are inducible at will, and so repeatable and testable.) Space follows as the aggregate of such possible experiences or spatial positions.

In the theory of *space from global experience,* local signs create the spatial field or feeling of extensity in relation to the 'here' of the mind. Within this field, particular sensations, such as the pain from the pin, are located. The relations between such particulars divide up the total field. Another way in which the field is divided is by the superimposition of bodily surfaces. Such divisions constitute the order of space.

SPACE AS PROCESS

James also establishes the experience of spatial relations from the perception of motion: "it is experimentally certain that we have the feeling of motion given us as a direct and simple sensation." [73] The motion *can* be considered a series of graduated differences in local sign feeling occurring as the moving body achieves successive positions. (Such feelings would be reinforced in the case of one sensitive bodily surface moving over another.) But James would insist that the "movement is originally given as a simple whole of feeling" and that its fragmentation into differences of sign feeling, or successive positions, is the work of sophisticated analysis.[74] Motion, like objects, is then wholistic; its fragmentations, like sensations, are the work of analysis.

James's theory is that the experience of motion (or, subjectively, process) *is* the experience of space and time. The case is closely analogous to that of the specious present. What is felt is not discrete units of sensation, but their *continuity, transition, or motion.* This phenomenon again raises the problem of the immanence of the just past in the present (see Chapter II). James's identification of the experience of space with the experience of motion offers yet another alternative to the Kantian theory of a full-blown a priori space.

SPATIAL SCHEMES

Finally, in answer to Kant, James maintains that schemes of space (and of time) are constructed, that there are many schemes, and that the work of their construction may or may not be undertaken. By contrast, Kantian space is necessary, a priori, singular, and given rather than formed. For James, as for Kant, the higher centers work at one stroke to produce feelings of extension. The difference lies in the fact that for James further schematization of these experiences depends on whether the mind has *constructed* (or is constructing) the schemes.

Sensations of the various senses, such as hearing and sight, need not be integrated; distant parts of the body need not be felt as interrelated. *"If a number of sensible extents are to be perceived alongside of each other and in definite order they must appear as parts in a vaster sensible extent which can enter the mind simply and all at once."* In short, they must form instances of a scheme. "The relative positions of the shops in a town, separated by many tortuous streets, have to be thus constructed from data apprehended in succession." [75]

One such scheme can be Newtonian space, but it is by no means necessary. James's views open up the possibility of there being various types of psychological space, as well as there being various theories for the depiction of so-called physical space.[76] Such alternative schemes for space correspond to those mentioned above for time, for example, the form of the opera, play, or book. A single scheme for space is then no more necessary than the Gregorian calendar is for time.

What remains to be explored is how the experiences of time and space express how the individual is in the world, how the world is *his* world, and how he makes himself *out* of his world. This is the subject of the next two chapters.

II Causality, Perception, and Self

CAUSALITY AND PERCEPTION

JAMES'S PHENOMENOLOGY

James generally begins an inquiry with the empiricist question "What is it known as?" Indeed, particularly in his later work, he becomes preoccupied with explaining the world *as* experience, rather than explaining how it is known *through* experience. Along these lines, a room is a subject's experience of a room describable in terms of that experience.

The subjectivist principle, according to Whitehead, is "that the datum in the act of experience can be adequately analyzed purely in terms of universals." [1] If the experience of the room were considered a complex universal, the condition for subjectivism would be fulfilled.

James believes that "pure experience" can become "subjective" or "objective" depending on how it is taken. Thus the "pure experience" of a room can be the *thought* of a room, part of one's biography, and a physical *thing,* part of the history of a house. The room is both the "thought-of-an-object" and the "object-thought-of." Subjectivity and objectivity are "functional attributes only." [2]

This is indeed subjectivism, and at one point James goes so far as to say that the experience (that is, the room) "has occupied that spot and had that environment for thirty years." [3] It is doubtful that James would care to defend the solipsistic implications of this statement. If, on the other hand, he is simply saying that the experience of the room can be fitted into the context of other experiences of the room, and, in that way, the sense of the room can be expanded to one of solidity and duration, he is asserting no more than did J. S. Mill. Here James would be analyzing a human experience purely in terms of universals, but he would not be committing himself to the adequacy of his description, because he would be ignoring the source or situation in which the universals arose.

Within this kind of analysis, James maintains that objects are discrete sections abstracted from the stream of consciousness. And he also says that experience is just what it appears to be; it has extension, is hot, and so on.[4] But at this very point, James deviates from a subjectivist position. There is a difference, James maintains, between real and fanciful things. Real things, he says, act, have independence; real fires burn, but fanciful fires do not.[5] But this independence begs the question, as James ultimately knew it did, of the adequacy of a purely subjectivist explanation. He is thus confronted with the problem of how to maintain a phenomenological explanation which is not solipsistic.

James early (1873) sought to solve the problem by holding that physical nature is *more* than any experience of it.[6] By the time he wrote "A World of Pure Experience" (1904) in *Radical Empiricism,* James was willing to credit this "beyond" with experience itself:

"we at every moment can continue to believe in an existing *beyond* . . . The beyond must, of course, always in our philosophy be itself of an experiential nature. If not a future experience of our own or a present one of our neighbor, it must be a thing in itself . . . that is, it must be an experience *for* itself whose relation to other things we translate into the action of molecules, ether-waves, or whatever else the physical symbols may be. This opens the chapter of the relations of radical empiricism to panpsychism." [7]

But the problem remains; for if we experience the beyond, what is that experience known as? The doctrine of sensations will not do. A ball is known as a round, red shape; but how do we know it is something out there which is *causing* us this experience? What is *that* experience?

James is clear enough that causality must be experienced, for unless something is experienced or experienceable, it is nothing. "Nothing," James says, "shall be admitted as fact . . . except what can be experienced at some definite time by some experient." [8] Whitehead states the issue when he says that "Descartes' discovery on the side of subjectivism requires balancing by an 'objectivist' principle as to the datum for experience." [9] The problem then is to find in human experience the experience of cause.

FEELINGS OF CAUSAL EFFICACY: WHITEHEAD'S CRITIQUE OF HUME

As has been seen, Hume denied that there was any direct experience of casuality *as such*. Accordingly, Hume thought that the only way to distinguish a causal agent was by reflection on habitual, sensory experience. Thus, in a variety of contexts, if one observes that factor A is followed habitually by factor B, one concludes that factor A is the "cause" of factor B.[10] Whitehead and James make clear that what Hume is concerned with is the *identification* of the cause, its distinct separation from the total experience so that it can be named. Finding that the cause cannot be clearly identified or isolated in a single experience, Hume denies that the direct experience of causality exists.

Kant was equally aware of this difficulty, and to "rescue" causality, he maintained that it was an a priori category of the understanding: "If, therefore, wax, which was formerly hard, melts, I can know *a priori* that *something* else must have preceded (for instance the heat of the sun) upon which this melting has followed according to a permanent law, although

without experience I could never know *a priori* definitely
either from the effect the cause, or from the cause the
effect." [11]

What is at issue is the nature of the evidence. If there is a
direct experience of cause, the Kantian solution is superfluous.
In Hume's examples, the philosopher observes causal interactions, such as those between billiard balls; he is not himself
involved as one of the agents. Accordingly, in attempting to
refute Hume, Whitehead turns to experience in which he, the
observer, rather than a billiard ball, suffers the effect. Whitehead is concerned with the relation of his subjective experience to something "out there"; Hume is concerned with the
relation among themselves of things "out there," regarded as
appearances.

Consider, Whitehead says, the following reflex action: "In
the dark, the electric light is suddenly turned on and the
man's eyes blink." [12] There are, according to his explanation,
two types of experience. The first includes the flash of light,
the feeling of eye-closure, and the instant of darkness. These
are the clear-cut experiences, or sensations, with which Hume
deals. These, according to Whitehead, are percepts in the
"mode of presentational immediacy" (see below). But there
is another nonsensory type of percept, for the man will say,
"The flash made me blink." This *feeling* of causality, however vague, Whitehead calls a percept in the "mode of causal
efficacy." Hume can either deny the man's feeling of causality
or attribute it to his feeling of the habit of blinking after
flashes; Whitehead rejects both positions as absurd.

Consider a second example, that of a man hit on the head
from behind. As he falls from the blow, he does not just feel
pain but influence. Something has done him in; the feeling of
causal efficacy is primitive and massive; the fear he experiences
is not just fear of the pain but fear of the influence. In this
case, it may be assumed that there is no "habit" of feeling
pain after being slugged. Here Hume must flatly deny the

man's feeling of causality. Whitehead is thus appealing to the empirical facts; they either sustain his argument or they do not.

Whitehead argues further that if causal feeling, according to Hume, follows our association of sensa (or ideas based on sensa), we should have few such feelings when we have few sensa. But such is not the case: "An inhibition of familiar sensa is very apt to leave us a prey to vague terrors respecting a circumambient world of causal operations. In the dark there are vague presences, doubtfully feared; in the silence, the irresistible causal efficacy of nature presses itself upon us." [13] A related instance of this is that in prison the terror of being beaten, beyond the mere pain, consists of entering a world whose causes are neither known nor controlled.

Whitehead calls upon another type of evidence, that of the efficacy of parts of our bodies in the production of sensations. He points out that Descartes' metaphysical separation of bodies and minds is based only on consideration of the mode of presentational immediacy, or appearance, and excludes the sense of efficacy from the body:

"all that is perceived is that the object has extension and is implicated in a complex of extensive relatedness with the animal body of the percipient . . . [I]f this be all that we perceive about the physical world, we have no basis for ascribing the origination of the mediating sensa to any functioning of the human body. We are thus driven to the Cartesian duality of substances, bodies and minds . . . We thus reduce perceptions to consciousness of impressions on the mind, consisting of sensa with 'manners' of relatedness."

For Descartes, an impression *of* the hand would be equal to an impression of a chair, both epiphenomenal accidents of the substantive mind. But for Whitehead, the evidence is plain that we *feel* the surface of a chair *with* our hands. But why correlate the "projected" surface with our hands; why not attribute it to our foot? Whitehead says because we have a feeling of efficacy *from* our hands: "Our bodily experience is primarily an experience of the dependence of presentational immediacy upon causal efficacy." [14]

We are immediately reminded of James's and Lotze's "local sign," that distinct feeling of origination from every point in the nervous system. This feeling *from* a part of the body is the reason why Whitehead calls such experiences "vectoral." Whitehead's alternate term is the "withness" of the body, that is, our feeling the sensation *with* our hands. Given a normal situation, what is important is that an external event affects the surface of the body, be it the light of a star or a flashlight. In either case, we will see the light *from* our eyes. [15]

But both Whitehead and James are perfectly willing to admit that the case may not be normal and that "delusions" are possible. They are clear that if the external organs or appropriate nerves are stimulated in a certain way, we will perceive a chair image, whether there is a chair or not. They are also clear that if parts of the brain are properly stimulated, or, for example, we take drugs, we can perceive a chair image when there is no chair. But we can also, according to Whitehead, *appear* to have feelings of derivation, that is, feelings of causal efficacy, when there is no flow of data from other parts of the body to the brain. An instance is the well-known feelings of amputees *from* their lost limbs. The problem here is that human perception is so complicated that such feelings of "pseudo-determinants" may arise due to secondary conceptual mechanisms; [16] with the simpler organisms, however, such delusions seem, for Whitehead, less likely.

These simpler organisms furnish Whitehead with still another proof of causal feelings. Despite their lack of varied sense perception, they *act as if* they felt causal relations: "A jellyfish advances and withdraws, and in so doing exhibits some perception of causal relationship with the world beyond itself." [17]

It will be seen that the idea of causal efficacy is closely analogous to Locke's notion of power. For both Locke and Whitehead, a perception is the experience of the power of something to give us particular sense data. This power is analogous to the power of an inanimate object to effect the physical alteration of another object. Thus Whitehead can say that "the problem of perception and the problem of power are one and the same." [18] But Whitehead does not assume, as do Locke and Hume, that the cause must be identified in the causal feeling. On the contrary, causal feelings for Whitehead do not necessarily entail consciousness.

JAMES AND CAUSAL FEELINGS

In discussing James's phenomenology, it became apparent that if James were not to lapse into solipsism, he must endorse an experience of causality. James seems to be doing just this when he says, "The 'original' of the notion of causation is in our inner personal experience, and only there can causes in the old-fashioned sense be directly observed and described." [19]

Despite this clear statement, James's position on causality is frequently not clear; on probably no problem does he twist and turn more. But one line of thought does run consistently through every phase: that there is something in experience which we feel escapes our control and which we feel makes its own contribution: "If it be a sensible experience it coerces our attention." For James, to know the truth about something is to seek it out, come into contact, and so reap *from it* the harvest of sensations which are the *"terminus a quo* and *terminus ad quem* of thought." [20]

What the thought knows are ultimately the sensational predicates from such experiential subjects: "there is something in man that accounts for his tendency towards death, and in bread that accounts for its tendency to nourish." [21] The truth *about* something is either a description of predicative experience—"it is red"—or directions telling how to get such experience—"the tigers in India." In either case, there is a felt independent source of experience. This thought, which is expressed by James dualistically and, later, phenomenologically, is what Whitehead means by perception in the mode of causal efficacy.

FEELINGS OF PRESENTATIONAL IMMEDIACY

For Whitehead, there is another mode of perception, that of presentational immediacy. This is the world as the play of mere appearance; it is what is meant conventionally by sensation. "This appearance is effected by the mediation of qualities, such as colours, sounds, tastes, etc., which can with equal truth be described as our sensations or as the qualities of the actual things which we perceive. These qualities are thus relational between the perceiving subject and the perceived things." [22] In the mode of presentational immediacy, we are only concerned with these qualities. However, the qualities may also be considered relational in that they are the way *we* experience the object. Locke explains this dual role when he says: "Thus a snowball having the power to produce in us the ideas of white, cold, and round—the power to produce those ideas in us, as they are in the snowball, I call qualities; and as they are sensations, or perceptions, in our understandings, I call them ideas." [23]

Both Whitehead and James at various times point to the fundamental difference between subjects and predicates. Whitehead expresses the distinction by attributing adjectives, such as 'gray', to the mode of immediacy, and substantives, such as 'stone', to our "dim percepts in the mode of efficacy." [24] But, it may be asked, if our experience of the stone is merely 'round' and 'gray', isn't this experience, according to the Cartesian view, completely expressible in those universals?

OBJECTIFICATION: WHITEHEAD'S CRITIQUE OF DESCARTES

Even as early as 1690, Locke knew that for an object to be seen something normally had to go from the object to our eyes and nerves, and from there to our brain. That Locke's "singly, imperceptible Bodies" have been described by modern physics as photons merely affirms Locke's fundamental truth. In short, perception has to do in some way with the taking into the constitution of one thing what was in the constitution of another. This is what Whitehead calls "objectification" from the causal past. The absorption of single photons may provide a clear-cut example, but it probably falsifies the general case Whitehead had in mind, which is the flows of energy in the physical field.[25]

In Whitehead's theory of perception, it means that seeing gray represents an alteration of one's energy state which results from the absorption of energy from something in one's causal past. That something is the gray stone. The gray stone is thus a constituent of one's being, in however a trivial way. But one's experience of the outside world, of which the experience of the gray stone is a fraction, is essential experience. (Indeed, high-level perception trivializes the causal input but does not eliminate it.) In this sense, the percept is not merely "representative" of outside entities, as Descartes and (usually) Locke maintain; the percept is the result of what outside entities have contributed to the percipient.[26] Whitehead's critique of Descartes rests on this fundamental point. He writes, "Descartes' notion of an unessential experience of the external world is alien to the organic philosophy." [27]

At the root of the trouble, as Whitehead points out, is Descartes' upholding of the substance-quality mode of thought. This view assumes that as a substance the mind is "a thing which so exists that it needs no other thing in order to exist." Thus a mind does not require the stone in order to exist, and can simply exist in a vacuum happily entertaining itself with its own universals or qualities. But Whitehead insists that the constituent supplied by the stone is an element, however trivial, of the mind's existence, and he holds with Locke that without the entire supply of causal inputs, including blood and gravitational forces, the mind cannot exist at all.

The mind's entertainment of its own universals is, more-

over, not an adequate characterization of experience. Whitehead writes that "the truism that we can only *conceive* in
terms of universals has been stretched to mean that we can
only *feel* in terms of universals. This is untrue." [28] We do
have feelings of causal efficacy, feelings of causal inputs contributing to our present being. This experience of what Whitehead calls prehension is the most primitive experience of all
being.

THE EXPERIENCE OF PREHENSION: A THEORY OF TIME

In his effort to frame a general theory, Whitehead begins
with the simplest case, the prehension of an electronic occasion by its immediate successor (a series of such electronic
occasions is an electron), and devises a general explanation of
the quality of this basic prehensive experience. His analysis
concerns the mediating role of eternal objects. "Eternal
objects" he calls, variously, "eternal ideas," "universals,"
"forms of definiteness," or "pure potentials for the specific
determination of fact." They are similar to Platonic forms.
Whitehead assumes that the electronic occasion is describable
by an eternal object (as will be the series of such occasions,
the electron). This eternal object is the form of the feeling of
an electronic occasion *for itself,* that is, a "subjective form." [29]

In the case under consideration, that of the prehension of
an electronic occasion by its successor a moment later, "the
subjective form of [the] physical feeling is re-enaction of the
subjective form of the [original] feeling." The eternal objects,
which are those forms, have a direct mediating role between
the cause and the effect: "Thus the cause passes on its feeling
to be reproduced by the new subject as its own, and yet as
inseparable from the cause. There is a flow of feeling. But the
re-enaction is not perfect. The . . . demands of the concrescence [the process of becoming of the new electronic
occasion] require adjustments of the pattern of emotional
intensities." The electronic occasion is almost, but not quite,
the same as its predecessor, which has perished. It is different,

first of all, because it has constituted itself a new entity. But, in addition, its predecessor is only one causal input, and probably does not exhaust everything that has "gone into" the constitution of the new occasion. These other elements must be integrated into the new unified occasion. (An even clearer example of this aspect would be the reenaction of an electronic occasion in an atom, or, less technically, the absorption of an electron into the unity of an atom.) This new unified occasion forms a subjective unity of experience, analogous to the conscious field discussed in Chapter I above. Thus the introduction of an electron in an atom is analogous to that of a patch of green in a painting: it is transformed in its values by virtue of its position in the total unity or composition. The vectoral form of feeling having to do with its reenaction in the atom is the *feeling of the passage* from the electronic occasion as cause to the new pattern of intensities as effect. Whitehead adds that this passage of cause into effect is the "cumulative character of time." [30]

In the case of a unicellular organism, a similar mode of analysis might well apply. Although the organism is simple, it nonetheless appears to have something in it which imparts to it central direction. That something can be called the central occasion. It would then appear that the experience of the central occasion is what constitutes primitive perception. For the simplest organisms, inflowing energy might be fairly directly prehended by the central occasion. (For man, this central occasion would be the conscious field, and the influence of energy flowing into the organism would only be quite indirectly felt in the brain.)

Whitehead seems to maintain that the experience of perception would in some way reflect the passage of its component feelings, feelings which are also inflowing components of the organism itself and which have been integrated into the central occasion. In other words, because what integrates these feelings into the central occasion are also these feelings themselves, there is an experience of passage or duration in the central occasion. As Whitehead puts it, "Feelings are 'vectors'; for they feel what is *there* and transform it into what is here." [31] This appears to be the basis in Whitehead for the retention of the vectoral character of perceptual experience in the mode of causal efficacy. It would account for the primitive feelings of time or passage.

Now James, in his discussion of the specious present (see Chapter I), maintains that the movement from the just past to the present is felt. It then becomes necessary to explain how the just past is immanent in the present. Whitehead's explanation is essentially that the organism's prehension, or grasp, of its causal inputs is felt vectorally as connecting the just past (the causal inputs) with the present (the organism as causally influenced). His analysis strongly suggests that time is an experience of primitive organisms, and is not dependent on the flux of higher sensory experience, which they do not enjoy. This view does not appear to be held in this form by James, although he does not controvert it.

But when we come to "high-grade" organisms, such as man, the situation becomes complicated. Take the feelings *from* our hands. In the normal case, this flow of feeling constitutes a route of responses, that is, the hand, the nerves, the brain, each of which contributes character to the final product, the conscious central occasion. Thus, the eternal objects of the original data (the stimuli) will not be simply reenacted; they will be utterly transformed (although even here, what the eternal objects of the stimuli are for themselves helps determine how they will be realized in the central occasion). Moreover, the actual physical components, that is, the energetic particles, or waves, of the stimuli, will be completely different in the central occasion from those that were initially absorbed by the body. It would thus appear that man's nervous system is designed primarily to mimic external forces rather than to reenact them more directly.

The experience of felt transition, then, cannot refer primarily to causal inputs from the "outside." What man experiences are energetic compositions of his own central occasion which have *reference* to external things.[32]

Conscious feelings of transition and, similarly, of motion remain to be explained. The discussion so far suggests that these feelings must relate to energy in transition and that this energy must be in the central occasion. This is strongly suggested by Whitehead when he says, "Time is known to us as the succession of our acts of experience, and derivatively as the succession of events objectively perceived in those acts."[33]

Part of this energy in transition would be that in the primary memory, and would, for example, account for the types of transitional, or durational, feelings involved in attended sensory perception. But our acts of experience are neither all sensorial nor all caught in attention. There are feelings of transition, James and Whitehead maintain, which have to do with aspects of experience involving more basic layers of our being. These are discussed in the section "Perception and Self," below.

HIGHER PERCEPTUAL EXPERIENCES

SYMBOLIC REFERENCE

Whitehead maintains that the preoccupation of philosophers with presentational immediacy is apt to render them blind to the more basic aspects of existence, as brought to us by causal efficacy. Nevertheless, presentational immediacy is what most people think of when they think of perception. It is a higher phase of existence, Whitehead believes, occurring in the final process, or "supplementary phase," by which we, as complex organisms, produce our central occasions.[34]

The final process, or "supplementary phase," must somehow simplify "that black and jointless continuity" which James writes about, else there will be no useful perception. There must then be a process by which useful abstractions are derived from basic physical experiences, such as the reception of photons. Whitehead writes: "It is a procedure of simplification. For example, in Appearance the one Region supersedes the many individual occasions which compose it." [35] There are a welter of incoming data and an almost infinite complexity of bodily occasions; nevertheless what we see is a simple patch of gray. Whitehead calls the process by which this patch is produced "transmutation" and the final effect "appearance."

A stone is made of atoms and molecules packed together which send countless individual emissions. The stone is what Whitehead calls a nexus. Transmutation makes us feel a fairly simple predicate or quality as characterizing a nexus, that is, transmutation makes it possible for us to feel the stone, or patch, as gray or rough. "It seems," Whitehead says, "as though in practice, for human beings at least, only transmuted feelings acquire consciousness, never simple physical feelings." [36]

What Locke and Hume refer to as "simple" ideas, such as 'green', would, in Whitehead's view, be high-level abstractions of central occasions, that is, products of transmutation. This difference in description may well cover the objections raised by William Ernest Hocking that Whitehead's theory of perception is dualistic. Hocking writes, "If we only perceive the qualities and not the qualities-as-enjoyed, we are not, according to the theory, perceiving them as they are;—the appearance lifts away from reality." [37] But what Whitehead is affirming is that the supplementary phase of concrescence introduces novelty of subjective experience. Take the case of a green tree. The photons which are absorbed or reenacted by an organism perceiving the tree have subjective experience for themselves, but that experience is not the 'green' of the perceiver. Whitehead's theory of perception means that "appearance" is the "reality" of the perceiver and that the perceiver uses the "realities" of his incoming components to create a new existential fact, the novel experience—'green'. Whitehead's theory does not create *two* classes of ideas, but it does uphold the subjectivity of experience.

According to Whitehead, ordinary perception is based upon transmutation.[38] Take the case of feeling a stone. The hand grasping the stone, Whitehead would say, transmits data, which, in the complex processes of the brain, give rise to a sense of derivation from the hand. The sense of derivation from the hand is similar to James's "local sign."

Whitehead goes on to say that in their function as sense data the data from the hand are transmuted or simplified into feelings of roughness characterizing a region. He also says that the data from the hand in their more primitive function as vectors give rise in the brain to feelings of geometric strain which are projections from the hand to an external region. When the transmuted sense data are integrated with these feelings of strain, we have feelings of roughness characterizing a region *out there*.

There still remains the problem of how that region is felt as spatially related to us. Whitehead's explanation seems remarkably close to James's. According to Whitehead, what is felt, the rough patch out there, is felt as "straight-away in such-and-such direction." This occurs because "strains," or feelings of straight lines, are projected *from* the brain into regions beyond. Such projection occurs "irrespective of the particular character of the external events." [39] The brain from which these feelings come is the "geometric standpoint" of the percipient. This spot will be remembered in James's thought as the 'here' which "the mind has chosen for its own post of observation . . . from any portion of which it may send forth its various acts of attention." Thus when the feelings of the rough patch out there are projected as felt from the geometric standpoint, the result is a tactual image of a rough surface out there with a particular relation to the percipient. This is perception in the mode of presentational immediacy.

There is one final step: We take the feelings of causal efficacy from the hand and attribute them to the region beyond, the region, as distinguished in presentational immediacy, which appears as a rough surface. The result is that we feel 'a rough *stone* out there'. Such a region is for us contemporary, but as a truly efficacious region, that is, as a sender of data, it lies in our past. This transfer of efficacy to the contemporary region also entails attributing to it all the additions, distortions, and adjustments of the "supplementary phase." [40] (For example, if our hands are sweaty, we may feel the region as smooth.) This step Whitehead calls "symbolic reference." [41]

For Whitehead, symbolic reference is the usual mode of human perception. He joins James in pointing out that we are so built that "our projected sensations indicate in general those regions which are the seat of important organisms." [42] We can spot a leopard in the bush—it is important for our survival that "symbolic reference" be correct.

However, we can be wrong. In "symbolic reference," we call a quality the product of a region. In other words, the epiphenomenal 'gray patch' becomes the 'gray stone', or more primitively and closer perhaps to Whitehead's intention, the 'causally efficacious something out there seen as gray'. But what if the gray patch doesn't come as an inheritance from that area to our sense organs and hence to our brains? In this case, we have an error. The check (see Chapter IV) is that of James, the test of leading to the object by sensory experience; it is what Whitehead, following James, calls "the appeal . . . to the pragmatic consequences, involving some future state of bodily feelings which can be checked up." [43] The final arbiter is, then, James's independent element in experience that is the basis of our perception of causal efficacy; it is the things out there to which we assign at least partial responsibility for the way to feel.

IMPRESSIONISM

In presentational immediacy, we feel a region as a mere appearance. We see, for example, a gray patch, but simply that, neither a cloud, nor a stone, nothing which is efficacious. This kind of feeling is less primitive than symbolic reference and less usual. It is what might also be called impressionism.

Whitehead opposes the sensationalists because they are preoccupied with appearances and ignore the efficacy of objects. In so doing, they consider normal a mode of perception which in its pure state can only be practiced by a highly trained artist.[44]

The impressionist movement in painting of Monet and Pissarro exactly corresponded to this mentality: the slighting of deep space, the equal concern for all colored surfaces, regardless of the importance of objects, the general placidity, graphic and social. But there is also a timeless quality to impressionist work, not the timelessness of the "classics" which stand forever, but the timeless charm of fleeting irrelevance. Whitehead writes that "a vivid enjoyment of immediate sense-data notoriously inhibits apprehension of the relevance of the future. The present moment is then all in all. In our consciousness, it approximates to 'simple occurrence'."[45] It may be added that the irrelevance heightens the feeling of perishing, and so gives to impressionist work that deeper, almost tragic feeling of which the viewer is hardly aware. The beautiful moment—passes!

MEASUREMENT, SPACE, AND TIME

For Whitehead, the basis of measurement is straight lines, "forms defined by projectors from the 'seat' of the strain and irrespective of the actualities which constitute the environment."[46] Because the projectors define space irrespective of real things, measurements are concerned with potentialities of extensiveness, in which real things, such as stones, are "actualized."

The type of perception of space upon which measurement is based is that of presentational immediacy devoid of content. It is essentially the perceptive field without the sensations. "Our direct perception of the contemporary world is thus reduced to extension, defining (i) our own geometrical perspectives, and (ii) possibilities of mutual perspectives for other contemporary entities *inter se,* and (iii) possibilities of division. These possibilities of division constitute the external world a continuum." [47]

This conception of space has a preformed, geometric character. James would no doubt sniff a bit at Whitehead's space, call it "machine-shop" and "Kantian," and accuse Whitehead of being in indecent haste to apply theoretical mathematics. Whitehead, in referring to space, does often jump to a geometric abstraction, but, as he made clear, even presentational immediacy, upon which the abstraction is based, must be abstracted from normal psychological experience. He would thus agree with James that space must be weaned away from its original qualitatively varied experiences. These, Whitehead says, come normally in the mixed mode of "symbolic reference." This is the perception of a world of significant individuals, that is, a world no longer potential but real, a world in "actual atomic division."

But such a world is in the causal past of the percipient. What is needed is an explanation of how individuals from the causal past are felt as significant in the present. This is the task of a theory of perception.

Consider, Whitehead would say, the light of a star. Although this light left, say, a million years ago, and, therefore, the star is by a million years in the causal past of the percipient, there is a way in which the star is in the percipient's present. After all, the percipient is perceiving the star. This present Whitehead calls the percipient's "presented duration." The presented duration is what is perceived in an occasion of presentational immediacy; Whitehead says "presentational immediacy gives positive information only about the immediate present as defined by itself." [48] This presented duration, revealed in sense perception, is the *relevant* world for the percipient; it is his "reality."

In symbolic reference this reality of the percipient is objectified. What is felt are those things actually influencing him;

what is tasted are the very things which are incorporated into his substance; what is seen is a vision of the factors, diminishing with the square of the distance, whose structured order is the very order from which he rises as a being. This, then, is a view, although highly incomplete, of the external world as it "fashions the actual occasion in question." [49] Seen from the point of view of the organism, perception "is the appropriation of the datum by the subject, so as to transform the datum into a unity of subjective feeling." [50] This unity of subjective feeling is what James means by "intelligible perspective"; for man it is the arrangement of the conscious field, with its background and foreground, accent and emphasis.

PERCEPTION AND SELF

The preceding discussion of causality and perception has dealt chiefly with the relations between our subjective experience and an "outside" world. In addition, there are the relations between our present subjective experience and our past or future experiences.

DERIVATION, CONTINUITY, AND CHANGE

The feeling of continuity from one occasion to the next is, for Whitehead (and for James), a feeling of causality, "the sense of derivation from an immediate past, and of passage to an immediate future; a sense of emotional feeling, belonging to oneself in the past, passing into oneself in the present, and passing from oneself in the present towards oneself in the future." [51]

The previous discussion suggests that such feeling should take the form of feelings of transition in the central occasion. These feelings should involve the passage of data from the central occasion of the organism's immediate predecessor to the central occasion of the present occasion. Because what transforms these data into the central occasion of the present organism are the dative feelings themselves, these feelings experience passage.

For both James and Whitehead, the flow of the past into the present is reflected in the stream of consciousness. Part of this stream is made up of the constantly changing feelings of derivation from the body, the fluctuations of perceptual objects and sense data, and evanescent thoughts—conceptual novelties or memories. Many of these experiences will be transmitted to the new occasion and will, according to Whitehead's theory of prehensions, experience passage.

Owing to the introduction of this material, the subject or central occasion will be continually changing. And yet we have a sense that we are more than these ephemeral elements, that they do not exhaust what we are, but are rather the surface of a deeper and more stable current which we call the self. Should this self be found, its passage from occasion to occasion would give rise to feelings of transition more massive than those occasioned by the ephemeral feelings. Time, Whitehead says, is known as a "derivation from state to state, with the latter state exhibiting conformity to the antecedent." [52]

There also remains the problem of how the subject knows ephemeral parts of the stream are his experience. How does he know that what he sees is his hand, or what he remembers is his memory, or what he desires is being desired by him? In other words, if the ephemeral elements of the stream of consciousness are what appear in awareness, how is he aware of his own identity? What is it in the central occasion which performs these functions? Again, we must look for more stable elements in the central occasion, and we must examine what constitutes the nature of the self.

The ultimate percipient subject is what Whitehead also calls the "central occasion" or "presiding personality." "The brain," he writes, "is coordinated so that a peculiar richness of inheritance is enjoyed now by this and now by that part; and thus there is produced the presiding personality at that moment in the body." This presiding personality is what is meant by a living person. Whitehead maintains that "self-consciousness is direct awareness of ourselves as such persons." But the implication is clear in Whitehead that self-consciousness does not *exhaust* the presiding personality. For him, the presiding personality, or central occasion, in its formal character in man is ideas (as are also the central occasions in lower organisms), but such ideas do not need to be conscious. Whitehead remarks: "Locke always supposes that consciousness is consciousness of the ideas in the conscious mind. But he never separates the 'ideas' from the 'consciousness.' The philosophy of organism makes this separation, and thereby relegates consciousness to a subordinate metaphysical position." [53]

The matter was far less clear to James. His preoccupation with consciousness, which he shares with Locke, would lead one to suspect that for him the central occasion in man must be conscious. And, in fact, in contrast to Whitehead, he vehemently denies the existence of unconscious ideas.[54] Were James to hold this position in its naked form, it *might* mean that the entire mentality of a man would have to be available from moment to moment. But the position is highly qualified. Dreams, for example, are, according to James, consciousness forgotten. More significant, most mentality is simply structures of the brain, "collocation of molecules." Such structures seem to determine our actions, but apparently *because* they are not conscious, they are not considered ideas. This leaves a large area for "simple cerebral association," instinctual actions of the nervous system, and so on.

James also maintains that what is conscious is not necessarily self-consciously known. "When I decide that I have, without knowing it, been for several weeks in love, I am simply giving a name to a state which previously *I have not named,* but which was fully conscious; which had no residual mode of being except the manner in which it was conscious." According to James, this is a case of attributing what you know subsequently about a state to the subjective state itself.[55] James says that the stream of thought is "objective." "Instead, then, of the stream of thought being one of *con*-sciousness, 'thinking its own existence along with whatever else it thinks' . . . it might be better called a stream of *Scious*ness pure and simple." [56]

Despite such disclaimers, James's restrictions on *unconscious* ideas could be serious, for they could leave him practically helpless to explain cognitive structures which are not in the ephemeral stream of consciousness, but which are inherited from occasion to occasion. However, James argues, perhaps inconsistently, that at least some of the cognitive structures *are* part of conscious life, even if they are not easily attended to. James tries to distinguish between "unconscious" states of mind and states "to which no attention had been paid, and of whose passage recollection could afterwards find no vestiges." These are transitive and intentional states of mind, such as prepositional feelings or urges; these are also schemes of intention, memory, and time. James describes them as "unnamed states or qualities of states" which are "important" and "cognitive," but which are "unrecognized by the traditional sensationalist and intellectualist philosophies of mind." [57]

If consciousness includes such schemes, and other aspects of experience are explained as molecular and structural, James's differences with Whitehead about the limits of consciousness appear largely semantic.[58] What remains to be determined is the self which passed on from occasion to occasion.

THE SELF

When James comes to consider what the *agent* of mentality is, his answer is dramatic: "how would it be if the Thought, the present judging Thought, instead of being in any way substantially or transcendentally identical with the former owner of the past self, merely inherited his 'title,' and

thus stood as his legal representative now?" [59] Whitehead
suggests the same answer: "the basis of all experience is this
immediate stage of experiencing, which is myself now." [60]
In James's analysis,[61] the scholastic theory of the soul declared
"that the principle of individuality within us must be *substantial*, for psychic phenomena are activities, and there can be no
activity without a concrete agent." This was also the position
of Descartes. But James and Whitehead reply that the soul is
itself an activity, unified by subjective feeling, and is related
from occasion to occasion with an identity. In James's famous
words: "To deny plumply that 'consciousness' exists seems so
absurd on the face of it—for undeniably 'thoughts' do exist—
that I fear some readers will follow me no farther. Let me then
immediately explain that I mean only to deny that the word
stands for an entity, but to insist most emphatically that it
does stand for a function . . . That function is *knowing*." [62]
James maintains that if all the qualities of a soul are fulfilled
by its functions, its "substance" would serve no purpose and
should be dropped as a concept.

On the empiricist side, Hume and Locke tried to develop
a theory of identity based on the connection felt between
present thoughts and thoughts just past and thoughts remembered. But Hume admits that all hopes for his theory "vanish"
when he "comes to explain the principles that unite our successive perceptions in our thought or consciousness." He
cannot reconcile or renounce his two theories that *"all our
distinct perceptions are distinct existences, and that the mind
never perceives any real connection among distinct existences."* [63] Hume falters because he cannot accept either the
unification of ideas in the conscious field or the immanence
of the just past in the present; James and Whitehead accept
these and proceed.

To explain the feelings of personal continuity, James
postulates a common link between the moments, something
which makes material in one moment appear to belong to

another moment, so that it may be appropriated *as belonging to it*. This quality James calls the material's "warmth and intimacy."

"Each pulse of cognitive consciousness, each Thought, dies away and is replaced by another. The other, among the things it knows, knows its own predecessor, and finding it 'warm' . . . greets it, saying: 'Thou art *mine,* and part of the same self with me' . . . It is this trick which the nascent thought has of immediately taking up the expiring thought and 'adopting' it, which is the foundation of the appropriation of most of the remoter constituents of the self."

James says that the "Thought is a vehicle of choice as well as of cognition; and among the choices it makes are these appropriations, or repudiations, of its 'own.' " [64]

James makes clear, however, that what appropriates is not what is appropriated: "But the Thought never is an object in its own hands, it never appropriates or disowns itself." [65]

James continues:

"It appropriates *to* itself, it is the actual focus of accretion, the hook from which the chain of past selves dangles, planted firmly in the Present, which alone passes for real, and thus keeping the chain from being a purely ideal thing. Anon the hook itself will drop into the past with all it carries, and then be treated as an object and appropriated by a new Thought in the new present which will serve as living hook in turn." [66]

That is, at the moment of appropriation, the past is *data,* and the present agent or thought cannot appropriate its past thought as such, but only the past thought's *objects*. This strongly implies that there is a difference between the objects and the thought. If this were not so, it would be difficult to imagine from what the present thought could arise. It appropriates the objects of the past to itself, but if it is not different from the objects to what could the objects be appropriated?

What are the objects from the past which are appropriated

by the present thought? These, it would appear, are sensory experiences and evanescent thoughts which appear in the primary memory or awareness. (Whitehead and James are both agreed on the feelings in the present of derivation from the body.) In this sense, then, the past exists as data for the present.

Whitehead suggests, however, as has been seen, that perception of *cause,* rather than the specious present or primary memory in the Jamesian sense, is the basis for the experience of the past. If "appropriation" is directly experienced, it would be involved with causal feelings, that is, direct feelings of derivation. These, Whitehead says, result from feelings in the central occasion which are passed on to the next central occasion, and feelings from the body. While such feelings might appear in the primary memory, I take Whitehead to mean that feelings of *derivation* are *not* dependent on the primary memory. As in the case of James's and Whitehead's critique of Hume, experience of cause is different from *identification* of cause. In this case, experience of derivation is primitive and comes first, and does not depend upon identification; rather identification of elements of the past self or selves which are part of the present self is a secondary operation.[67] Such identification is what James seems primarily concerned with, and would seem to be his usual meaning of "appropriation."

James continues his analysis by saying that the appropriations of the present moment of consciousness are "less to *itself* than to the most intimately felt *part of its present Object, the body, and the central adjustments* which accompany the act of thinking, in the head. *These are the real nucleus of our personal identity,* and it is their actual existence, realized as a solid present fact, which makes us say, 'as sure *as I exist,* those past facts were part of myself.' "[68]

As for the body, Whitehead offers a concrete explanation for the identity: We feel our bodily *inheritance* or derivation in the present moment so strongly that we identify our momentary selves with the body. The reason we do not include the entire world in this identity, although we might, is that the body's "spatial and temporal connections obtain some definition in the experience of the subject." [69] In other words, placed parts of the body are felt components in each perception. And James points out that when we cannot recall bodily feelings, for example, when we remember ourselves as little children, a memory becomes "cold and foreign." [70]

Although it is clear why we identify ourselves with our momentary bodily feelings, because in large part we are these feelings, it is not clear from this explanation why we make an identification between past bodily feelings and ourselves. Why do we find such bodily feelings, including primarily sensations, to be "warm and intimate"? Why, for example, when a man looks at his hand, does he feel it to be his hand, or, in other words, why does he feel the warmth and intimacy of that image, even considered as a memory?

Again, there must be something which finds past facts warm and intimate, something which is more stable than the flux of sensations, feelings of bodily derivation, thoughts and memories, and so on. This will be the basis of identity. To find this factor, James looks within the stream of thought for an inner self, or self of selves, "felt by all men as a sort of innermost centre." His language is worth citing in detail:

"It is what welcomes or rejects. It presides over the perception of sensations, and by giving or withholding its assent it influences the movements they tend to arouse. It is the home of interest,—not the pleasant or the painful, not even pleasure or pain, as such, but that within us to which pleasure and pain, the pleasant and painful, speak. It is the source of effort and attention, and the place from which appear to emanate the fiats of the will."

James adds: "It is as if all that visited the mind had to stand an entrance-examination, and just show its face so as to be either approved or sent back. These primary reactions are like the opening or the closing of the door." But when we look for the perception of these functions, all we find, according to James, is their *effects,* what is furthered and inhibited; of the functions themselves, all we feel is the central adjustments which accompany the act of thinking in the head, "a *collection of these peculiar motions in the head or between the head and throat."* [71]

Now if the bodily feelings be things which are appropriated from the past, just as are other elements from the stream of consciousness, one must look to something in the present thought which does the appropriating. This James says, is the present thought itself and, within it, the inner self. This is the factor which is concerned with conveying a sense of identity from occasion to occasion.[72]

What is the self? Looked at one way, James says, *"a man's Self is the sum total of all that he* CAN *call his,* not only his body and his psychic powers, but his clothes and his house, his wife and children, his ancestors and friends, his reputation and works, his lands and horses, and yacht and bank-account." [73] This empirical self does not come fully developed. It is built up piece by piece. Like Freud, James insists that love is cathected to experiences (generalized and conceptualized as "objects") which produce gratification. In the beginning, objects, like parts of one's own body or the mother's breast, are connected to instincts, and are the source of instinctual gratification. These are objects which are primordially exciting, and we attend to them without reflection. Like Freud, James also believes that the self is then the accretion of *identification* with these loved experiences or objects, and that all other components of the self (or experiences we love) are experiences *associated* with these.[74] While the instincts remain the basic components, all the things secondarily associated with them unite to form the self. In this way, as one matures, one acquires a material, social, and spiritual self, but all the objects of the self have, with the

instincts with which they are associated, the *"power to produce in a stream of consciousness excitement of a certain
peculiar sort."* [75] Our interest in these objects thus reflects our
love, and our self is simply what we love.

James implies that a conception of what we love is carried
into every momentary experience, in the direct sense suggested by Whitehead.

"In what capacity is it that I claim and demand a respectful
greeting from you instead of this expression of disdain? It is
not as being a bare I that I claim it; it is as being an I who
has always been treated with respect, who belongs to a certain
family and 'set', who has certain powers, possessions, and
public functions, sensibilities, duties, and purposes, and merits
and deserts." [76]

Such a conception is not an active part of the stream of consciousness in the same way as, say, the first part of a sentence.
It is transmitted from occasion to occasion, and yet is not
realized, and may not even be recognizable. It seems to be
like an inherited "complex eternal object," that is, a conceptual, though not necessarily conscious, scheme. [77] (For
example, part of this scheme would be our conception of the
body, a sense of its spatial distribution and feelings, its potential movements, and so on.) The transmission of the conception of the self, as modified, from occasion to occasion may
account in part for our feelings of continuity from the past,
as Whitehead's theory of primitive vectoral transmission
would suggest.

James points out that a sense that an experience is ours, is
a *two*-term relation. "It is the sense of a sameness perceived
by thought and predicated of things *thought-about*." [78] What
are these terms? One, it seems clear, is the concept of the self.
James offers some help in identifying the second term, the
"things *thought-about*," when he says of the present moment
of consciousness that "nothing can be known *about* it till it
be dead and gone." [79] But what is "dead and gone" must be

in the present; accordingly, James would most likely say that it resides in the primary memory, and it is from here that identity is predicated of things thought about.

This analysis of James indicates, then, that the conception of the self is one of the terms of the relation, and that the "just past" experiences of the stream is the other. That is, the experiences of the stream would be checked for their relation to our self conception. For example, A calls B a 'bum'. B compares 'bum' with his conception of identity and "rejects" it, which may mean that he reacts emotionally or initiates a planned action.[80] More simple, A sees an image of his own hand and knows it is his because it corresponds to the schematic sense he has of his own body, which is part of his concept of the self.

It will be recalled that attention is one of the functions James attributes to the inner self. He also writes that *"an object once attended to will remain in the memory,* whilst one inattentively allowed to pass will leave no traces behind."[81] This suggests that the inner self helps determine which things get in the primary memory, that is, are put in a position to be accepted or rejected. (Strong sensations and objects which have "aesthetic interest," that is, are clear gestalts, will also be attended to, and will also reside in the primary memory.)

James supports such an analysis when he writes that *"all* that is experienced is, strictly considered, *objective;* that this Objective falls asunder into two contrasted parts, one realized as 'Self', the other as 'not-Self'." He agrees with Whitehead that the experience is a *that* until it is decided *what* it is. (Thus a chair and the *image* of one's hand are objective until differentiated.) This analysis requires that the objects in order to be differentiated must be attended to and so be held in the primary memory. Their "warmth and intimacy" would then be their relation of sameness with the concept of the self. This I take to be James's primary meaning of "warmth and intimacy."[82]

James himself strongly suggests this interpretation in his

discussion of schemes of intention. These, it will be remembered, *are* passed on from occasion to occasion, just as the conception of the self must be. Like the conception of the self, they do not show up clearly in the stream of consciousness, being neither sensations nor words, and yet they are operative. Such schemes, and the others of which James gives examples, such as schemes of memory or time, are employed in "test phases" in which the material they are structuring or controlling is checked against them.[83] In Neisser's phrase, these are "executive routines" [84] which control more detailed, lower-case experience. The similarity between James's description of schemes and the self is evident in his language:

"And has the reader never asked himself what kind of a mental fact is his *intention of saying a thing* before he has said it? . . . how much of it consists of definite sensorial images, either of words or of things? Hardly anything! Linger, and the words and things come into the mind; the anticipatory intention, the divination is there no more. But as the words that replace it arrive, it welcomes them successively and calls them right if they agree with it, it rejects them and calls them wrong if they do not."

"Each pulse of cognitive consciousness, each Thought, dies away and is replaced by another. The other among the things it knows, knows its own predecessor, and finding it 'warm', in the way we have described, greets it, saying: Thou art *mine,* and part of the same self with me."

"Each of us when he awakens says, Here's the same old self again, just as he says, Here's the same old bed, the same old room, the same old world." [85]

To sum up: James's self is a scheme, and partially a scheme of intention, and it is partially responsible for controlling attention. Further, "warmth and intimacy" is a relation of sameness between the concept of self and objects held in the primary memory, and is a primary basis for feelings of personal continuity or identity.

James indicates that the self may be difficult to define. He says, for example, that a man "identifies himself with this body because he loves *it,* and that he does not love it because he finds it to be identified with himself." This might mean that instincts, and experiences associated with them, are somewhat independent of a more integrated conception of the self. But James implies that this analysis may apply more to children, whose loves, as opposed to those of adults, are more unintegrated and objective (see Chapter III). The problem is complex, for as James also says, we have not one self, but many, and James is extremely vague in defining what is the conception of the self and what are the specific things we love. He suggests that such an analysis may be fruitless, and that *"one's mere principle of conscious identity"* may be a Kantian ghost well dismissed.[86] The problem then is how we organize the things we love into schematic conceptions and how these influence specific experience (see Chapter III).

But the ghost continues to haunt. What does the feeling "I am thinking this" mean for James? Does consciousness exist? His answers are various, sometimes profound, and sometimes a little sophistic. "I am as confident as I am of anything that, in myself, the stream of thinking (which I recognize emphatically as a phenomenon) is only a careless name for what, when scrutinized, reveals itself to consist chiefly of the stream of my breathing. The 'I think' which Kant said must be able to accompany all my objects, is the 'I breathe' which actually does accompany them." [87] Kant's 'I think' is "the formal unity of our consciousness in the synthesis of the manifold in our representations." James agrees that such integration, which he calls the unified conscious field, must be presupposed. What he is saying in opposition to Kant is that self-consciousness is not a necessary accompaniment of consciousness.[88]

Self-consciousness does occur, and would appear, according to the above interpretation of James, to be some relation between the concept of the self in the primary memory and the concept of the self in the present moment. Put another way, it is the concept of the self caught in attention.

James's attack on the ubiquity of the Kantian ego has another basis, and is similar to his attack on the Kantian conception of space. He would not deny the ego, as he does not deny Newtonian space; nor would he even deny that they are experienced, despite his bebunking of the experience of "consciousness" as human breath. What he is saying is that these conceptual experiences are not a priori, but constructed, a posteriori, intermittent and imperfect.

But in another sense, James would say that Kant is right: Experience, or conceptually, I 'think', is the basis for all our construction of the world, and so does accompany all our objects, as Kant says. This positing of experience as a precondition of our world is the basis for James's phenomenology.

There is another objective dimension to this ubiquity of experience. James says of the beyond or external world that if it is "not a future experience of our own or a present one of our neighbor, it must be a thing in itself . . . that is, it must be an experience *for* itself." [89] Whitehead expresses the same view when he says, "To be an actual entity is to have a self-interest." [90] In this sense, 'I am thinking this' characterizes all actual entities.

Finally, 'I am thinking this' may be taken as some ultimate expression of egoistic concern. James writes:

"The unsharable feeling which each one of us has of the pinch of his individual destiny as he privately feels it rolling out on fortune's wheel may be disparaged for its egotism, may be sneered at as unscientific, but it is the one thing that fills up the measure of our concrete actuality, and any would-be existent that should lack such a feeling, or its analogue, would be a piece of reality only half made up." [91]

Whitehead puts it this way: "At the base of our existence is the sense of 'worth' . . . It is the sense of existence for its own sake, of existence which is its own justification, of existence with its own character." "The discrimination of detail is definitely a secondary process, which may or may not assume importance." [92] This is precisely the position of James. Self-consciousness, the self, the ego, are secondary experiences; but self-value, the feeling of destiny, of being at the clutch of existence, are primary. These represent the ultimate experiences of existence for itself.

The "pinch" of existence may be taken as the feeling of transition, that is, of receiving causal inputs, including one's previous existence, and of pushing ahead into the future. But both James and Whitehead indicate that it is not the self which is exclusively the subject of these basic feelings. The sense of importance, Whitehead says, "is not exclusively referent to the experiencing self," but "differentiates itself into the disclosure of the whole, the many, and the self." [93] And for James, as well, it is the objective which "falls asunder into two contrasted parts, one realized as 'Self', the other as 'not-Self'." [94] This is why I suggested that James's "appropriation," to the extent it is concerned with identity, is a secondary mechanism, and that it is founded upon more basic processes of transition.

THE PERSPECTIVE-INTEREST

For both James and Whitehead, the process of existence is the working out of what James calls a "perspective-interest." For Whitehead, it is "concrescence." It is the way in which the many influences of the world, including the prior self, are integrated into a particularly located, single individual. It is how, at the highest level, the subjective field is united by feeling in some cognitive, purposeful, personal way. Whitehead writes:

"It follows that in every consideration of a single fact there is the suppressed presupposition of the environmental coördination requisite for its existence. This environment, thus coördinated, is the whole universe in its perspective to the fact. But perspective is gradation of relevance; that is to say, it is gradation of importance. Feeling is the agent which reduces the universe to its perspective for fact." [95]

This is the position in philosophy which James pioneered. In the following passage, he sums up the argument of this chapter, uniting perception, causality, and personality, as well as position and value.

"The body is the storm centre, the origin of co-ordinates, the constant place of stress in all that experience-train. Everything circles round it, and is felt from its point of view. The word 'I', then, is primarily a noun of position, just like 'this' and 'here'. Activities attached to 'this' position have prerogative emphasis, and, if activities have feelings, must be felt in a peculiar way. The word 'my' designates the kind of emphasis . . . the feeling of perspective-interest in which they are dyed." [96]

The stress of these last pages has been on activity, as opposed to more "passive" reception of causality, perception, or identification of self. Both James and Whitehead are philosophers of activity, and the outcome of this activity is the individual with his "perspective-interest." This is the theme of Chapter III.

III Organic Purpose

The Universe, with every living entity which her resources create,
creates at the same time a call for that entity, and an appetite
for its continuance,—creates it, if nowhere else, at least within
the heart of the entity itself.[1]—James

The primary meaning of "life" is the origination of conceptual novelty—novelty of appetition.[2]—Whitehead

THE WILL

TELEOLOGY OF IDEAS

The discussion of causality up to now has been concerned
with passage from the past to the present, either as perception
or as inheritance of identity, personality or the self. But
causality is experienced in yet another way, for the process
must go forward into the future. Were the future a blank
repetition of the present, this shift would create no problems.
And even if the future *were different* from the past, there
would be no problem so long as such differences were attributable, as some scientists say they are, to the blind working of
physical laws; in such cases, our task would be clearly cut out
for us: learn the physical laws.

But when we look at human experience, we find, according to James and Whitehead, factors at work which the physical sciences have not envisaged. Whitehead writes: "The
conduct of human affairs is entirely dominated by our recognition of foresight determining purpose, and purpose issuing
in conduct." [3] Examples Whitehead gives are the words

"policy" and "intention" and the construction of a ship, with its plan and its implementation and its finished product.

For Whitehead, purpose is a component of causality, just as inflowing physical forces or personal inheritance are components of causality, for we *cause* things to happen. For James, knowledge of purpose comes as "an original perceptual experience of the kind of thing we mean by causation." "What we feel is that a previous field of 'consciousness' containing (in the midst of its complexity) the idea as a result, develops gradually into another field in which that result either appears as accomplished, or else is prevented by obstacles . . ." James admits that the path of this kind of causality is often difficult to identify. For example, we think we move our limbs, and "ignore the brain-cells whose activity that will must first arouse." [4] But for James and Whitehead, the problems involved in identification do not invalidate the fact that purpose effects an issue.

The opposite point of view was stated by T. H. Huxley, who claimed that mentality is "epiphenomenal," that it merely accompanies, and does not influence, physical changes. Whitehead calls the ignoring by scientists of the evidence of purpose "a colossal example of anti-empirical dogmatism arising from a successful methodology." [5]

The rationalists also object, claiming that purpose effecting an issue means getting out of one's self and being one's other, which they say is self-contradictory. At issue is Descartes' belief in the self-sufficiency of primary substances. But for James and Whitehead, the belief must give way to the evidence, for "each of us actually *is* his own other to that extent, livingly knowing how to perform the trick which logic tells us can't be done. My thoughts animate and actuate this very body which you see and hear, and thereby influence your thoughts." [6]

The body which the thoughts animate is the whole body. Whitehead writes, "In the case of an animal, the mental states enter into the plan of the total organism and thus modify the plans of the successive subordinate organisms until the smallest organisms, such as electrons, are reached." [7] Whitehead maintains that the entertainment of thoughts without action, the typical case in the philosophies of Descartes and Hume, is a "figment of the learned world." [8] Rather, James assures us, mental facts are always *accompanied or followed by a bodily change.*" [9] Thus mentality affects the entire organism, and, in fact, the degree of the coordination of the effects of mentality might be taken as a measure of the organism's integration.

Finally, James says, "When they [ideas] add themselves to being, they partly redetermine the existent, so that reality as a whole appears incompletely definable unless ideas also are kept account of." [10] In Aristotelian terms, the position of James and Whitehead is that ideas function as final causes. James writes:

"The way in which we feel our successive fields continue each other in these cases is evidently what the orthodox doctrine means when it vaguely says 'in some way' the cause 'contains' the effect. It contains it by proposing it as the end pursued. Since the desire of that end is the efficient cause, we see that in the total fact of personal activity final and efficient causes coalesce." [11]

For Whitehead final causes are "ideals proper to the organism in question." They are a necessary reaction to the "over-stressing of the notion of 'efficient causes' during the modern scientific period." [12]

But while continuing to emphasize final causes, he is not unaware of their hazards, for the idea "introduces a dangerous mode of facile explanation." [13] For example, anything an organism does or is can be explained as a result of a hypothetical final cause. Despite the fact that Whitehead clearly recognizes the danger of explanations by final cause, he often commits the fault. For example, Whitehead calls an advance toward order or greater complexity of experience in the universe the "teleology of the Universe." But in so doing, he is merely assigning purpose to a phenomenon. This is a real problem in Whitehead, and to some extent in James. And even if we assume that the world does advance by final causes, we are still left with the pragmatic question, what are they experienced as? Both Whitehead and James must answer this question because both ultimately hold that anything real in the universe is an experienced fact. Accordingly, final causes must be felt.

APPETITIONS AND THE IMPULSIVE QUALITY OF IDEAS

In his use of final causes, James lays more stress on specific actions, Whitehead on organic construction, though Whitehead agrees with James as far as James goes.[14] The common ground is perhaps expressed by Whitehead when he says, "The lowest form of mental experience is blind urge towards a *form* of experience, that is to say, an urge towards a *form for realization*." Whitehead's phrase, "form of experience," is here taken to mean either organic construction or action.

It is important to make explicit just what Whitehead's forms are: "These forms of definiteness," Whitehead says, "are the Platonic forms, the Platonic ideas, the medieval universals." The task that Whitehead sets for himself is to explain how these ideas are implicated in process. The key concept is appetition: "In physical experience, the forms are the defining factors: in mental experience the forms connect the immediate occasions with occasions which lie beyond. The connection of immediate fact with the future resides in its appetitions." An example is hunger or thirst. There is a physical feeling, and there is a conceptual form which the physical feeling takes. This form is an urge toward the future realization of a fact, such as drinking water or eating food, a change which will involve the absorption of new elements into the constitution of the organism. This will further result in the alteration of the organism's constitution. Appetition thus illustrates how unrealized abstract form can be relevant for process.[15]

Appetition may also be demonstrated by aggression, for example, the process which may be set in motion by an insult. One of the factors of anger is a greater than normal supply of adrenalin in the blood stream. The idea, or insult, has here caused a somatic change. An angry man may also strike out with his fist. Such a motion changes the environment supplying data for that man. In this case, it may put his fist in contact with another man's jaw, or, more indirectly, it may result in inciting a dangerous adversary.

James is generally more concerned with the conscious and transitory; Whitehead embraces the permanent and structural as well.[16] But for both, ideas work in the world. James indicates his feeling that he is at the clutch of a basic metaphysical fact, when he says, "The *impulsive quality* of mental states is an attribute beyond which we cannot go." [17] This is what he calls the "ideo-motor theory" of action.

TELEOLOGY OF CONSCIOUSNESS

For Whitehead, all existence is characterized by mentality, but at the level of inorganic nature that mentality is confined to mere passive registration in subjective form of the inputs of physical energy. But with the appearance of organic life, there is a growth of novelty, the creation of goals which go beyond mere passive registration; there is growth of appetition, of ideal ends.[18]

James agrees exactly with this line of description. In an early review, dated 1878, of an article by Herbert Spencer, James seeks to show that intelligence not only supplies the means by which the organism survives, but itself creates the *end* of survival. The end of survival is a "final purpose" or "subjective interest," and James confesses his inability to formulate the matter in nonmental terms. In the *Psychology*, he uses this early example, declaring that with the appearance of life, "*Real* ends appear for the first time now upon the world's stage." In tracing the evolution of mentality, James shows that consciousness itself must serve a purpose, else it would not have evolved. The purposes it serves are often the very ends it proposes, and James holds that its "powers of cognition are mainly subservient to these ends, discerning which facts further them and which do not." [19]

What the mind conceives are "possibilities." It will be recalled that, for Whitehead, conceptual experience is of "eternal objects," or alternatively phrased, "pure potentials." These, as in James, are deficiently real; in appetition they envision a reality, such as food or the eating of food, without that reality yet being actualized. But some possibilities are more *probable* than others: water, or drinking, is more probable at a fountain than in a desert. One is what James would call a "live hypothesis," or "live option," and the other a dead one. For Whitehead, the distinction is between "relevance" and "irrelevance."

The creation of ends, if actualized, introduces real novelties into the world. This for Whitehead is the basis of the "creative advance."

For both James and Whitehead, novel ends, or conceptual novelty, are the criterion of advance up the philogenetic scale.[20] Inert things, such as stones, passively receive the physical inputs of their environment. The influences are received as they come individually, and are organized only at the lowest level of physical adjustment. But organic things organize what is perceived, and the highest-grade organisms have presentational immediacy, in which data are transmuted to characterize whole regions. In the conscious field, as experienced by human beings, the presentation is organized with its simplifications, its background, foreground, abstractions, distortions, enhancements, and suppressions according to the very interests which James says are the products of consciousness.

Thus the growth of ends is paralleled by the evolution of organized conscious presentation. Both sense perception and ends are usually involved in action, for the "object" of an act, such as food, must be both perceived and wanted. The conscious field is thus the scene where perception and ideality are unified; it is the supreme expression of the organism's pulling himself up from the bootstraps of his own data to become a purposeful individual. This then is the common doctrine of consciousness which lies behind James's philosophy of action and Whitehead's philosophy of organic construction.

Both are philosophies of transcendence. Perception gives knowledge of what lies beyond the individual; action passes beyond into the world; and organic construction rises from the data of the past to fulfill the present, and thence to create the future. Both action and organic construction involve the realization of ideal ends, ends which at once transcend the individual and fulfill him. Whitehead writes:

"The conception of knowledge as passive contemplation is too inadequate to meet the facts. Nature is ever originating its own development, and the sense of action is the direct knowledge of the percipient event as having its very being in the formation of its natural relations . . . For this reason perception is always at the utmost point of creation . . . The forward moving time exhibits this characteristic of experience, that it is essentially action. This passage of nature—or, in other words, its creative advance—is its fundamental characteristic." [21]

ACTION AND THE OBJECT OF THOUGHT

James was concerned with those actions in which the role of mentality seems evident. Purely routine action of the body, its "vegetative" or "housekeeping" functions, such as the heart beat, he relegated to the physiologists. What generally interested him were actions in which the conscious field was somehow involved.

Considered one way, the basic unit was the passage of action from the sense organ to the brain and thence to the voluntary muscles or the glands and autonomic system. Particularly in his earlier years, James claimed that this unit, essentially the reflex, accounted for virtually all mentality. "The theory of evolution," he once said, "is beginning to do very good service by its reduction of all mentality to the type of reflex action." [22]

But James's description of the reflex revealed problems of which he became increasingly aware: "The current of life which runs in at our eyes or ears is meant to run out at our hands, feet, or lips. The only use of the thoughts it occasions while inside is to determine its direction to whichever of these organs shall, on the whole, under the circumstances actually present, act in the way most propitious to our welfare." However, the "sense-data" or the "current of life" could not explain the reaction. "Objects," James said, "are certainly the primitive arousers of instinctive reflex movements." But what are "objects"? "In my nomenclature it is the total situation which is the 'object' on which the reaction of the subject is made." Thus it is not a stimulus, but a situation as conceived, and "in the last resort" it is "one of its elements which strikes us for the time being as most vitally important." [23]

James gives the example of a bear coming toward us. "The same bear may truly enough excite us to either fight or flight, according as he suggests an overpowering 'idea' of his killing us, or one of our killing him." The situation is the *total* one of the perceiver, his position in the woods, the presence or absence of a gun, and so forth. (And indeed that brown shape must be *conceived* as a bear.) Thus, it is only out of this total situation, or object of thought, that the idea of flight or fight arises. [24]

But this "total object of thought" was not the specific stimulus demanded by the general reflex scheme. And yet throughout the opening chapters of the *Psychology,* James talked as if this difficulty hardly existed. He was, in short, willing to accept a discrete object or stimulus, much as did the sensationalists, against whom he continually inveighed. The obvious use of reflexes is that they fit in so well with the associationist scheme.

Associationism entails several key assumptions: "The same cerebral process which, when aroused from without by a sense-organ, gives the perception of an object, will give an *idea* of the same object when aroused by other cerebral processes from within." [25] The further assumption here is that the original process by which the perception was created leaves a "trace" in the brain which can be continually reproduced. But James, as has been seen, denied that the same idea could ever be reproduced: it would be in a different brain, in a different situation and mental context, the rememberer would be older and more experienced, and so on. Nevertheless, James never directly challenged the belief that "traces" could provide the basis for standardized reactions.

The second key assumption is the so-called law of association. "If processes 1, 2, 3, 4 have once been aroused together or in immediate succession, any subsequent arousal of any one of them (whether from without or within) will tend to arouse the others in the original order." The further assumption here is that a stimulus which activates the trace need have nothing in it which could create the trace in the first instance, that is, nothing in common with the original object.

The classic example, developed by the Austrian anatomist Thomas Meynert, is that of the child and the candle flame. The child, following a reflex, grasps a flame, is burnt, and following another reflex, withdraws his hand:

"The effect on the child's conduct when the candle-flame is next presented is easy to imagine. Of course the sight of it arouses the grasping reflex; but it arouses simultaneously the idea thereof, together with that of the consequent pain, and of the final retraction of the hand; and if these cerebral processes prevail in strength over the immediate sensation in the centres below, the last idea will be the cue by which the final action is discharged." [26]

In this example, one of the associative links is the previous burning, but the sight of the candle flame has nothing itself to do with the sensation of burning. Such links are the basis of Pavlov's experiments on conditioned reflexes.[27] Although James could not fully accept the Meynert scheme, he never developed a satisfactory critique based on his deeper philosophical ideas. John Dewey, however, did.

In the example of the child and the candle, Dewey points out that the candle flame is not just a sensation, but an "act of seeing," in which *both* sensation and coordinated movement are "inside" the act. The act of grasping is not only stimulated but controlled by the seeing, so that the so-called stimulus and response are part of a larger coordination. This emphasis on control and action is thoroughly in the Jamesian spirit. The explanation of the reaction to the burn is even more Jamesian: "The burn is the original seeing, the original optical-ocular experience enlarged and transformed in its value. It is no longer mere seeing; it is seeing-of-a-light-that-means-pain-when-contact-occurs." [28] The "seeing-of-a-light-that-means-pain-when-contact-occurs" reminds one of James's "thunder-breaking-upon-silence-and-contrasting-with-it." Dewey appears to take James one step further by having the agglutinated thought be the present moment of the organism in control of action. But James's analysis of intentional schemes, such as "the-pack-of-cards-is-on-the-table," controlling the sentence at each point, has the same effect. Dewey's innovation consists in having the agglutinated thought itself *arise in* the situation *and* control it.

INSTINCTS

Although James did not evolve a thoroughgoing criticism, he did ask why the child grasped the candle in the first place. Disagreeing with Meynert, he thought that the explanation was a reflex in the hemispheres, rather than the lower centers. The hemispheres, far from being unorganized at birth, as Meynert assumed, had "native tendencies to reaction of a determinate sort." These are the instincts, which are built-in reactions to "special sorts of objects of *perception* . . . [T]hey take place the first time the exciting object is met, are accompanied by no forethought or deliberation, and are irresistible." [29] At least, James said, the instinctual reactions occur in this automatic way the first time, though subsequently, he pointed out, they could be modified.

Instincts, and for that matter, all other action, could be conceived as the result of energized paths or wiring in the brain. (In instincts, the paths or wiring would be preestablished.) But the inciting "object" would be no less than the "total object of thought," that is, the appropriate object in the right perspective, under the right conditions. Thus, James writes that "objects of the same class arouse reactions of opposite sorts in consequence of slight changes in the circumstances, in the individual fact, or in the agent's inward condition." [30] Combining a rigid morphology and a highly specific mental field in one analysis proved understandably difficult.

Instincts, James also maintains, are teleological: *"Instinct is usually defined as the faculty of acting in such a way as to produce certain ends, without foresight of the ends, and without previous education in the performance."* [31] James, however, qualifies this view of instincts by saying it is not an end but a "particular sensation or perception or image which calls them forth." [32] But it must be pointed out that if this is so, the end *as such* is not experienced as a mental fact.

In any case, according to James, one purpose which instincts accomplish is to get the organism started. Without some built-in mechanism which fixes objects in the welter of the environment and *acts* on them, the organism would have no basis of survival. "When a particular movement, having once occurred in a random, reflex, or involuntary way, has left an image of itself in the memory, then the movement can be desired again, proposed as an end, and deliberately willed. But it is impossible to see how it could be willed before." Unless the child starts feeding instinctively, it will die before it knows what it must do to live. But once the action is completed, James says, the pleasure which it occasioned will itself acquire impulsive power.[33] What then is left as a legacy of the first instinctively determined act is the inciting object or class of objects, the memory of the kinesthetic action which followed, and the resulting pleasure or pain as an enhancer or inhibitor now associated with the object.

A main difficulty with James's theory of instincts is that there are so many of them. Unlike Freud's modest count of instinctual drives, James's total numbers as the sands: "Thus, greediness and suspicion, curiosity and timidity, coyness and desire, bashfulness and vanity, sociability and pugnacity . . . are all impulses, congenital, blind at first, and productive of motor reactions of a rigorously determinate sort." [34] James has in addition such items as a "hunting instinct," an "instinct to imitate sounds," and an instinct of "constructiveness." His list of instincts, whatever else its charms, lacks the inner simplicity of creditable scientific theory, and appears, like the Ptolemaic epicycles, as a series of ad hoc descriptions of otherwise unexplained fact. Instincts for James are final causes. In explaining types of behavior by calling them instincts, James is, in Whitehead's words, introducing a "dangerous mode of facile explanation." Moreover, it may be pointed out that many of James's instincts, for example, "acquisitiveness" and "kleptomania," lose their ad hoc quality in psychoanalytic theory and become absorbed in Freud's larger schemes of explanation.

In any case, James's instincts, with their high specificity, seem quickly to lose their identifiability, if they do not fade away altogether. James concludes in typical Darwinist fashion that *"most instincts are implanted for the sake of giving rise to habits, and that, this purpose once accomplished, the instincts themselves, as such, have no raison d'être in the psychical economy, and consequently fall away."* [35] The "as such" is an interesting escape clause. James plays with the idea that

the instincts themselves continue, *after* they have apparently
faded away, as the base character of noninstinctual behavior,
which he calls the "superstructure." [36] The implications of
this idea for James's theory of attention and the self have in
part already been explored (see Chapter II).

HABITS

Although James maintains that habits, such as eating, may
appear as the continuation of instinctual activity, he says that
habits may also arise through conscious choice. Instead of the
individual components of an action being parts of a preestablished instinct, they can be chosen, and the wrong alternative
action-components rejected. Thus a young pianist only painfully learns to play a scale.

But, according to James, a habit once learned is the same
as an instinct: "The most complex habits . . . are . . .
nothing but *concatenated* discharges in the nerve-centres, due
to the presence there of systems of reflex paths, so organized
as to wake each other up successively—the impression produced by one muscular contraction serving as a stimulus to
provoke the next, until a final impression inhibits the process
and closes the chain." James says that the object of thought
initiates the chain of actions and implies that at a lower level
the action may be guided by "plans." For example, James
would say that the playing of the scale on the piano is a two-
level operation. At one level would be the intention to play
the scale thought of in a highly schematic way, and at the
other level would be the mental equivalent of the notes themselves, which would "guide" the process of the scale being
played. Some equivalent split-level operation also seems indicated in James's example of "the pack of cards is on the
table." James indicates that the "concatenated discharges" are
subject to some kind of test because the individual movements
of the chain are "accompanied by consciousness of some kind.
They are *sensations* to which we are *usually inattentive,* but
which immediately call our attention if they go *wrong.*" [37]

The point of habits is that the higher centers are involved in only a minimal degree, and our attention can be absorbed elsewhere. ("In action grown habitual, what instigates each new muscular contraction to take place in its appointed order is not a thought or perception, but the *sensation occasioned by the muscular contraction just finished*.") The resources of conscious attention are limited; also, because they are involved in making choices, they are indecisive. Thus the object of education, according to James, is early to make automatic and habitual as many actions as possible.[38]

Although Whitehead wrote no general work on psychology, the similarity between his *Aims of Education* and James's *Talks to Teachers* reflects the fact that their concepts of psychology concerning the matters discussed above are virtually identical. Like James, Whitehead endorses the need for early training of the nervous system in skills. And, like James and Dewey, he stresses learning through doing, work in the shop and laboratory, which fix processes in the mind through active engagement. Whitehead also accepts James's ideas of attention and interest (see below), and shares with James the idea that they, not repetition, determine what will be learned and acted upon. And along Jamesian lines, Whitehead maintains that the appearance of instinctual interests at various ages should be reflected in the curriculum.[39] Where James holds that information is integrated by interest and can only be held in nets of association, Whitehead similarly inveighs against what he calls "inert ideas," by which he means isolated informational bits that have no place in any arrangement. Both consider mentality more abstract, more self-generating, more nurtured by leisure and less dependent for its creativity on the exigencies of immediate situations than does Dewey (although the differences should not be overworked). They both believed that the mind, if relieved from tedium, could indeed fly.[40]

THE IDEO-MOTOR THEORY

Both Whitehead and James embrace what James called the ideo-motor theory—if an exciting idea is brought before the conscious attention, an action will automatically follow. The same principle, which James and Whitehead apply to instincts and habits, holds for emotions: *"the bodily changes follow directly the perception of the exciting fact."* The emotion, James says, is *"our feeling of the same changes as they occur."* James explains that "we feel sorry because we cry, angry because we strike, afraid because we tremble," and not the other way round. Of equal importance are internal changes in the viscera which, along with the movements, have been triggered by the exciting idea. This explanation of the emotions, published by James in 1884, and, independently, a year later by the Danish psychologist Carl Lange, became known as the James-Lange theory.[41]

For years after the James-Lange theory was published, a debate raged among psychologists about whether emotional feeling necessarily depends on somatic feedback. Current evidence would indicate that emotions do not necessarily depend on such feedback.[42] But whether they do or not, the ideo-motor theory stands—that somatic changes follow directly from the perception.

As for voluntary acts, the principle is the same: *"there is nothing else, in the mind but the kinesthetic idea, thus defined, of what the act is to be."* James says, however, that while in the beginning this is true, once the movement is learned, only the ends which the movement is to attain need come strongly before consciousness.[43]

James argued that a "feeling of innervation" (command signal), or a "feeling of the outgoing discharge" into the motor nerves, does not exist. In so doing, he challenged Wilhelm Wundt, Alexander Bain, Hermann von Helmholtz, Ernst Mach, and, in fact, most of the psychologists of his day. If it could have been demonstrated that feelings of innervation were consciously experienced, James's ideo-motor theory would have had to be radically changed; fortunately for the theory, James could find no evidence that such feelings were so experienced.[44]

For James, the vital matter remained what commands our conscious attention, because *that* is what we will do or emotionally react to. Our actions are determined by what appears in consciousness, and thus by what operations we perform in creating the conscious field so that objects are enhanced or inhibited, accepted or dismissed. The key factor is interest.

ATTENTION AND INTEREST

James wrote:

"If one must have a single name for the condition upon which the impulsive and inhibitive quality of objects depends, one had better call it their *interest*. 'The interesting' is a title which covers not only the pleasant and the painful, but also the morbidly fascinating, the tediously haunting, and even the simply habitual, inasmuch as the attention usually travels on habitual lines, and what-we-attend-to and what-interests-us are synonymous terms." [45]

Interest, it will be recalled, is the basis upon which the subjective field is organized. It is what determines which object holds the foreground and how it relates to all the other items in the field. It is this subjective organization which determines our acts and, Whitehead says, our constitution to the extent that this can be consciously decided. Indeed, for Whitehead, "consciousness is a mode of attention." [46]

James finds that when we attend to a perceptual object two processes usually go together: "(1) *The accommodation or adjustment of the sensory organs;* and (2) *The anticipatory preparation from within of the ideational centres concerned with the object to which the attention is paid.*" Following G. H. Lewes, James calls this anticipatory preparation "pre-perception." Although it is "impossible to tell how much of the

percept comes from without and how much from within,"
James finds that "the *preparation* we made for it always partly
consists of the creation of an imaginary duplicate of the object
in the mind, which shall stand ready to receive the outward
impression as if in a matrix." [47] It is, for example, the preperceptual image which accounts for the tendency to see
objects in standard positions—a table which "appears" oblong
but is "seen" as square—and to take the sign of an object for
the "whole thing"—a distant glow as a whole house.

Then, in a highly significant shift, James writes: "The
image in the mind *is* the attention; the *preperception* . . .
is half of the perception of the looked-for-thing." Moreover,
*"the only things which we commonly see are those which we
preperceive."* [48]

Under this analysis, instincts would consist of preperceptual
images with associated motor responses. But instincts relate to
classes of objects. The word "matrix" for the preperceptual
image suggests that the image might well be abstract, involving perhaps a limited number of related features. Moreover,
the image is being constructed *while* it is being seen. James
suggests this when he says, for example, that "even in mere
sense-impression [where there is no preperceptual image] the
duplication of the object by an inner construction must take
place." [49] The argument tends to support the hypothesis that
the preperceptual image, abstract and schematic, determines
where we focus our attention. The attention would then be
the process of "seeing" or "hearing", that is, constructing the
detailed image or sound pattern in the mind.[50]

Recall James's point that *"an object attended to will remain
in the memory"* and his conclusion that because attention is
one of the tasks of the self, the latter helps determine which
things get in the primary memory, that is, the self helps
determine which things are put in a *position* where they can
be remembered. Now once we have perceived an object, its preperceptual image may figure again as a memory to effect our
perception. It then becomes crucial to determine how we

achieve the preperceptual image which guided our early perception. Instincts supply one group; the other group, James says, is the memory of strong sensations. James remarks: "The native interests of children lie altogether in the sphere of sensation." [51] The reason for such attention, James suggests, is that without it, the organism could never have survived.

Interest is then transferred from strong or instinctive materials to materials connected with them. But at another level of analysis, it would seem that this process is the development or modification or transformation of the *early* preperceptual images—those of instincts and strong sensations—into preperceptual images of new material. (The capability for such development assumes the schematic or abstract character of the initial preperceptual images.) For example, interest in knobs might derive from modification of preperceptual sets for nipples. The relation between the new preperceptual image and the base, generative instinctual image would be like that between a branch and a trunk. This metaphor implies both homology and dependence of the new image for energy upon the old.

"The passive sensorial attention is *derived* when the impression, without being either strong or of an instinctively exciting nature, is connected by previous experience and education with things that are so. These things may be called the *motives* of the attention. The impression draws an interest from them, or perhaps it even fuses into a single complex object with them; the result is that it is brought into the focus of the mind." [52]

James here suggests a growing set of images, sensory and symbolic, which picks things out of the field for conscious attention. James does not explain how such preperceptual images fuse into complex objects with what is picked out; nor does he say how the preperceptual images themselves develop from early material of instinctual interest. The process is no doubt quite complicated. Both analogue and digital, or symbolic, types of relations would seem implied in this extension of attention to "connected" objects.[53]

Both Whitehead and James indicate that we generally perceive those objects in the environment which are important for our survival. But such objects, like food or enemies, are precisely those with which, James would say, we have instinctual relations. Visual angularity, for example, is related to dangerous objects, and is a factor to which we are extraordinarily sensitive in the sensory environment.[54] James's theory thus opens up for study the relation between factors in our preattentive mechanisms which signal in our focal attention and our instinctual or emotional interests.[55]

INTEREST AND THE SELF

James's conception of "motives" for the attention relates cognitive and Freudian (or dynamic) ways of thought. In the following, he shows the egoistic base from which conscious attention grows:

"My own body and what ministers to its needs are thus the primitive object, instinctively determined, of my egoistic interests. Other objects may become interesting derivatively through association with any of these things, either as means or as habitual concomitants; *and so in a thousand ways the primitive sphere of the egoistic emotions may enlarge* and change its boundaries . . . This sort of interest is really the meaning of the word 'my.'"* [56]

Whether this "interest" signals in the object for conscious attention or keeps it in attention once it is there, James is clear that the self is an objective designation *"meaning* ALL THE THINGS *which have the power to produce in a stream of consciousness excitement of a certain peculiar sort."* [57] But as Freud points out, ego identity represents in part what we have gotten from the world to fulfill our instinctual needs. Our bodies are given, but the food to feed them, our wives or mistresses, houses or bank accounts we must get. These objects of our instinctual needs, and those associated with them, coalesce conceptually into James's self; and as objects, they emerge with special salience from the sensory field, and with memory are recalled from the past. (For the moment, I ignore the opposing role of the Freudian superego, which would also control attention. For Freud, the superego represents a *secondary* reactive identification founded upon more basic instinctual needs.)

DREAM FORMATION

James says that in order to be remembered, objects must interest us and so be attended to. With this assumption, the Freudian system of symbolic dream construction might be conceived as a function of James's system of preperceptual sets. During the dream day, the preperceptual sets would partially control attention. For example, one might hold in attention some aspect of a man which formed part of the preperceptual set for one's father. In this way, one would remember either the aspect or the man associated with it. (Standard Freudian symbols, such as snakes and jars, might be already remembered objects, related to instinctively determined preperceptual sets.) During the dream work, the preperceptual sets would pick out remembered objects or symbolically related aspects from the dream day or from the more distant memory for incorporation into dreams. But Freud would maintain that the preperceptual sets—the instinctual drives or the concept of the self—need not themselves be consciously realized, as James himself half admits (see Chapter II). With this qualification, James's analysis does suggest a bridge between a cognitive and dynamic theory of dream formation.[58]

INTEREST AND BELIEF

Both the factors of instinctual interest and strong sensation combine to provide the basis for "belief." James writes: "Whichever represented objects give us sensations, especially interesting ones, or incite our motor impulses, or arouse our hate, desire, or fear, are real enough for us. Our requirements in the way of reality terminate in our own acts and emotions, our own pleasures and pains." Accordingly, James says, "Nothing which I can feel like *that* can be false." The analogy to the ideo-motor theory, that action follows directly the exciting idea, is clear: James says that in the absence of a stronger relation, or reasons for not believing, any relation to the mind at all is sufficient to make an object real. Belief thus follows directly the exciting idea. "As a rule we believe as much as we can. We would believe everything if we only could." And when we believe, when the idea is in sole possession of the field, "motor effects are apt to follow." [59]

Like James, Whitehead holds that in the absence of contradiction belief results automatically if there is interest. "It is more important that a proposition be interesting than that it be true. This statement is almost a tautology. For the energy of operation of a proposition in an occasion of experience is its interest, and is its importance." Here "energy of operation" means ability to determine the future, either as emotion or as action. Whitehead points out that interesting propositions whose truth is irrelevant are frequently entertained, for example, 'If I could drink . . .' or 'To be or not to be, that is the question'. Such propositions are "believed" and incite action or emotion, and yet the truth is hardly at issue.[60] These arguments perhaps help to explain the hold of art, which is not "true," and to account for the fact that in the development of civilization myth precedes factual history.

Whitehead maintains that propositions of the type 'If I could drink . . .' or, more basic, 'If drinking . . .' are quite primitive, and entertained by simple organisms, although not, of course, in linguistic form. Belief here is merely another name for appetition or feeling.

When the truth of a proposition is at issue, we are dealing with a more sophisticated phenomenon. There must be negative propositions in the form 'It is not true that . . .'; and a belief which results from the rejection of such negative propositions is probably a function performed only by the highest grade of organisms, possibly only by man. Such belief, Whitehead says, adds salience or strength to the proposition, and thereby adds to its ability to guide the future.[61] This added strength, based on a decision to believe, is also expressed by James when he says that adding reality or belief "fixes" the picture and "stamps it in to *us*." [62]

ATTENTION WITH EFFORT

James indicates that were we the simple products of our instincts, as, to a great extent, are animals, we would attend without effort to whatever in the conscious field attracted our instinctual interests, like a fish taking bait, and so act without further ado. But man makes an effortful choice to attend to some objects and not others. Within broad lines, James and Freud have the same analysis. In Freud, the ego has two mediating roles: between instinctual objects and between these objects and the superego. In James, these are the functions of what he loosely calls "reason" and, elsewhere, the "will":

"there is no material antagonism between instinct and reason. Reason, *per se,* can inhibit no impulses; the only thing that can neutralize an impulse is an impulse the other way. Reason may, however, make an *inference which will excite the imagination so as to set loose* the impulse the other way; and thus, though the animal richest in reason might be also the animal richest in instinctive impulses too, he would never seem the fatal automaton which a *merely* instinctive animal would be." [63]

But impulses may exist at birth or develop later or be acquired by assiduous habit; they may be basely instinctual, or "refined" and "moral," the type of impulses which constitute the Freudian superego. The will's mediation between impulses therefore subsumes both Freudian categories.

James seems to assume that, in comparison with baser instinctual impulses, impulses of the refined, abstract, or moral type have necessarily little direct energy behind them. If they prevail, they do so only with effort. Accomplishing this effort is the task of the will: *"The essential achievement of the will, in short, when it is most 'voluntary,' is to* ATTEND *to a difficult object and hold it fast before the mind. The so-doing is the fiat."* [64] But when stronger impulsive material is also present, holding the object before the mind is not easy. The problem is that the difficult object is easily crowded out by the emotionally strong one which surrounds itself with "congruous" images.

How then do we get the wise or difficult object or action to stay before the mind? Putting aside for the moment the question of energy (see below), James says that the wise object can call up its associates and result in a change of "disposition" of the man's consciousness. This change of disposition can be understood when it is recalled that the wise "object" is really the total felt situation in which the reaction is made, and the object itself is only an element of the "total object of thought." The associates of this element form an "interest-perspective" which enables the subject to act.

Now the effort to attend or to keep one thing in the mind in opposition to another is felt. James explains the feeling of effort in an example which is at once so explicit and charmingly Victorian that I quote it at length:

"Effort is felt only where there is a conflict of interests in the mind. The idea A may be intrinsically exciting to us. The idea Z may derive its interest from association with some remoter good. A may be our sweetheart, Z may be some condition of our soul's salvation. Under these circumstances, if we succeed in attending to Z at all it is always with expenditure of effort. The 'ideational preparation,' the 'preperception' of A keeps going on of its own accord, whilst that of Z needs incessant pulses of voluntary reinforcement (or effort) at each successive moment in which the thought of A flares brightly up in our mind. Dynamically, however, that may mean only this: that the associative processes which make Z triumph are really stronger, and in A's absence would make us give a 'passive' and unimpeded attention to Z; but, so long as A is present, some of their force is used to inhibit the processes concerned with A. Such inhibition is a partial neutralization of the brain-energy which would otherwise be available for fluent thought . . . But what is lost for thought is converted into feeling, in this case into the peculiar feeling of effort, difficulty, or strain." [65]

Here James comes as close as he ever gets to describing the process by which the will operates. The "incessant pulses of voluntary reinforcement" suggest a unified, monotonous process by which the main idea would be energetically repeated and so sustained that it would call up emotionally charged associates; in this way, it would commandeer the field. Thus simply repeating the name of one's wife (Z) might call up associations sufficiently powerful to provide the basis of remaining faithful to her, as opposed to having an affair with A. But another tactic might be to evoke the associates of Z in order to lend support to the idea; James suggests that these "reinforcing and inhibiting ideas" might then be termed the "reasons" for the eventual action connected with Z. But the fight to construct a sustaining structure for a single "desire or thought of purpose" involves real conflict among ideas. Elsewhere, James suggests that the members of "mental activity trains" actually work on each other: "they check, sustain, and introduce," both when the activity is associational and when "effort" is there. The conversion of mental energy ("what is lost for thought is converted into feeling") reminds one again of Freud. [66]

James also states that although the "associative processes which make Z triumph are really the stronger," the preperception of A—it is the more exciting idea—keeps A going. In this situation, Z must be lent support by incessant pulses of energy. Where does the energy for Z come from? If it has stronger "associative processes," the logical way would be by association. In this sense, association may be described as a coupling or borrowing of energy of one idea by another. "If, for instance, I think of Paris whilst I am *hungry,* I shall not improbably find that its *restaurants* have become the pivot of my thoughts." [67] Thus the energy may flow from hunger to Parisian restaurants, and from there possibly to plans for getting to Paris.

CONCLUSION

Do all these separate ideas work into anything like a coherent theory? In Chapter II, I interpret James as saying that the same objects which elicit our interests and compel our attention make up the self and that the self is a scheme or schemes carried over from moment to moment in the life of the individual. It is now clear that this scheme or schemes is for James a preperceptual image or images and that it is the self, seen in this cognitive way, which directs attention. [68]

As interpreted in Chapter II, James also implies that the experiences of the stream of consciousness are checked in a two-term relation by our conception of our self. It is the self, as the director of attention, which determines which things get in the primary memory, that is, are put in a position to be accepted or rejected. Thus the self determines what is attended to, and it also determines what is accepted or rejected. But James says that acceptance or rejection will be automatic if the relation between the object and our instinctual interests is clear and not in conflict with other instinctual interests, that is, if the object is attended to without effort. The action or emotion will follow directly, according to the ideo-motor theory and the real possibilities of the situation. The example given was that of a man being called a "bum." Rejection here means an emotional reaction of anger or the action of hitting the giver of the insult.

James's discussion of ideal ends and means suggests that the ideal end of the organism is the self, at least to the extent

that the end functions in what James would call consciousness. The self as an ideal end might well be what James
means by the end of "survival," or what he means when he
says, "The Universe, with every living entity which her
resources create, creates at the same time a call for that entity,
and an appetite for its continuance,—creates it, if nowhere
else, at least within the heart of the entity itself."

This ideal end, or self, is fully implicated in the daily problems of existence. It is, for James, not only what directs attention, but what compels belief and commands volition:

"although attention is the first and fundamental thing in
volition, *express consent to the reality of what is attended to*
is often an additional and quite distinct phenomenon involved
. . . When an idea *stings* us in a certain way, makes as it
were certain electric connection with our Self, we believe that
it *is* a reality. When it stings us in another way, makes another
connection with our Self, we say, *let it be* a reality." [69]

This second reaction, this "express consent to the reality,"
would most likely result from a defined positive relation or
congruence between the self and the object as it continued in
the memory. The audit or search fixing this relation would be
an "executive routine" of the organism, and represent one of
its highest cognitive functions.

What the executive routine would do would be to connect
the object with the self. At the cognitive level, there would
be the merger or "fusion" of the appropriate preperceptual
image in the self with the image of the object, for example,
being "religious" with going to church. This "fusion" would
eventually account for the energy needed to trigger the act. In
this analysis the storehouse of psychic energy is the self. The
"executive routine" is what throws the switch releasing the
energy. It is a cognitive function based on determining a relation of like to like. This "executive routine" is probably what
James means by the "Self of Selves." [70]

Were the relation between the object and the self in doubt,

and the doubt then resolved, the "express consent" would then be psychologically felt. The effort to attend would be felt when several objects appealed simultaneously to components of the self. Acceptance by one component of the self would mean a fusion of the emotional energy of that component with the object and, at a lower cognitive level, the energy behind what plan of action that object carried.[71] But the same component of the self would reject the other object, and although it is not clear from James what form that rejection would take, it might well be inhibition of that second object's implementation. James's "incessant pulses of voluntary reinforcement (or effort) at each successive moment," which kept the object in attention, would in this analysis draw their energy from the connection between the object and the emotionally charged self.

In the case of the A and Z example, suppose that our subject wishes to be a priest and also wishes to be a lover. A is going to a girl's house and Z is going to church. The decision whether to do A or Z will involve conflict. Part of the process going on when A and Z are in the primary memory or in attention is to make the connections clear between A and being a lover and being a priest, and the same for Z. Meanwhile, according to this interpretation of James, the energy behind being a priest would inhibit going to the girl's house. The energy not available for "fluent thought" is energy not available for action. This energy, neutralized by the inhibition, would be converted into feelings, such as frustration or anxiety.

Let me now return to James's statement that the "essential achievement of the will" is to attend to a difficult or moral object and hold it fast before the mind in the face of a competing and more energetic instinctual object. The logical problem is this: If the instinctual object has more energy, how can the higher object prevail? An explanation can be based on James's belief that instincts can retain autonomy, whereas "higher impulses" tend to become parts of the *integrated* conception of the self. The integrated self would then be the source of energy and would account for the ability of higher impulses to prevail over more base instincts, once a connection with the self was established.

It would seem that preperceptual elements which are conscious are those which probably are *integrated* components of the self and that those which are unintegrated are probably unconscious. A man can live with some irresolution in his character, but the other possibility, which Freud explores and James ignores, is repression of unintegratable elements. (It is the task of psychoanalysis to integrate such elements in consciousness.) The integration of the conscious elements would mean in practice that a man faced with a decision between A and Z, and knowing consciously that Z is connected with the self, could use certain psychic resources available to consciousness to call up associations to make the connection strong. Without such conscious knowledge, the strategy, in James's analysis, would be impossible.

Thus, according to the above interpretation of James, one of the tasks performed in the primary memory or the maintained attention is to trace connections with the self. The decision made is *always* a decision of character, however trivial. James indicates that most men maintain subplans of action based on their character; thus the issue of character need not be opened as a primary consideration: "The moment we hit upon a conception which lets us apply some principle of action which is a fixed and stable part of our Ego, our state of doubt is at an end." [72]

But there are moments in which the ego itself must be decided from among its many possibilities.

"The ethical energy *par excellence* has to go farther and choose which *interest* out of several, equally coercive, shall become supreme. The issue here is of the utmost pregnancy, for it decides a man's entire career. When he debates, Shall I commit this crime? choose that profession? accept that office, or marry this fortune?—his choice really lies between one of the several equally possible future Characters . . . The problem with the man is less what act he shall now choose to do, than what being he shall now resolve to become." [73]

This is the task of the unification of character: we are deciding what we will be within the limits of our existence. The self is then a scheme of intention. What it is intending is its own future. In Whitehead's phrase, what it achieves is its "satisfaction," what it seeks is its "subjective aim." [74]

FREEDOM

FREEDOM OF THOUGHT AND RESPONSIBILITY

The decision of what to be is the point where James's philosophy of action merges into Whitehead's philosophy of becoming. Such decisions are at the summit of the world's spontaneity. Below lie massive inheritance and massive routine.

And yet, though routine predominates, even at the level of human life, it is not the whole story. There is, Whitehead believes, a measure of spontaneity of thought. The interplay between this spontaneity and the self, or, in Whitehead's phrase, the "whole," is described by Whitehead entirely along Jamesian lines:

"Most of us believe that there is a spontaneity of thought which lies beyond routine. Otherwise, the moral claim for freedom of thought is without meaning. This spontaneity of thought is, in its turn, subject to control as to its maintenance and efficiency. Such control is the judgment of the whole, attenuating or strengthening the partial flashes of self-determination. The whole determines what it wills to be, and thereby adjusts the relative importance of its own inherent flashes of spontaneity. The final determination is its Wisdom or, in other words, its subjective aim as to its own nature, with its limits set by inherited factors." [75]

For Whitehead as for James, the agency of spontaneity, the means by which mentality at the highest level controls process, is a composition, essentially the conscious field. Objects in the field, Whitehead says, work as catalytic agents do in chemistry: "They modify the aesthetic process by which the occasion constitutes itself out of the many streams of feeling received from the past." [76] This is information control at a high level of representation and a low level of energy. In Aristotelian terms, it is the creation and modification of final causes as they operate in an organic system.[77]

James offers, as has been seen, a full description of how the self arises as an ideal end and of how it "determines what it wills to be" through its decisions of character. Like Whitehead, he assumes that processes, such as those that take place in a frog or a man, create flashes of spontaneity and novel ideal ends, including the integrated concept of the self. But at times he seems to ignore them,[78] and he is willing to have the voluntary life consist solely of how much attention we give to rival motor ideas, regardless of how they arise. This becomes for him *the* vital factor in answering the metaphysical question of whether or not there is freedom.[79]

James finds the answer to this question impossible on "strictly psychological grounds." On the one hand, he cannot know how feeling actually works in the brain. If "the feeling which coexists with the brain-cells' activity reacts dynamically upon that activity, furthering or checking it, then the attention is in part, at least, a *cause*"; but such an effect is not measurable. On the other hand, he cannot decide whether or not more or less of the crucial attention might have been given. "To tell that, we should have to ascend to the antecedents of the effort, and defining them with mathematical exactitude, prove, by laws of which we have not at present even an inkling, that the only amount of sequent effort which could *possibly* comport with them was the precise amount which actually came." [80] Again, the same problem: the effort cannot be measured. With exact evidence unavailable, James accepts the evidence of introspection—he feels that his will works effects; and he credits the a priori dictates of his own desire—he wills to believe in free will.[81]

James considers the arguments of the associationists that the mind works according to strict associational laws. But, James argues, even if this were true—and at times he seems perhaps too eager to admit it—the spontaneity would still be preserved because ideas, however mechanically brought forward, could still be selected for extra attention. Because such selection would influence the subsequent associations, and hence the developing conscious field, it would help determine a man's acts.[82]

FREEDOM AND HISTORY

Whatever the process, the individual in James's universe feels he has agency. History in retrospect looks inevitable. But for the individual, who creates history through his own decisions, it seems far from inevitable:

"To *yourselves*, it is true, those very acts of choice, which to me are so blind, opaque, and external, are the opposites of this, for you are within them and effect them. To you they appear as decisions; and decisions, for him who makes them, are altogether peculiar psychic facts. Self-luminous and self-justifying at the living moment at which they occur, they appeal to no outside moment to put its stamp upon them or make them continuous with the rest of nature. Themselves it is rather who seem to make nature continuous; and in their strange and intense function of granting consent to one possibility and withholding it from another, to transform an equivocal and double future into an inalterable and simple past." [83]

Determinism argues the other way, and it gains strength by reconstructing events which seem to issue inevitably into known events. For example, Richard Pipes of Harvard University reports that nineteenth-century Russian history is viewed in the Soviet Union as preparation for the events of October 1917, and that as a consequence Soviet scholars greatly neglect conservatives, such as Karamzin. What Dr. Pipes stresses is that such figures offered in their time a live option in Russian history. Switches were thrown the other way, and the option was not exercised, but it *might have been.*

The career of Lenin was perhaps such a switch. Determinists argue that the "great man" only *seems* to influence history, but that he is really an epiphenomenon in a stream of events controlled by historical laws. But James and Whitehead would maintain that to the man himself his decisions seem real and that indeed they are. He decides to throw the switches, and when he does, history proceeds smoothly to its accomplished result.[84]

FREEDOM AND SELF-CAUSATION

Believing with James in the freedom of the individual to determine historical effects, Whitehead seeks to find that freedom in the process by which the individual constitutes himself. This process he calls its concrescence. As through evolution the organism rises in complication, say, from a mollusk to a man, its mentality expands to the various possibilities open to it. For Whitehead, these are the various eternal objects, the forms of definiteness in the world, which are proposed for it by its mentality. It must decide. But, as James indicates, one cannot be a bon vivant as well as a philosopher, a saint, and an African explorer. These are not all possible within the aesthetic limits of an integrated human being. There *are* limits, both psychological and physical: pure seeking cannot coexist with sordid exploitation; and one cannot usually write metaphysics on a wild game hunt. Accordingly, aesthetic decisions of compatibility must be made.

Whitehead also points out that changes in character cannot easily be effected at once. Acts which seem to do this are usually conditioned by a long series of rejections and selections.[85] James would also maintain that the creation of character is accomplished only gradually in rejections and selections, where the "will" chooses between rival motor ideas. Such decisions not only are made by the self, but also help to create it.

Whitehead points out that when such decisions are made, causal inputs, which might have figured in the emerging character, are cast aside into irrelevancy. To a young man deciding to be a philosopher, the gift of *Process and Reality* might be a significant causal input, to a playboy, an irrelevance. The ability to cast causal inputs into relevance or irrelevance is a measure of freedom.[86]

Another measure of freedom is the creation of novelty, although both James and Whitehead allow that novelty can also result from accident.[87] For Whitehead, novelty issues from the "intensity," or integration, of organic purpose seeking a result in the universe. The result may be either a future act or a future being. An example is an angry man who knocks his neighbor down. Whitehead says that the same kind of mathematical formalities which explain how a stone falls to a patch of ground also apply to the man, but that the man's action is *only* explainable if his individual satisfaction is also taken into account.[88] James draws the same distinction between the physical nature of a stone and human life, and makes the same connection between purpose and novelty. Our feelings, he says, must be taken as real facts in the universe, even if their appearance depends on molecular arrangements. He points out that scientists themselves, when they forget their positivistic theories, believe that purpose creates new things and helps to determine the future.[89]

But it can be argued that purposefulness as such does not fully indicate freedom. A man may intend to eat, but because he is hungry, he has no choice. Moreover, some causes cannot be rejected. Hunger is a cause (of eating), and only a saint can long withstand it; not even the saint can withstand the effects of gravity. Likewise, selection may also not fully indicate freedom. A hungry man, faced with a roast beef and a steak, will make a choice, but the choice seems somehow irrelevant.

For Whitehead, and often for James, freedom consists in absorbing causal inputs into the integration of a wider purpose. A hungry man can grab at a piece of meat, but he can also integrate eating or food into a wider pattern of life, his social affairs, business plans, and growing reputation. This is the freedom of the individual as it is created by the wider integration of his novel subjective purposes or ends. Simple causes, such as the pull of gravity or hunger, are not so much rejected, since this is often not possible, as taken up into the wider, novel integration.

For Whitehead, freedom emerges in the world with mentality; and mentality is the product of complex organic organization, at the apex of which is the conscious field. Thus, the laws of physics are "obeyed" at the molecular level, but each human being has a measure of freedom to integrate his molecules in the peculiar way that becomes his character. Freedom is the product of concrescence, which is in part its own cause; in other words, the actions of the organism cannot be explained without reference to conceptual novelties introduced by itself. At the highest level, these novelties are the concepts of self and the life plans of an individual.

JAMES AND FREE WILL

For James, his supreme philosophic insight was that his youthful assertions of free will were not really necessary; for freedom, the freedom to work real effects in the world, was already given in consciousness. This is his final doctrine of freedom. The complex composition which determines what a man will do and how he will feel is itself a unique creation in the world. "A 'principle' of free will," he wrote, "if there were one, would doubtless manifest itself in such phenomena, but I never saw, nor do I now see, what the principle could do except rehearse the phenomenon beforehand, or why it ever should be involved." [90] In the end, he thus looked to the facts of experience, and resisted the Kantian temptation of establishing an independent (a priori) principle.[91]

James had to defend free will against two sets of opponents, the scientific determinists and the rational monists. To the former, James said (1) that deterministic knowledge, even if metaphysically possible, was not immediately at hand, and (2) that the immediate experience of purposeful causality could not be discounted by more abstract explanations involving molecules and atoms. To the monists, who claimed that free will derogated from God's omnipotence, James posited a less than omnipotent God, if any (see Chapter V), and a world of partially free individuals. Pragmatically, he defended free will as the basis of moral responsibility, rejecting a "blocuniverse" in which everything is already preordained.

Today many scientists are content to explain what can be explained in energetic terms and to let lie the sleeping dogs of metaphysics. In addition, they are becoming increasingly sophisticated in describing mental functions, like memory and control, in physical terms, owing, in large part, to the development of cybernetics and computer science.

Psychologists, except a few remaining behaviorists,[92] generally affirm James's notion that actions can only be explained if experience subjective to the actor is taken into account. But it may be asked how much our later experience is conditioned by our genetic endowment and by our earlier experience. Freud, for example, established a second order of determinacy within the subjective experiences in the very area of "voluntary" action where James sought freedom. There are the oedipal complex, the effects of trauma, the stages of sexuality—the whole mechanism of the unconscious. The large remaining question is how extensively and how usefully Freud's scheme can be translated into James's theories of the creation of the self through time and of the training of the nervous system. The problem of the limits of freedom is thus still with us, the freedom of man to restructure his personality and his life.

THE ORGANISM IN CREATION

CONCRESCENCE

In the most general sense, the world of a moment ago is very similar to the world now. Descartes' doctrine of substance, by which identity is preserved from occasion to occasion, has an obvious appeal to common sense. The philosophy of organism, the doctrine which Whitehead proposes, is less obvious.

Whitehead's philosophy is primarily concerned with organisms, from electrons and atoms to human beings. It should be pointed out, however, that for Whitehead objects such as stones are technically nexus and *not* organisms. They may be capable of massive simplifications of their physical inputs, as are shock waves and average heat, but they are not capable of purpose. The agents for the science of mechanics are nexus; their relations are expressible in differential equations. However, the components of nexus are organisms, such as atoms, and so fall under Whitehead's organic analysis.

Now the doctrine of substance accounts very well for the continuity of real things from the immediate past to the present. They are what they are. Their movements are accidental, their subjective experiences, if any, are accidental. The substantial identity endures. But what the doctrine of substance cannot account for is that the *subjective* accidental experience *changes* an organic substance itself. In Whitehead's philosophy of organism, this is done by the "purpose" or "subjective aim." The great innovation of Whitehead's philosophy is that *in each* occasion of the organism's history, this aim emerges from its data, including its previous self, and guides the organism to what it finally becomes: "The philosophies of substance presuppose a subject which then encounters a datum, and then reacts to the datum. The philosophy of organism presupposes a datum which is met with feelings, and progressively attains the unity of a subject." [93]

In other words, the philosophy of substance stops with high-level sensory perception. The philosophy of organism is concerned with how the entire organism emerges from its immediate facts. There is no dead a priori hand laid on existence. The entire pluralistic structure of the world is utterly dependent on the moment. The greatness of Whitehead lies in his explanation of how the present absorbs all the past and, creating itself of that material, transmits itself into the future. Whitehead writes: "And the foundation of reverence is this perception, that the present holds within itself the complete sum of existence, backwards and forwards, that whole amplitude of time, which is eternity." [94]

SUBJECTIVE AND OBJECTIVE

The subjective experience of an organism has this quality, that to the extent the organism is unified its experience characterizes its entire being. In an animal, such a feeling can be 'hunger' or 'green'. Unification of the organism means that the experience itself is not divisible. One cannot chop 'green' in half by decapitating the man experiencing it. (A plant, however, has no such central experience.) The subjective experience is, according to Whitehead, defined by eternal ideas. These are the Platonic forms which participate in the individual occasions. 'Green' is such an eternal object, and eternal objects are also elements of purposes, or appetitions, such as 'hungry' and 'want to be a doctor'.

These are clearly subjective forms at the apex of an organism's unified experience. At the bottom are the many particles of energy, which, regarded as localized experiences or intensities, Whitehead also considers subjective forms. The philosophy of organism maintains, as does James, that in the animal body the behavior of these many particles of energy is in part influenced by the higher subjective forms, such as 'hungry' and 'want to be a doctor'.

Whitehead points out that if these influences are considered "epiphenomenal," then "the gap must be supplied by the introduction of arbitrary laws of nature regulating the relation of intensities." [95] What Whitehead objects to is the arbitrariness of the laws: He believes that the laws of nature (see Chapter V) are in fact the relations which real things, such as these intensities, or particles of energy, establish among themselves. There is nothing for Whitehead which is arbitrary about the "laws of psychology." But because each human being is unique, the patterns of interrelationship which his intensities, or particles of energy, exhibit are different from those of other human beings. The most individual such pattern might be the peculiar way a man 'wants to be a doctor', or what James would call his "total object of thought." And both James and Whitehead would go on to say that such patterns exercise a causal influence on the future behavior of the organism—the man becomes a doctor because he wants to be one; men of the Huxley and Clifford sort would call the pattern "epiphenomenal."

But private feelings in themselves do not explain for Whitehead how things function as data for each other, or, in other words, as *efficient* causes. In addition to the subjectivity of existence, there is transition, the flowing of data or energy into the organism from past time and distant space, and the passing on of data or energy from the organism to existences outside itself. Whitehead believes that the world in its function as a medium for these transitions has characterizations which are *not subjectively felt*. These characterizations are the *external* eternal objects, or, otherwise phrased, the Platonic mathematic forms.[96] They define the world as a physical fact. For example, the spatial relation between a light source and a man can be specifically characterized by eternal objects, including, for instance, the distance between them; also, the light itself can be given a specific wavelength.

Whitehead does not make clear why these objective matters of fact may not also characterize subjective experience. Thus 'square' and 'two feet long' *can* in fact be experienced. Moreover, there is nothing certain about the particular mathematical forms which may be thought to characterize a given situation.

For example, when three objects are held in the hand, they may be felt as three, but they may also be felt as two or one, as James points out. How they are felt depends on subjective factors.[97]

Thus the external eternal objects may be said to define experienceable factors in all fact, whether these factors are actually *experienced* or not. In any case, these form for Whitehead the spatiotemporal continuum (alternatively phrased, the "extensive continuum"), which is the expression of *all* physical relationships, including those within organic compositions.

Whitehead offers two grounds for giving to the spatio-temporal continuum this fundamental character: (1) Mathematical abstractions represent an ultimate ground of abstraction to which much experience can be reduced. Thus colors can be reduced to wavelengths; the visual field can be reduced to its complex geometrical relations. In particular, experiences in the mode of presentational immediacy (see Chapter II) can be so reduced, although in all cases the reduction means elimination, the exclusion of emotional tone, association, feelings of purpose, and so forth. In "real" experiences, as opposed to ideal ones, this exclusion, however, is never total. (2) Whitehead makes the more basic point that extension "is the first determination of order—that is, of real potentiality—arising out of the general character of the world." Or again: "It provides the general scheme of extensive perspective which is exhibited in all the mutual objectifications by which actual entities prehend each other." Accordingly, the "objective" character of mathematical forms is grounded for Whitehead on the ultimate character of extension.[98]

If external eternal objects are not subjective experiences, it might be asked *where* they are. If they are the matrix in which real things are related, as might seem to be indicated above, they would not only not be subjective experiences, they would not be dependent on things in any way. Accordingly, external eternal objects would be nowhere (except perhaps, somewhat improbably, in the mind of God), and so would violate Whitehead's principle of ontology. This principle says: "That every condition to which the process of becoming conforms in any particular instance, has its reason either in the character of some actual entity in the actual world of that concrescence *or* in the character of the subject which is in process of con-crescence." [99]

An interpretation of Whitehead which avoids these diffi-culties is that of Victor Lowe, who maintains that Whitehead's theory of space is completely relational. Despite some signs which appear to the contrary in *Process and Reality*, this in-terpretation seems most acceptable. Physical bodies, Professor Lowe says in his explanation, "are in space because they inter-act, and space is only the expression of certain properties of their interaction." [100] Such interactions are prehensions, or, in other words, the way various bodies contribute to the existence of other bodies within quantum requirements. The spatiotemporal continuum is the expression of how such con-tributions can occur.

As a prehension, the spatiotemporal continuum *is* an expe-rience of the organism so contributed to. Such experience, for Whitehead, is vectoral and is the most basic experience in the universe. If I am not misinterpreting Whitehead, the experience of the spatiotemporal continuum abstracted from the specific content of a prehension is what he means by a "strain." [101] In any case, human spatiotemporal experience, to the extent that it is conscious, does not occur at the level of individual prehensions.

Human spatial and temporal experiences are rather the final abstract precipitates of such real physical prehensions. From such abstract residues in the brain, man painfully constructs a final picture of the world, a Newtonian space or a more sophis-ticated spatiotemporal continuum. The connections, however remote, between his physical prehensions and his final, central experiences are usually mediately causal, and so enable man to construct schemes which make additional experience predicta-ble. Experiences may be, in Helmholtz's phrase, merely symbolic, but they are, as he said, delicately adjusted to reality. This is Whitehead's answer to Kant, why it was necessary for Whitehead neither to posit an independent physical matrix of space, which Kant denied, nor an a priori category of the mind, which he affirmed.

The differences between the objectivity, or externality, of *things* and their subjectivity, or internality, can be described in physical terms. According to Whitehead, the first represents their vectoral character, the second their scalar. In the "supplemental stage" with the incoming appetition in the concrescence of an organism, "the 'scalar' form overwhelms the original 'vector' form: the origins become subordinate to the individual experience. The vector form is not lost, but is submerged as the foundation of the scalar superstructure." [102] This is why human spatial experience, for example, is related only indirectly to the vectoral prehensions which originally incite it. Human spatial experience of the "external" world is thus a product of the "supplemental stage," an experience of the organism as a complex scalar.

However established, the eternal objects of the objective series concern the world as a field; the "morphological scheme" they define is geometrical and accordingly is divisible; it accounts for the relations of time and space, both relations "internal" to the organism, for instance *inside* an atom or the conscious field, and "external" to the organism, that is, relations involving how the *rest* of the world enters into its nature.[103] The scheme involves such ideas as whole and part, of overlap and disjunction, and of routes of abstraction by which geometrical elements are defined.

The details of the extensive continuum will not be discussed here. What is of concern is not the external relations of the organism, but its internal processes of self-formation, the concrescence in which the psychological values of existence emerge. The extensive continuum, which accounts for the transitions between past and present and between present and past, must be presupposed.[104]

SPACE, TIME, AND SOCIETIES

Organisms which are negligible in their extent of time and space are describable for the most part in terms of their causal inputs, the most important usually being their previous existences. The creative aspects of concrescence, however, demand an extensive organization in which to take place. Within this "breadth" of time and space, the organism can be its own cause; that is, it can achieve a certain local independence, by virtue of its unity, or integration, within its breadth, of the many separate causes pouring into it from its causal past. This is its "elbow-room within the Universe." Within this breadth, any cause, such as an incoming parcel of energy, is relevant only to its place in the integrated scheme of the entire organism.[105]

Whitehead maintains that the time in which concrescence occurs is the specious present. "Within this specious present the event realises itself as a totality, and also in so doing realises itself as grouping together a number of aspects of its own temporal parts." [106] Whitehead thus makes of the specious present a basic biological unit. He further reenforces this view by identifying the specious present with his concept of duration, the length of time required by "actual entities" to constitute themselves.[107] The implication is that the duration is repeated, that there is a swing from existence to existence in single units, or quanta, of this duration.

There seems little doubt that Whitehead's argument for an organic duration is based on an analogy from particle physics, with its vibratory description of the existence of matter. In *Modes of Thought*, Whitehead maintains that there is a profound difference between the "passive, instantaneous existence of bits of matter," postulated by Newton and Democritus, and the "agitations of experience" that are assumed by modern field theory. He goes on to say, "*Analogous* [italics mine] notions of activity, and of forms of transition, apply to human experience and to the human body." [108]

Whitehead finds a quantum of time necessary to define an organism, just as a quantum of time is necessary to define a particle: "In biology the concept of an organism cannot be expressed in terms of material distribution at an instant. The essence of an organism is that it is one thing which functions and is spread through space. Now functioning takes time. Thus a biological organism is a unity with a spatio-temporal extension which is of the essence of its being." [109] It may be pointed out, however, that the time which an organism takes to function depends on how much and what kind of functioning one wishes to consider. What unit do we use? Do we use the unit of the breathing cycle, "reaction time," the conception and implementation of short-range or long-range plans? What about the processes which take place below the level of centrality, such as protein synthesis, oxygen absorption by the red blood cells, and so on? Whitehead is clear that greater processes, with their respective times and spaces, enclose lesser ones, for example, becoming a doctor encloses taking a breath which, in turn, encloses the absorption of oxygen by a red blood cell. But this analysis indicates that no one quantum of time applies at every level throughout the organic world.

Both James and Whitehead affirm quanta of existence for another reason: to account for the passage of nature. If the present is a mathematical limit to zero, and it is the only real thing, how does existence acquire the duration which we know it has? In other words, if there is not some least extensive unit of time (and space, too), how does the race of life get run? This is the paradox of Zeno, who maintains that if the unit is infinitely divisible, the division may proceed indefinitely before the unit is exhausted. The quanta of particles may be such least durational units, but it would seem more likely that the organism could exhibit a steady front or wave crest of in-phase existence. Thus the organism could have statistical maintenance *derived* from its lower units, or particles; and its higher experiences, such as consciousness, could be without phase.

It will be recalled that James talks of "incessant pulses of voluntary reinforcement" in maintaining attention with effort. Such pulses, if indeed they occur, might be somehow related to a vibratory existence of the self. In his last work, he says that experience comes in quanta, and that the intellect only makes it continuous, although elsewhere he argues on the other side.[110]

In any case, an "actual entity," by repeating its character in succeeding durations, becomes an enduring object. Such an enduring object is, for example, an electron. Living things, however, change, and Whitehead indicates that they cannot be enduring objects in any strict sense, although his analysis of actual entities and enduring objects can be of use in understanding living things.

When an actual entity succeeds itself, it establishes a *line* of succession; such a line of entities showing more or less the same character is what Whitehead also calls a "society." In such a society, each member shares characteristics and contributes them to other members, that is, its successors. (Thus, an electronic occasion passes on its character to its immediate future selves.) These linear societies are what metaphysicians called "substances"; their changes are the traditional accidents.[111] This means that when Whitehead talks of an actual entity he does not mean an enduring object, but simply one thing through a single duration. Although rough analogies to human life are apparent, Whitehead's formal model, based as it is on atomic particles, is difficult to apply strictly.

PREHENSIONS

In his analysis of concrescence, Whitehead is concerned with how organisms achieve unity of feeling out of the multiplicity of their incoming data. The data as such are public, but when they are integrated into the organism, they are private. This privatizing of data Whitehead calls "prehension"; another name for it is "feeling"; still another is "objectification." [112] This feeling is always defined by eternal objects.

For example, a light in our eye is how we *feel* the light; it is our *prehension* of the light; the eternal object, such as green, has "ingression" into that occasion of feeling, that is, participation in the Platonic sense. Such feelings are positive prehensions; they can be as simple as the absorption of an electron or, in the case of a human being, the seeing of light as green.

A prehension is positive because the datum is itself transformed into the feeling, however mediately; when this does not occur in an organism enjoying an experience, Whitehead speaks of negative prehensions.[113] One type of negative prehension is a definite decision of exclusion. An example would be an artist's saying "No, not green!" In Whitehead's language, such a negative prehension "adds to the emotional complex, though not to the objective data." The more basic case would be an organism excluding a possibility of development on grounds of organic incompatibility. At the highest level, it would be James's example of a man who, realizing the incompatibility of being a bon vivant and a saint, rejects being a bon vivant. At the lowest level, it might be a "decision"—this is speculation—of an atom to emit (or exclude) a photon rather than to disintegrate.[114] Such negative prehensions are basically aesthetic adjustments in the concrescence of an organism.

Another type of negative prehension is the conception of an eternal object not realized in the datum. Thus a boy who says "I want to be a doctor" is rising above his datum as a boy, or, in other words, is entertaining an idea which negates his immediate reality. Another example might be the "mental phase" of a crystalline virus preceding its conversion into a living organism. A variety of such negative prehensions is the imagining of a red light or the thought 'not red' after seeing a green light. Negative prehensions which are conceptions not realized in the data are conceptual novelties. Such novelties form the basis of progress in the world, whether they originate in the conscious field or at lower phases of existence.

CONCEPTUAL NOVELTY AND SUBJECTIVE AIM

Organisms survive, as James pointed out, following Spencer and Darwin, because they can adapt to changing conditions. If they are too "specialized" for their environment, they perish when that environment becomes unstable. As organisms, men are "specialized" for a narrow range of temperature. But the range is larger than it might be owing to heating and cooling by various homeostatic mechanisms of the body; and also because, as human beings, we put on and take off clothes, heat or air-condition our buildings, and so forth. James viewed evolution as the adaptation effected by the introduction of novel ends or purposes. Whitehead's analysis is the same: the adaptation effected by the novel end, or negative prehension, is an aesthetic adjustment by the organism to the novelty of the environment. For Whitehead, "the primary meaning of 'life' is the origination of conceptual novelty—novelty of appetition." [115]

There is always the question: How does the aim or negative prehension arise? Whitehead points out that "a cell gives no evidence whatever of a single unified mentality, guided in each of its occasions by inheritance from its own past." And yet there is a "certain originality in the response of a cell to an external stimulus." This novelty Whitehead believes is "introduced conceptually and disturbs the inherited 'responsive' adjustment of subjective forms. It alters the 'values,' in the artist's sense of that term." [116] It is clearly not the inheritance which produces the guidance, but rather the complexity of the material cell which introduces the aim: *this is the origin of life in each moment* from its inert materials. The life that emerges, with its novel direction or aim, is that immediately relevant to the changed conditions of the inert physical particles: while it guides their organization, it reflects their interaction. The soul, being a substance, cannot explain how novel aims are introduced which change its basic character. Its very stability would rule out such an explanation: It is static, unimaginative, a dead hand from the past.[117]

Life is another word for innovative mentality, the mentality of organisms; another term Whitehead uses is the presiding, or central, occasion. Whitehead says that although "mentality is non-spatial, mentality is always a reaction from, and integration with, physical experience which is spatial." In a sense, it has a focus, but the ambiguity which infects its location is the same as that for an electron: is it where it is focused or is it throughout the entire energetic field? Thus for Whitehead, life has no particular location; it is merely where the inorganic experiences focus which elicit it into being. "Life lurks in the interstices of each living cell, and in the interstices of the brain . . . [I]ts more vivid manifestations wander to whatever quarter is receiving from the animal body an enormous variety of physical experience." [118] The nervous system can be seen as a way of producing this variety of physical experiences requisite to the growth of the "subjective aim" or mentality.

Consider a cell. At the lowest levels, it is compatible with Whitehead's scheme that its reactions are explainable as the way its molecules or particles, put in certain positions and given certain inputs, adjust to each other. Such adjustments, however, are for Whitehead only explainable as qualitative adjustments of eternal ideas of the vectoral and scalar intensities involved. The question arises: Does the central occasion in man represent the aesthetic synthesis of these ideas? Such a description might mean that so-called simple eternal objects of the central occasion, such as 'green', or more complicated subjective aims, such as 'want to be a doctor', are actually complex integrations of eternal objects characterizing the experience of the cells. In higher organisms, however, as Whitehead points out, the central experience does not sum up the experiences of its components, that is, the cells and, even further down, the molecules; the cells contribute to the central experience in only a very special way, that is, as impulses of the nerves. In that way, the central experience is only the highest abstraction of the experience of the entire body. (This process of abstraction as it functions in perception is what Whitehead calls "transmutation." [119]) According to this view, the qualitative adjustment of the eternal ideas of the abstract elements (impulses) contributed by the cells, as mediated and reenacted by the nerves and the brain, and of the eternal ideas of the impulses generated by the brain without direct relation to the rest of the body is what produces the body's purpose and subjective aim, to the extent that these are centrally controlled.

The power of man's presiding occasion to control his organism is clearly limited. At the lowest level, there are the inorganic compounds, and next, the millions of cells, all of which maintain their quasi-independence. And there are whole organs, such as the heart, and systems, such as the digestion, which go on functioning more or less "on their own." But control is achieved in part. The nervous system which produces the physical experience for the growth of subjective aims also provides the mechanisms for this control. And through this control the presiding occasion stamps on man's organism its distinctive "character." [120]

THE ORIGINS OF CONCEPTUAL AIMS

Two interrelated questions naturally arise: What are the origins of the novel conceptual aims? And what is the process by which these aims impose their character on the organism? In the answer to these questions lies the answer to the question of whether or not there is freedom and how it operates. In exploring this problem, Whitehead goes deeper than James: James is concerned only with voluntary, conscious means of supporting freedom; Whitehead seeks the grounds of all freedom, conscious and unconscious. In Whitehead's analysis, James's will becomes simply an aspect of subjective aims in their highest phase of intellectuality.

Whitehead seeks the origins of freedom in the process by which an organism constitutes itself, that is, its concrescence. The first stage of this process is that of mere reception. The data flow in, including the data of the preceding occasion of that organism. This process is the world being received as an efficient cause: the data are felt as many feelings and alien. In the second stage, the final cause, or subjective aim, gradually emerges "shaped in the process itself"; it is this subjective aim, or private ideal, which transforms the many alien data into a final unified subjective experience. The subjective aim Whitehead also calls "appetition" and, at the highest levels, "vision."

If the vision exceeds the data, it may be asked from where else it comes. Whitehead gives two answers. The first emphasizes the individual responsibility of the organism for its own measure of creativity; the second indicates that the creativity is God's valuation of the organism as a result of his immanence in its subjective aim.

In the first answer, Whitehead stresses that the aim results from the coalescing of the conjoint feelings of the organism itself into a unified view: "Emotional feeling is still subject to [Whitehead's] third metaphysical principle, that to be 'something' is 'to have the potentiality for acquiring real unity with other entities.' " [121] The novel aim simply emerges from the interaction of feelings. James wavers on this point. When arguing against the associationists, he states that ideas cannot be combined, only things. But usually, agreeing with Whitehead, he tends to go the other way: "We say . . . a higher state *is* not a lot of lower states; it is itself. When, however, a lot of lower states have come together, or when certain brain-conditions occur together which, *if they occurred separately, would produce* a lot of lower states, we have not for a moment pretended that a higher state may not emerge. In fact it does emerge under those conditions." [122] Such a higher state would be the subjective aim. The word "state" here bridges the gap, because it is a mental fact reflecting a physical reality.

With Whitehead, James emphasizes the relevance of the aim to the data of the organism. For him, a relevant aim is a "live option" or a "live possibility." To be realized, James maintains that the option must not only have an agent or champion, but also that there must be "complementary conditions." [123] This suggests that some aims, because they arise, may in some way be relevant to the aimer but not be practicable or relevant to the larger world. Thus a solitary madman may aim at universal peace, but be unable to effect it. Novelty of subjective aim is a measure of freedom; it is also a producer of frustration.

In his second answer, Whitehead emphasizes God's role. Here, the aim, instead of emerging from an integration of feeling, comes first and guides the organic constitution from the outset. The aim *can* come first because it represents God's initial judgment of the total datum. "Thus an originality in the temporal world is conditioned, though not determined, by an initial subjective aim supplied by the ground of all order and of all originality." [124] James also swings between a higher state emergent from lower feelings and ideals which come from an "unseen or mystical" world. He writes:

"The further limits of our being plunge . . . into an altogether other dimension of existence from the sensible and merely "understandable" world . . . So far as our ideal impulses originate in this region (and most of them do originate in it, for we find them possessing us in a way for which we cannot articulately account), we belong to it in a more intimate sense than that in which we belong to the visible world, for we belong in the most intimate sense wherever our ideals belong. Yet the unseen region in question is not merely ideal, for it produces effects in this world." [125]

The unseen world would here correspond to Whitehead's primordial nature of God.

For Whitehead, God's primordial nature is a graduated order of appetitions (see Chapters IV and V). All eternal objects are included in this structured order of God's nature, which forms the basis of all potentiality in the world. Whitehead asks: How can novelty enter the world if it is not already somewhere? Accordingly, the "proximate relevance" of eternal objects to a given concrescence, that is, what the organism might become, "means relevance as in the primordial mind of God." [126]

The freedom which Whitehead seems to find is the freedom of Plato [127] and the scholastics. It is the freedom, conditioned only by the limits of understanding, to be the Good, the freedom to obey God and merge with His nature. "In this sense," Whitehead writes, "the captive can be free, taking as his own the supreme insight, the indwelling persuasion towards the harmony which is the height of existence." [128]

Let me here ask some pragmatic questions. What does the doctrine explain? How can one set of eternal objects, or appetitions, be known as more relevant to an emerging organism than another? Who can know the mind of God?

Whitehead seeks answers from several sources. God, he finds, works in definite ways. He seeks intensity of experience; He seeks beauty.[129] He is persuasive, for despite the tendency of the world to unwind into chaos, it does not; and organic evolution and human civilization achieve still greater complexities or intensities of experience.[130] James also notes this "upward thrust":

"The result of life, however, is to fill the world more and more with things displaying *organic unity*. By this is meant any arrangement of which one part helps to keep the other parts in existence. Some organic unities are material,—a sea-urchin, for example, a department store, a civil service, or an ecclesiastical organization. Some are mental, as a "science," a code of laws, or an educational programme." [131]

Whitehead would assign to some such effects a theological cause, although it is not immediately clear why, or how he would distinguish which effects are godlike and which are not. The problem is that God would appear not to be the warranty for the effects, but the effects the warranty for God. What moves Whitehead, what commands his respect, what elicits his participation he holds to be godlike. In this sense, he believes with James that man helps God in his unfinished work of creation.

But Whitehead maintains that man can intuitively discern what is godlike. He holds that in direct experience we can have some grasp of what is suitable for occasions, including ourselves, and that such grasp represents insight into the divine nature, and hence, how it is relevant to those occasions.[132] James, as has been noted, also believes in direct intuition of ideas emanating from a mystical world. The source of such ideas, according to Freud, might better be sought elsewhere. He would disagree with James, and probably Whitehead, by attributing our "ideals" to our identification with our parent figures (or society) in the superego, rather than to our communication with divinity.[133]

Whitehead's ultimate argument for God's persuasive power, like Plato's, is thus the intuition which artists know as art, and moralists know as right, and workmen know as effective, and statesmen know as just, and organisms know, or feel, as healthy—the basic, unjustified assumptions of life. All men seek the Good, Plato says, and all men choose it, if they know what it is; for when they find it, it is utterly persuasive.

To put these ideas to work, consider a painting by, say, the American Mark Rothko. Whitehead may be interpreted as saying that the idea of the painting was a potentiality before it became a conception in Rothko's mind. As a potentiality, it was part of God's primordial nature. But every potentiality waits for its time and place and mode of concretion, in this case a moment in the life of Rothko. God's judgment of the occasion of Rothko's existence helps shape the idea of the painting—Rothko's "inspiration" would thus be the conceptual judgment of God who is immanent in Rothko.

Now suppose Rothko has just completed a painting with a large red area surmounted by a large blue one; and before beginning a new painting, he watches a twilight sky and hears some bad news. His next potential painting is, say, virtually the same as the last one, but more somber, using more purple. Whitehead would analyze the similarity in two ways: (1) the two paintings have similar but not identical patterns of eternal objects—this is a logical analysis without reference to process; and (2) the "potential" painting is a possible option for the painter, and needs but a few new factors in order to emerge. Such factors could be the twilight and the bad news. But these would not have to be directly reflected in the painting, because, at the moment of conception, the painter has his freedom to make just one, total, integrated, aesthetic decision, discarding causal influences which are not compatible with an emerging conception of the painting. The subjective aim, so considered, is a decision among alternatives. Moreover, the new elements, or complex eternal objects, must be fitted into a composition of ideas which creates depth of contrast, just as the last painting, with *its* elements, did. Thus Rothko uses the twilight, but does not *particularly* use his supper. What Rothko is totally at that moment, his immediately past thoughts, the state of his body, his physical surroundings, his personal life, the prevalent mode of civilized life, the entire physical world, all these go into the painting, but under selection and adjustment.

AESTHETICS IN PROCESS

The other question I raised about novel conceptual aims was: What is the process by which the aims, or ideals, impose their character on the organism? In other words, how do the aims guide the process of organic formation? One way Whitehead analyzes this process, suggested above, is aesthetic. Whereas in the *Symposium,* Plato ends with a beauty independent of process, Whitehead believes that beauty which is not realized in process is "deficiently actual." Because there are unrealized beauties in God's nature, God needs the world to give Him plenary being, and, specifically, He needs the individual occasions of the world in which His beauties can be actualized. Conversely, this means, for both James and Whitehead, that there are "special" truths and beauties which are relevant only to those actual occasions·which alone are the realities. Anything which leaves the ground of these actual occasions is, to that extent, less real. Metaphysics, for instance, loses in *real* particulars what it gains in scope. This view is at the heart of empiricism. For Whitehead, things are beautiful by gift of metaphor in the Aristotelian sense, that is, by *sharing the ideas* of the source of all beauty. But things are beautiful in themselves, as they *are* the beauties which they display—they are not deficiently real, a mere stage for beautiful ideas, as Plato holds—they are the very play itself.

Beyond beauty, which Whitehead uses as a synonym for the Good, there is no appeal, for "the teleology of the Universe is·directed to the production of Beauty." [134] It seems clear that Whitehead's thinking is based on the beauty of organic integration and that all other forms of beauty derive from this. There is something approaching an absolute standard here which looks not to relative "standards of taste" but to the organization of the material.

Whitehead believes that what the universe is directed toward is "balanced complexity." "Here 'complexity' means the realization of contrasts, of contrasts of contrasts, and so on; and 'balance' means the absence of attenuations due to the elimination of contrasts which some elements in the pattern would introduce and other elements inhibit." [135] Whitehead might render an explanation as follows:[136] Take the simplest case, that of an electron. An electron is a physical fact; it also has an eternal object as its private or subjective form of definiteness. This eternal object is an abstract possibility, as well as a realized form, and thus *contrasts* with the physical fact. Whitehead says that a value is given to the contrast, which determines whether and how the electron will endure in its present form in the future.[137] With the electron the emphasis is on "balanced" rather than on "complexity," and balanced here probably means unitary and not incompatible.

Put the electron in a larger context. According to Whitehead, a thing is a product of the inputs of the entire universe at that thing's standpoint. The environment so considered may prove hostile to the electron's continued existence; the inputs may give rise to a contrast between eternal objects and the real physical fact which issues in a feeling for destruction —in this case, the electron will break up. Here "balance" is not possible, because complexity is not realizable.[138]

A larger organized complex, a virus, for example, also originates eternal objects. In the crystalline form of the virus, these objects will be more or less the same as those it had on a previous occasion of its existence. But the virus may also originate new eternal objects, or, in other words, negative prehensions; it is not just the new physical inputs which determine that the eternal objects will arise (although they may be the stimulus for their coming), but the aim of the universe toward intensity of experience. These eternal objects, or negative prehensions, will give rise to physical changes productive of richer contrasts, that is, more intense experience, than the virus entertained before. Such experience is characteristic of life, as opposed to crystalline structure. The result of further novelties of conceptual experience originated by life will be new changes in the physical existence of the virus, productive of still new adaptations in the *succeeding* occasions of the virus's existence. The eternal objects, or negative prehensions, are thus anticipations of the future; they are urges, or appetitions, with their characteristic hold on physical reality. In this case, "balanced complexity" *is* possible, and is productive of greater richness of experience.

Whitehead's theory of meaningful contrasts provides the link between beauty and intensity of experience. The aim of the universe is beauty; the form is meaningful contrasts. But all things do not go together: some clash rather than contrast; some explode, break, fritter away as a result of their relations to other things. The means of rescuing beauty, or meaningful contrast, from the danger of incompatibility are various. Through negative prehensions, the organism can dismiss, ignore, or repress elements which would destroy desirable effects. Another way is to accept clashes, such as pain or horror, as the price for higher experience. Still another is to adjust magnitudes of intensity, for example, lifting into the foreground or shoving into the background. All these methods can take place at the lowest levels. The crystalline virus, for example, becomes part of the energy transfer system of a bacterium. The changes in the "internal constitution" of the virus necessary to effect the accommodation are aesthetic in the sense used here.

In the higher organisms, the methods to obtain meaningful contrast are characteristics of "appearance," or, in other words, the "field of consciousness." For Whitehead, aesthetics is allied to purpose: "The danger of a street-crossing is for the pedestrian a regulative factor in the aesthetic values of the apparent scene. The concept of completely passive contemplation in abstraction from action and purpose is a fallacious extreme." [139] The processes of adjustment of the conscious field are thus dictated by interest, or the "subjective aim," which emerges out of the life experience. Through the conscious field, interest creates its effects, subtly altering the organism, imposing its character and ordering its actions. This is to return full circle to the position of James.

Whitehead's analysis of art parallels his discussion of consciousness. In consciousness, the highest feelings come not in conformity to physical fact but in novelty, novelty of imagination and aim. In art, the summit is reached in "discovery." This is the "final stretch of beauty" whereby "appearance summons up new resources of feeling from the depths of Reality." The aim of art is twofold. First, Whitehead says, we cannot wait indefinitely for reality; therefore, some beauty, however insubstantial, must come now: "Art neglects the safety of the future for the gain of the present. In so doing it is apt to render its Beauty thin. But after all, there must be some immediate harvest. The good of the Universe cannot lie in indefinite postponement." But in "summoning up new resources of feeling," art also helps create in real fact the beauty which it envisions. Whitehead says, "It requires Art to evoke into consciousness the finite perfections which lie ready for human achievement." [140]

This aesthetic analysis offers us a description, if not an explanation, of how the process of concrescence proceeds. James, though he devotes little time to aesthetics, presents an analysis startlingly close to that of Whitehead.

For James, there is something sui generis about aesthetic judgments: "The aesthetic principles are at bottom such axioms as that a note sounds good with its third and fifth, or that potatoes need salt." Like Whitehead and Plato, James regards morality and aesthetics as basically similar; neither can be explained away entirely as habit or social convention. Something more basic is clearly involved: "The *moral* principles which our mental structure engenders are quite as little explicable *in toto* by habitual experiences having bred inner cohesions." What then determines an unhabitual moral or aesthetic decision? James's answer is the theory of internal relations among ideas, of novelty rising out of the data: it is the theory of organism. "The forces which conspire to this resultant are subtle harmonies and discords between the elementary ideas which form the data of the case." [141] This same explanation of aesthetics and purpose is the heart of Whitehead's scheme.

PROPOSITIONS IN PROCESS

Whitehead offers another explanation, or description, of concrescence—his theory of propositional feelings. This is Whitehead at his best, seeking in the most general aspects of the universe the foundation of mental operations which have conventionally been relegated to specialists.

For Whitehead, "propositional feelings" are internal processes in the constitution of all organisms; only secondarily, as "propositions," are they formal statements of philosophy, and so material for logicians. A propositional feeling is a proposition being felt and so a real occasion in the existence of an organism; a proposition, as a formal statement, is thus an abstraction from occasions of experience. An example is 'Socrates is a man'. According to logicians, the essential thing about a proposition is whether it is right or wrong. Whitehead disagrees. Many propositions are merely entertained, such as 'To be or not to be . . .'; and their rightness or wrongness is consequently irrelevant. Moreover, judgment is a function of only the highest organisms, possibly only of man, whereas, Whitehead maintains, propositional feelings are felt by all organisms.

A propositional feeling is what Whitehead calls a "lure for feeling." It is a conceptual form proposing ideas which beckon the organism toward their realization in feeling, action, or reorganization.[142]

In his analysis of the way propositions are involved in process, Whitehead divides propositional feelings into two groups, conformal and nonconformal, true and false. A conformal propositional feeling would be the feeling of hunger in the propositional form—'I (a particular organism) am hungry (an eternal object)'. A nonconformal propositional feeling would be an appetition in the propositional form—'If I (a particular organism) could be full (eternal object)'. The "subject" is the organism and the "predicate" is the eternal object; the subject is "determinate," but the predicate is "potential"; the subject is a positive prehension, the predicate is a negative prehension. The proposition 'If I could be full' is a lure for feeling, and when it is fully felt, it is "realized."[143]

In a conformal propositional feeling, the eternal objects conform to the physical facts. But this "conformity" is really an aesthetic product, the result of the integration of feelings, which, Whitehead says, guides the process of its realization into full physical fact, that is, the completed physical organism.[144] In the successive durations of an enduring object, there is thus a swing between conception and realization, a swing which can become a mere repetitive vibration, as in the case of an electron. A failure to achieve integration can, as already indicated, lead to destruction. This can be the result of new physical inputs, which cannot be assimilated into harmony. But new facts can simply result in altered conformal propositions. Such would be the case in "stable" but changed atoms or crystalline viruses.

A nonconformal proposition introduces eternal objects which do not conform to the physical facts, or, in other words, negative prehensions. This is the introduction of novelty of conceptual aim. When such a proposition is "admitted into feeling," new things issue into the world. An example of this process would be the transition from crystalline virus to living organism.

At the highest level, novelty of conceptual aim, or negative prehension, takes the form of imagination. The experience of imagination is, for Whitehead, the contrast felt between what ideas actually conform to the physical facts and what ideas are imagined for those facts. An example would be a hungry man being aware of both his real hunger and his possible eating.[145] Another example would be Browning's "Home-Thoughts, From Abroad," which begins "Oh, to be in England / Now that April's there." Still another would be the wish to be a doctor or to establish international peace.

The supreme value of nonconformal propositions in promoting novelty in the world points up the limitations of the traditional view of propositions: "The conception of propositions as merely material for judgments is fatal to any understanding of their role in the universe. In that purely logical aspect, a non-conformal proposition is merely wrong, and therefore worse than useless. But in their primary role, they pave the way along which the world advances into novelty." [146]

CONSCIOUSNESS IN PROCESS

Imagination forms a limited case of what Whitehead calls "consciousness." For Whitehead, consciousness is an awareness of the contrast between the eternal objects exhibited by the physical facts and whatever eternal objects are in a proposition about those facts. In Whitehead's language, it is "the subjective form involved in feeling the contrast between the 'theory' which *may* be erroneous and the fact which is given.' " [147]

Consciousness thus includes three types of situations: The first is exemplified by the proposition 'This ball *is* red.' Here there is an awareness of the conformity between the physical feeling of the ball and the proposition about it, that is, between an eternal object, in its "abstract capacity," and an actual fact. The second type is illustrated by the proposition 'This ball is not red.' Here there is an awareness of the lack of conformity between the physical feeling of the ball and the proposition about it. Finally, there is the type of consciousness which is imagination, represented by the proposition 'This red ball might be blue.' Whether there is conformity, negation, or difference, what is vital for consciousness, according to Whitehead, is that the contrast between the eternal objects exhibited by the physical facts and those in the proposition be felt.

It should also be pointed out that all three types involve the existence of a nonconformal proposition, that is, one containing a negative prehension. Cases of consciousness involving imagination and negative perception clearly contain nonconformal propositions. The dubious type of case might seem to be that involving conformity, as represented by the proposition 'This ball *is* red.' But even here there is a ghost of nonconformity, for in order for consciousness to occur there must be the realization that the red might be something else; there must be a felt contrast between the red as one among many possible colors, thus suggesting a difference, and just that red as felt in the ball.

The contrast can be felt between physical facts and a proposition, as above, or it can be felt between a conception and a proposition about it. The latter, conceptual consciousness, can be illustrated by the propositions 'It *is* number 2 (and no other)', 'It is not number 2', and, finally, 'It is number 2, but it could be number 3'.

Consciousness implies some way attention can take up its contrasted terms in succession, and yet together, and also some way that the terms to be contrasted can be held. This would be possible if the terms were held and contrasted in the specious present, or in what James also calls the primary memory. In the case of consciousness illustrated by the proposition 'This ball *is* red', both the perception of the ball and the concept of red relating to it would be held and contrasted in the primary memory. (It is possible that distant memory might be involved in the available concept of red, though Whitehead maintains, in opposition to sensationalist doctrine, that such a concept *can* arise as a novelty in the mind without either memory or immediate perceptual experience.[148]) In any case, Whitehead says, "Whenever there is consciousness there is some element of recollection." [149]

Whitehead also holds that consciousness is a primitive form of judgment.[150] This is so, in his view, because consciousness implies a judgment about the conformity of a proposition to a fact or a concept. "A judgment," Whitehead says, "is the critique of a lure for feeling." [151] As such, it can influence the effect of the proposition on future feeling or action. James's concept of judgment is generally the same as Whitehead's. For James, to judge something is to decide whether or not to keep it in the conscious field, that is, whether to allow it to be a lure for feeling or action. James, however, maintains that the conformity to perceptual fact may not be the criterion of judgment. We may judge something true because we believe the Lord says it is true, or because for one reason or another we feel it would be better if it were that way (see Chapter IV).

Unlike Whitehead, James does not provide a specific definition of consciousness. Consciousness, he says, connotes "a kind of external relation, and does not denote a special stuff or way of being." [152] The relation is to previous experiences, but how this relation functions to give conscious matter its peculiar quality, James does not definitely say. He does offer several useful hints.

For example, he maintains that naming what is in the field assuredly makes it conscious.[153] Naming would also involve consciousness for Whitehead, because using language would mean the realization of eternal objects in their "abstract capacity." But neither Whitehead nor James suggests that naming is the sole method of projecting feelings into consciousness. What words do seem to accomplish is to relate the eternal objects to systems of thought more easily than do associations of sensory states. Thus the word "gray" relates the impression immediately to other colors. Indeed, for James (see Chapter IV), one of the major functions of abstract systems, such as language, is to effect such relations.

James also finds that consciousness arises through the difference between the anticipated result of an action and what actually occurs. Awareness is the result of frustration. James here characteristically emphasizes action: "In every hindrance of desire the sense of an ideal presence which is absent in fact . . . is even more notoriously there." [154] Here frustration is the agent of conscious contrast.

Awareness would seem for Whitehead to be a necessary but perhaps not a sufficient condition for consciousness. Those things of which we are aware reside in the primary memory. There they are in a position to form one side of a contrast, the other being "thoughts-about" them, in James's phrase,[155] or, in Whitehead's, eternal objects.

James says that we are aware of things of which we have preperceptual images. In Whitehead's terms, such awareness would entail the conformity or contrast between the ideality of the preperceptual image and the physical experience. However, if the preperceptual image were not grasped in its "abstract capacity" or the conformity or contrast between it and the physical experience were not felt, Whitehead would hold that consciousness need not arise.

James says we are also aware of those things which give rise to strong sensations. These also reside in the primary memory, and could thus be contrasted with a concept of them in an abstract capacity or with associated experiences, such as 'not bright'. Again, in Whitehead's view, such contrasts need not be felt.

In any case, consciousness of the Whiteheadian type requires that one part of the relation wait for the other; it implies a key role for anticipation or memory. As felt comparison, it is essentially more restrictive than that of James. For James, what is conscious seems to be everything in the conscious field, attended objects as well as their unattended fringes and field. It is also the transitive elements of thought, and the deeper schemes which structure the field. Whitehead refers to such elements simply as ideas or conceptions at levels below consciousness. The terminology of both James and Whitehead on these matters is often loose.

For both, the structure of ideas, conscious or unconscious, which forms the "interest-perspective" is the agency of subjective aims at the highest level (see Chapter II). For Whitehead, it is the supreme manifestation of concrescence, emerging out of the process and guiding it to its final achievement, or "satisfaction." The organism is then completed and ready to begin again. As a realized fact, the organism will then act as an efficient cause in the world, both for its future self and for other things.

IV Concepts and Conceptual Operations

THE NOMINALISM OF JAMES

If ideas are to have agency in process, they must be implicated in process in a suitable way. Conversely, they must be the kind of things which can produce the effects they produce. These considerations are crucial for James and Whitehead. Any ultimate appreciation of their philosophies must be grounded on an understanding of their theories of ideas.

IDEAS FROM PERCEPTS

James purports, inconsistently with his views at other times, to find the origin of all ideas in percepts. He writes: "All conceptual content is borrowed: to know what the concept 'color' means you must have *seen* red or blue, or green . . . You can create new concepts out of old elements, but the elements must have been perceptually given." [1] He explains that concepts achieve their "universal" quality because we attach that quality to them; we give them an "intention" to refer to a class of objects, a particular "psychic fringe." Such a case is 'man' for men, or 'white' for white objects. [2]

The fixity of ideas is equally a matter of convention. We attribute a constant meaning to concepts like 'triangle', 'genera', 'red', 'left', and so on, to achieve ease in handling the perceptual flux. [3] In reality, ideas and even sensations are never the same twice (see Chapter I); they are different by being in different brain states and by being part of a new and total "object of thought."

163

"We think the thing now in one context, now in another; now in a definite image, now in a symbol. Sometimes our sense of its identity pertains to the mere fringe, sometimes it involves the nucleus, of our thought. We never can break the thought asunder and tell just which one of its bits is the part that lets us know which subject is referred to." [4]

One way of achieving *some* fixity is by abstraction, that is, by disassociating concepts from the different contexts in which they appear, and by making of them objects of abstract contemplation.[5] But again only limited success can be claimed; the fringe of relations which occurs because the concept appears in a particular state of mind can never be totally dissipated. With the enormous prestige given ideas in the Platonic and Aristotelian tradition, there is every incentive to having them as permanent fixtures in one's philosophy; and yet, for James, they were very hard to fix.[6]

JAMES'S CRITIQUE OF THE RATIONALIST THEORY OF IDEAS

The very effort which concepts require—their abstraction, their artificial fixity—makes them suspect. Strongly influenced by Bergson, James denied that ideas, as traditionally conceived by the rationalists, could say very much about process,[7] although the implication of ideas for process is precisely what he was concerned with. In despair, he maintained that "the relations between conceptual objects as such are only the static ones of bare comparison, as difference or sameness, congruity or contradiction, inclusion or exclusion. Nothing *happens* in the realm of concepts; relations there are 'eternal' only." [8]

What was at the base of James's objections was the substance-accident mode of thought. This held that the things, being static, had changeless definitions, which themselves seemed to deny change. The ideas, being discrete and fixed, seemed inappropriate for describing moving and continuous process.

"What makes you call real life confusion is that it presents, as if they were dissolved in one another, a lot of differents which conception breaks life's flow by keeping apart . . . Even so it is with all our experiences. Their changes are not complete annihilations followed by complete creations of something absolutely novel. There is partial decay and partial growth, and all the while a nucleus of relative constancy from which what decays drops off, and which takes into itself whatever is grafted on, until at length something wholly different has taken its place . . . Without being one throughout, such a universe is continuous. Its members interdigitate with their next neighbors in manifold directions, and there are no clean cuts between them anywhere." [9]

James's criticism of the rationalists' analysis of conception is systematic. He finds it unable to explain not only change, but causation, knowledge, and personal identity as well. For the rationalists:

(1) Causation is inexplicable because it can only be understood with concepts, and concepts, being "timeless," cannot be directly implicated in process; as tools of analysis, they can only be juxtaposed and compared in the style of Hume and Kant.

(2) Knowledge is inexplicable: because the knower and the known are different substances, they can never get into each other.

(3) Personal identity cannot be explained, because " 'ideas' and 'states of mind' are discrete concepts, and a series of them in time means a plurality of disconnected terms." The soul or ego is "but another discrete concept."

(4) Finally, motion and change are also beyond the pale of explication. As James explains, these are continuous phenomena, but a continuum is precisely the kind of thing which concepts cannot handle. Calculus can, for example, only break a continuum up into discrete units or stopping points. [10]

So conceived, ideas do violence to reality. Indeed, after a

long emotional stretch of writing, James is ready to give up "logic" altogether:

"For my own part, I have finally found myself compelled to *give up the logic,* fairly, squarely, and irrevocably. It has an imperishable use in human life, but that use is not to make us theoretically acquainted with the essential nature of reality . . . Reality, life, experience, concreteness, immediacy, use what word you will, exceeds our logic, overflows and surrounds it." [11]

To James, this kind of logic deprives nature of all that seems vital and interesting—of purpose, sensibility, and beauty. James's rejection of this kind of thinking is at the root of his distaste for science.[12]

James's reaction is in part to a caricature of science and rationalism which he built up himself under the stress of polemics. (It betrays a certain uneasiness with the rigidity of forms which haunts the late nineteenth century, and is most noticeable in impressionism and art nouveau.) "Another type of reaction," Whitehead writes, "is to assume, often tacitly, that if there can be any intellectual analysis it must proceed according to some one discarded dogmatic method, and thence to deduce that intellect is intrinsically tied to erroneous fiction. This type is illustrated by the anti-intellectualism of Nietzsche and Bergson, and tinges American Pragmatism." [13]

THE PRAGMATIC CONCEPT OF TRUTH

James's doctrine of pragmatism is largely concerned with epistemological questions which, in his view, rationalism could not answer. The most salient aspect is James's concept of truth, and, in his later years, James spent much of the time remaining to him futilely debating this question with his rationalist opponents. What impresses one about them is what a self-righteous crowd they were, constantly beating their chests about "Truth," like wooers of a maiden each outdoing the other in shows of devotion.

Briefly, James's concept of truth uses Occam's razor to cut away excessive rationalist terms. The rationalists saw three terms involved in knowledge: "the reality, the knowing, and the truth." [14] Thus, there would be a red book, or reality; the truth that the book is red; and finally the apprehension of this truth, or knowing. James asks, "What is 'the truth' *known as*—is it not the knowing of the reality?" Given this analysis, truth, like consciousness, drops out as an "entity," and reappears as a "function," or "process." Truth characterizes experiences, not objects. The truth of a previously held idea is the *process* of its verification. "The truth of an idea is not a stagnant property inherent in it. Truth *happens* to an idea. It *becomes* true, is *made* true by events. Its verity *is* in fact an event, a process: the process namely of its verifying itself, its veri-*fication*. Its validity is the process of its valid-*ation*." [15]

Whitehead's theoretical rendering of James's process of verification is this: a contrast between the pattern of eternal objects exhibited by a particular physical fact in immediate experience (the feeling of this something being red) and the pattern of eternal objects referring to that physical fact in a proposition ('This is red'). The result is affirmation or negation in the form 'It is true, or it is false, that *this* is red'.[16]

Take another example, that of a man in a drunken fit who thinks he sees a rat, what he takes to be a "causally efficacious" rat. 'There is a rat', he says, by which he means that he expects physical experience to corroborate this proposition, based, as it is, on his image. But when he reaches out his hand, the expected physical experiences do not come. Slightly sobered, he concludes he has made a mistake, his proposition 'There is a rat' was false.

True ideas for James are verifiable in this way. James also maintains that we can assume the truth of our ideas if we can assume that it can be verified at some future time. For example, I may have an idea of a gray stone there. I assume my idea is true, but after a while I check it, and I find that the gray stone *is* there just as I remember seeing it. In this way, "truth becomes a habit of certain of our ideas and beliefs in their intervals of rest from their verifying activities." [17]

A phenomenological interpretation cuts the three terms of the rationalists to one—pure experience—which then becomes the sole "reality." Verification is then simply the relations of one part of our experience to another: "Truth here is a relation, not of our ideas to non-human realities, but of conceptual parts of our experience to sensational parts. Those thoughts are true which guide us to *beneficial interaction* with sensible particulars as they occur." In this way, an idea, like 'Memorial Hall', leads to a sensory experience of the building. [18]

The rationalist notion of truth, as James defines it, ultimately depends on the idea of independent existences, or, in Whitehead's phrase, "simple location." Things are then true in themselves. The pragmatist position is ultimately relational. It says that "truth" is a relation of significance, that is, something is significant for us; otherwise it does not exist in our universe of discourse, or in our universe at all. It achieves this significance by entering into a relation with us—this is its verification.

STANDARDS OF TRUTH

James says that what we consider significant will be peculiar to our natures, dependent on our entire past, our particular constitutions, and so on. Not unexpectedly, James focuses on attention as a major differentiating factor: "Each thinker, however, has dominant habits of attention; and these *practically elect from among the various worlds some one to be for him the world of ultimate realities*." [19] For most men, this is the world of sense, but, as James pointed out, what we attend to must command our interest. To experience truth, which is

the act of knowing, we must put ourselves in practical relations with what is known. Our truths will depend on our
interests.

Another subjective element in truth, according to James,
is what we regard as objective evidence for it. There are so
many standards: sensory experience, revelation, public opinion,
organic coherence, common sense, the instincts of the heart,
and so forth. "No concrete test of what is really true has ever
been agreed upon," and, indeed, James points out, no philosophy has proved "objectively" convincing. Rather it finds
arguments for what the passions and mystical intuitions of its
proposers would have them believe. James also says that we
will believe what is in the line of our needs, and reject what is
not. To succeed, a philosophy "must not be one that essentially baffles and disappoints our dearest desires and most
cherished powers." [20]

TELEOLOGICAL IDEAS AND INSTRUMENTALISM

Both James and Whitehead, as nominalists, reject the idea
of independent essences which can be grasped, like Descartes'
"waxiness," only by the intelligence (*inspectio*). Rather than
essences, they hold that what is known about something is a
relation. Thus a man's perceptual knowledge of a tree is the
relation of the tree to the man.

For Whitehead, and I assume for James, the data which
the tree contributes to the man are the basis of the relation. But,
as James points out, different men drawing on similar data
can conceive of the tree under a variety of aspects which are
relational in character: a hot man will consider its shade; a
lumberer its cubic feet of timber; and so on. These are related
to their purposes, getting cool or selling wood. Accordingly,
James maintains that attributes are teleological; there is nothing *absolutely* essential about them; they are only *relatively*
essential to some purpose. On this basis, James lays down the
principle that *"the only meaning of essence is teleological,*

and that classification and conception are purely teleological weapons of the mind." [21] This is what he means by "instrumentalism."

James makes such "interested" abstractions the basis of classification: "Every way of classifying a thing is but a way of handling it for some particular purpose. Conceptions, 'kinds', are teleological instruments. No abstract concept can be a valid substitute for a concrete reality except with reference to a particular interest in the conceiver." [22]

Reasoning is another illustration of the theory. James rejects the classic concept of reasoning as simply a means of establishing a tautology, for example, 'All men are mortal, etc.' For James, reasoning is instead the means by which a purpose is achieved, "such as the means to a proposed end, the ground for an observed effect, or the effect of an assumed cause." [23] Technically, what happens is that one aspect of a thing is chosen as representative of it, and what applies to the aspect applies to the thing. For example, how do we answer the question, 'Is butter fattening'? We substitute for butter, the aspect 'having over 4,000 calories a pound'. *That* is fattening. Therefore, butter is fattening. The substitution 'something smooth to the tongue' gets us nowhere. The substituted aspect involving calories simplifies the object and suggests a useful relation.[24] Indeed, it often happens that the aspect which leads to the useful relation is precisely that aspect of the object which interests us. If we see a pair of scissors for the first time and wish to know if they will cut, we will search the instrument for a sharp surface, because this will be suggested by our interest in cutting. By selecting the numerical aspects of objects, we can hook into great systems of preestablished relationships, which give us results unattainable with objects considered in a more plenary way. Oranges can be added, subtracted, and multiplied, but only if they are considered numerically, not if they are considered as "round and nubbly in texture and orange in color and of such-and-such size." [25]

A PRIORI SCIENCES

The a priori sciences, such as mathematics, do not, for James, bear directly on reality, and so are more palatable than sciences such as physics. These, he sometimes felt, do violence to reality by claiming to describe its essential nature. The a priori sciences are more modest. They consist of vast schemes of "necessary and eternal" relations among fixed ideas, the relations being developed without reference to any possible description of reality.[26] But if a case in nature can be found in which real things can be substituted for the ideal terms, all the preestablished relations of the ideal system will hold for the things in the real world. For example, nine balls can be divided evenly into three groups of balls because '9', which can be substituted for the nine balls, is divisible by '3'. Although inadequate to describe real experience, the a priori sciences have their uses. Indeed, for James, the point of a science like chemistry is to find things, such as atoms or weight units, which will stay numbered, and so be able to hook into the a priori science of mathematics.

This view of ideas roughly corresponds to that expressed in Whitehead's writings around 1915–1917. Whitehead even seemed then to share some of James's animus, going so far as to call the world of science a "mere fairy tale." As the degree of abstraction increases, he says, logical relations among concepts, such as molecules, achieve a "peculiar smoothness," that is, the invariance of physical laws. But molecules *are* abstractions, as opposed to concrete percepts, such as chairs, and the physical laws relate to abstractions and not directly to concrete particulars.[27] With James, he finds the sciences immensely useful, but unmindful of main elements of experience, such as causality, purpose, and organic process.

PRAGMATISM AND SCIENCE

Once the sciences give up the pretense of describing reality and appeal only for their use, James is quite willing to embrace them. Indeed, pragmatism began as an attempt to use the practical consequences of scientific ideas as the basis of their meaning. Charles Peirce, whom James credited with originating pragmatism, was well versed in the physical sciences, and developed his theory on a scientific model.[28]

The model was that of experimental research, as Peirce conceived it: we observe an effect; we devise an explanatory hypothesis with its verifying experiment; we observe the "practical consequences" of the experiment; revise our hypothesis; perform a new verifying experiment; observe its results; and so on. The meaning of a scientific theory then becomes the predictable results from certain standardized actions.

Pragmatism would maintain that what is true of theories is true for concepts or words. Either they must be capable of operational definition or they must be dropped. For example, the term "substance" may mean that "a definite group of sensations will recur," a meaning which gives it an operational definition. But if "substance" is taken to mean a substratum for accidents in the medieval sense, James would ask what it is *known as:* what practical consequences or results does it speak for? And if these questions cannot be adequately answered, he would maintain that the term should be dropped.

Pragmatism represents an attempt to draw the implications of the meaning of meaning in science into other fields. James says, "The pragmatic rule is that the meaning of a concept may always be found, if not in some sensible particular which it directly designates, then in some particular difference in the cause of human experience which its being true will make." [29]

Psychologically, pragmatism conceives of ideas as the second stage of the reflex arc, following inputs and preceding action. Epistemologically, it represents a push to the stage of action, or practical relations, rather than a stasis at the stage of contemplation.

The corollary of a philosophy that sees ideas as directing action is that thinking is conceived as instrumental: *"Theories*

*thus become instruments, not answers to enigmas, in which
we can rest.* We don't lie back upon them, we move forward,
and, on occasion, make nature over again by their aid." [30] If
the "essences" of things depend on our means of observation,
and this in turn on our interest in what we can do with the
things, the systems of thought built up from the observations
will themselves be instrumental. "Ether and molecules may
be like co-ordinates and averages, only so many crutches by
the help of which we practically perform the operation of getting about among our sensible experiences." Theories and
laws, even in science, are not transcripts of reality but only
useful approximations. [31]

TRUTH AND CREATIVITY

In the sciences, at least as they are "for themselves," we
can afford to wait and let the evidence decide the "truth" for
us. James says that "in our dealings with objective nature we
obviously are recorders, not makers, of the truth; and decisions
for the mere sake of deciding promptly and getting on to the
next business would be wholly out of place." [32]

In "life," we do not have this option. Sometimes a decision
can be intellectually settled, as when, having resolved to marry
wealth, one determines whether in fact a particular girl has
sufficient funds. But otherwise, indecision is a decision. When
someone does not marry, he has "decided" the question of
whether or not to marry by remaining single. [33]

Philosophic and religious questions, which resist clear-cut
solutions based on passively received evidence, can still be
decided, James holds, according to the consequences of particular decisions. The matter is thus analogous to science,
where questions are answered according to the results of particular experiments. Take the question of the existence of
God. James would ask, "What difference would its being
true make in human experience?" If the consequences of holding the idea are more beneficial than not holding it, including
whatever difficulties the idea might make in the general

integrity of the questioner's thought, then, James maintains, it should be held.

James goes so far as to say that "the part of wisdom as well as of courage is to *believe what is in the line of your needs,* for only by such belief is the need fulfilled." James saves himself from wishful thinking by constantly maintaining a receptivity to the evidence, if there is any. But in its absence, he licenses belief which has "good" effects, such as good works and inner peace. In his encouragement of belief, he sometimes equates need with evidence, and loses track of what evidence he is looking for: "If religious hypotheses about the universe be in order at all, then the active faiths of individuals in them, freely expressing themselves in life, are the experimental tests by which they are verified, and the only means by which their truth or falsehood can be wrought out." [34] Despite a specious element, one that distressed Charles Peirce, it is a sympathetic view, a willingness to let people go their own way, with their private beliefs and their special truths.

James felt the same kind of thinking was valid for moral questions. One is here no longer concerned with questions of is, but with questions of ought. For James, "A moral question is a question not of what sensibly exists, but of what is good, or would be good if it did exist." [35] The thought precedes the act as its final cause, and the preception of the results is the verification, or validation, of the idea.

James asssumes that what are "good" effects of an idea can be known. This assumption is in part an empiricist act of faith, the faith that if matters are brought to the level of concrete particulars, they will be clear. It is a questionable assumption.

In any case, it follows, according to James's beliefs, that we thus engender truths in the world. Any act—picking up a pencil—will serve as an instance. But James's example, more remote, is too charming to pass up: "How many women's hearts are vanquished by the mere sanguine insistence of some man that they *must* love him! He will not consent to the hypothesis that they cannot. The desire for a certain kind of truth here brings about that special truth's existence." [36]

In concrescence, as depicted by Whitehead, the subjective aim brings about the organic construction or action. In this process, man and all organisms add to creation, or, in Whitehead's phrase, they participate in the "creative advance." James sums up: "In our cognitive as well as in our active life we are creative. We *add,* both to the subject and to the predicate part of reality. The world stands really malleable, waiting to receive its final touches at our hands. Like the kingdom of heaven, it suffers human violence willingly. Man *engenders* truths upon it." [37]

THE NOMINALISM OF WHITEHEAD

Whitehead's theory of ideas has two tendencies: one is nominalistic and is very close to James's, and the other is more realistic; it is embodied in his theory of the internal relations of ideas, which James merely suggests. Whitehead does not completely unify these two tendencies in his thinking, although the difficulties may be caused more by differences of emphasis than by basic contradiction.

IDEAS AND THE FIELD

Whitehead, as has been seen, attacks Descartes' subjectivism because it claims that universals are adequate to describe experience. Whitehead's attack on self-sufficient substances, or similarly on simple location, is based on the idea that an organism absorbs the rest of the world from its standpoint. Accordingly, the organism is only analyzable with reference to the rest of the world, that is, the things from the world which it incorporates into its nature.

The experience of the organism can, however, be abstracted from its relations with other things, from its place in the world, in which case this experience is what Whitehead calls an "abstract essence." [38] But an "abstract essence," such as a feeling of green, is deficiently actual. It does not include the feelings of participation of other entities, such as the green *tree,* or feelings by the subject of its own feelings of green in the preceding moment. These, Whitehead would say, are feelings in the mode of causal efficacy with their vectoral components. It follows as a corollary that "abstract essences" roughly correspond to our perceptions in the mode of presentational immediacy and to the "clear and distinct" ideas of Descartes and "impressions" of Hume.

Whitehead believes that experience is always peculiar to the experiencer. This belief is not solipsism, because Whitehead holds that the experiencer reenacts as a constituent of his nature some real elements from the nature of the prehended object. Consider, however, A. H. Johnson's proposal, put forth in a discussion with Whitehead, that an actual entity is really "restricted to the experience of its own component elements." Johnson maintained that although the elements come from other entities, *"as experienced,* these data are part of the constituent content of the prehending actual entity," that is, the subject himself. Whitehead admitted the danger, and said that he had not been careful in formulating his ideas.[39] I do not think he need have been so diffident. The process of concrescence, or of simple perception, is the process of "privatizing" the many data originally felt as vectoral and alien. Johnson's argument assumes the data have already been privatized; he is thus talking about the end of the process, not the process itself or, particularly, its early stages, when the organism feels in the clutch of the causal world. But this defense of Whitehead would hold only for very simple organisms. Where Whitehead does seem careless is in sometimes talking about man's perception of "external" things as if it were simple perception in the mode of causal efficacy, losing sight of the fact that in man causation of this type is mimicked rather than directly experienced.

In any case, to understand experience *always* involves going beyond the immediate subject. Whitehead writes, "Whenever we attempt to express the matter of immediate experience, we find its understanding leads us beyond itself, to its contemporaries, to its past, to its future, and to the universals in terms of which its definiteness is exhibited." [40]

The same analysis applies to argument. The only way in which adequate premises can be assumed is by presupposing independent existences which can be described by finite propositions. But existences are not independent, and thus premises can never be adequate. Behind any sentence there is always an infinite, indescribable background. For special purposes the background can be ignored—abstraction has its uses; but the procedure is always selective, and to the extent that the selection is taken to represent the whole, it is subject to error.

Consider the sentence 'John is happy'. It is an enormous abstraction which says nothing about John's previous thoughts, his organic functioning, the air he breathes, the conditions of pressure, gravity, temperature, and so forth—the whole causal environment, physical and historical. This is what Whitehead means by the "environment of a proposition." John *is* happy, but John and his happiness are, to use Whitehead's phrase, like "the grin on the cat." [41]

Invariance cannot be presupposed. One and one make two, but only sometimes. A spark and gunpowder make one explosion. We must know what kind of things are being combined, how they are being combined, and under what conditions. "When anything is placed in another situation, it changes. Every hostess takes account of this truth when she invites suitable guests to a party; and every cook presupposes it as she proceeds to cook the dinner." On this basis, Whitehead, like James, dismisses the pretensions of logic: "In fact, there is not a sentence, or a word, with a meaning which is independent of the circumstances under which it is uttered . . . The conclusion is that Logic, conceived as an adequate analysis of the advance of thought, is a fake." [42] Thus the adequacy and invariance of ideas are questioned by Whitehead in the same way as they are questioned by James.

TELEOLOGICAL IDEAS AND THE SUBJECTIVE AIM

Like James, Whitehead emphasizes the effectiveness of ideas in eliciting action. He maintains that it is their finitude which renders them effective. Inorganic matter absorbs the world without selection; living things reduce its infinity of causation to the determinate finitude of purpose.[43]

In the conscious field, the multiplicity of data is reduced to an intelligible finite order, that is, a limited selection of eternal objects.[44] The type of abstraction of which James speaks, the grasping of an aspect of an object according to our interest, is, in Whitehead's view, effected through what he calls transmutation.[45] The aspect of the object is what achieves salience in the field.

But its infection with purpose indicates that it is part of the subjective aim. Thus, the experiential abstraction 'paper to write with' is a prehension. It grasps the paper as part of the experience of the subject; and it is also part of the subjective aim, that is, to write, to be a writer, and so forth. James maintains that abstractions are teleological. Whitehead says that they are teleological because they are parts of the total, unifying subjective aim. This is what he means when he says that "each of them is its subject viewed in that abstract objectification." [46]

Like James, Whitehead holds that interest or importance determines why a particular abstraction is made. James, it will be remembered, said that interest is directed by the self, which may be defined as the subjective aim for the person. Thus, what we notice will reflect an aspect of our subjective aim. The combination of James and Whitehead might be summed up as follows: Prehensions or aspects of the datum which express peculiarly well the subjective aim will be prominent in the way the datum is conceived. Thus a thirsty man will see water as quenching rather than as chemical.

IDEAS IN PROCESS

The creation of subjective aims is one way Whitehead has of describing how ideas are implicated in process; other ways are aesthetics and logic or mathematics. The conventional view of mathematics, that of James, is of a morphological structure whose relations to process are welcome but in no way direct. Such structures, if accurately applied, can form the basis for scientific discovery, as, for example, in Newton's *Principia*.[47]

For James, statements expressing mathematical relations *suggest* processes in the world, or can *represent* such processes. Whitehead goes further and says that they are abstract statements of the processes *themselves*. Thus, Whitehead says that the "modern concept of an infinite series is the concept of a form of transition," and even 'twice-three is six' "considers a process and its issue." Whitehead offers a "belated reminder to Plato that his eternal mathematical forms are essentially referent to process." [48]

For Whitehead, mathematics is related to process in still another way: "activity means the origination of patterns of assemblage, and mathematics is the study of pattern." Organically such patterns appear as conscious fields, subjective aims and abstract essences. Because the aim of the universe, according to Whitehead, is the production of intensity of experience, and such intensity comes through the development of these patterns, mathematics, as the study of pattern, is related to the aim of the universe. "Thus the infusion of pattern into natural occurrences, and the stability of such patterns, and the modification of such patterns, is the necessary condition for the realization of the Good." [49] Although Whitehead's statement is rich with suggestion, he is unhelpfully vague in describing organic patterns, and says virtually nothing specific about how they might be related to mathematical patterns.

For Whitehead, aesthetics and logic are only secondarily separate branches of thought or of human activity; he sees them primarily as abstractions of real or possible organic processes. As such, they are closely related, and Whitehead declares that "the analogy between aesthetics and logic is one of the undeveloped topics of philosophy." [50] Logic is more abstract, according to Whitehead, and offers "possibilities" to the universe of how it might realize concretely the unity of abstract patterns. Art, on the other hand, is more concrete. It is the immediate harvest—we can enjoy the picture in its full detail—it offers a simulacrum of a completed reality which the universe has not made, or has not made *yet*. [51]

As abstraction from real process, both aesthetics and logic show a coerciveness which illustrates their real implication in process. Whitehead speaks of the "patch of red" which *ruins* the composition. And, indeed, any writer of fiction knows that in the development of a character a moment arrives in which there is what might be called a "critical mass"; it is the moment in which he realizes that the character is "on his own," that the character, not the writer, is now capable of dictating what he will further say and do and feel. This demand, like the rejection of the "patch of red," is coercive.

The unity of the painting or of the character is analogous to the unities of real organisms in the world. These unities are also analogous to mathematical systems. This means, for Whitehead, that from a set of abstract conditions or postulates involved in the unified system, an infinite number of other conditions can be derived which are also involved. In mathematics, if two angles of a triangle are equal so are two sides. Whitehead applies the same thinking to organisms: "This means that the thought can penetrate into every occasion of fact, so that by comprehending its key conditions, the whole complex of its pattern of conditions lies open before it." [52]

But with respect to real organisms, as Whitehead himself makes clear, abstractions are always limited, and their limitations can only be overcome by recurrence to the concrete, that is, to the complex experience of the organism itself. It may, however, be impossible to state *all* the controlling axioms in an organic system; [53] and in extending mathematical thought to organisms, Whitehead perhaps goes too far, although under the proper limitations the suggestion is rich with possibility. In particular, one thinks of the simulation of intelligence and organic systems by computers and information theory, developments in thought Whitehead would no doubt have warmly applauded.

INTERNAL RELATIONS OF IDEAS

THE INDEPENDENCE OF IDEAS

These considerations of Whitehead go beyond nominalism. They suggest a realistic theory of ideas whereby ideas create effects by their internal relations within organic concrescence. Purpose here plays the vital role of connecting ideas together as feeling. This was discussed by James as the basis for the unity of the conscious field.

James, it will be remembered, holds that ideas fuse into a single undivided object of thought; and that a higher state may emerge from lower states, or from conditions which would produce lower states. These are ideas in internal relations.

But James goes further, and suggests a theory of ideas, at once Platonic and nominalistic, which resembles Whitehead's. In referring to his dispute with Bradley, James says: "The entire *elenchus* and inquest is just as to whether parts which you can abstract from existing wholes can also contribute to other wholes without changing their inner nature. If they can thus mould various wholes into new *gestaltqualitäten,* then it follows that the same elements are logically able to exist in different wholes [whether physically able would depend on additional hypotheses]." [54] Whitehead seems to be expressing the same view when he says, "Each fact is more than its forms, and each form 'participates' throughout the world of facts." [55]

It would be a mistake to overrepresent the Platonic element

in James's thought. The main point of James's theory of the conscious field is that ideas are different by being in different compositions or brainstates. Further, he stresses that ideas are abstractions whose relative simplicity is only painfully reached. Whitehead would agree. As to the first point, Whitehead says that in concrescence feelings are "conditioned" by other feelings and by the subjective aim. As to the second point, he writes, "We may doubt whether 'simplicity' is ever more than a relative term, having regard to some definite procedure of analysis." [56]

But for Whitehead, and sometimes for James, ideas have an independent status in the universe. What ultimately defines that status are three factors: (1) their control of process, either action or concrescence; (2) the fact that they relate to other ideas only in determinate ways; and (3) the fact that out of this interrelation arise ideas which were not originally present.

RELEVANCE

The first point is the subject of Chapter III. As for the second point, Whitehead says that every eternal object is a possibility for realization in an actual thing.[57] What is the nature of this possibility?

It is James's view that a specific result is possible for realization in a thing (1) if appropriate conditions are in the environment, including the causal past of the thing; or (2) when the result is a "live option" for it, that is, if the thing has a choice and the choice is realizable. "Live options" are only for living things; dead things simply take what they get from their causal past, and so come under the first category. James writes with his usual specificity:

"Thus a concretely possible chicken means: (1) that the idea of chicken contains no essential self-contradiction; (2) that no boys, skunks, or other enemies are about; and (3) that at least an actual egg exists. Possible chicken means actual egg—plus actual sitting hen, or incubator, or what not. As the actual conditions approach completeness the chicken becomes a better-and-better-grounded possibility. When the conditions are entirely complete, it ceases to be a possibility, and turns into an actual fact." [58]

Whitehead would agree with this interpretation as far as it goes. The relevance of an eternal object to an actual entity must depend not only on the entity, but on the wider field from which that entity emerges. For "chicken" to be realized by the egg, skunks must be regarded as part of its field and so must air and gravity. Whitehead would also point out, in no contradiction to James, that the possibility of an idea being realized by an entity depends on the nature of the idea and the nature of the entity, and how those natures determine a relationship. These are *internal* relations among ideas.

RELATIONAL ESSENCES

Formally, Whitehead explains that how an eternal idea has ingression into an actual thing depends on the idea's "relational essence": "Since the relationship of *A* [an eternal object] to other eternal objects stands determinately in the essence of *A,* it follows that they are internal relations. I mean by this that these relationships are constitutive of *A.*" [59] This means, for example, that the relation of red to green stands determinately in the nature of red. There is that relation because red is red.

Whitehead goes on to say that if the relation of an eternal object *A* with *every other* eternal object is constitutive of *A*'s nature, then there is an interrelationship of all eternal objects. This interrelationship is the unity of the primordial nature of God, as Whitehead conceives it. (Most probably, Whitehead has in mind the structure of interrelationships conceived in mathematics and the metaphysics of Kant.[60])

The problem facing Whitehead is how *meaningfully* to relate this interrelationship of ideas to the world, that is, how to avoid the realm of abstract ideas, pristine and sterile, which characterizes the early Platonic dialogues. Whitehead's way is to say that the interrelation of ideas in God's primordial nature is a "graduated order of appetitions," and that this is the ground for the interrelation of eternal ideas *within* the real occasions of the world.[61] For example, red is related to all other colors, considered as eternal objects, in God's nature. The relations of red to other colors, say, in a painting being conceived by an artist, *by virtue of* red's eternal relations to all other colors in God's nature, will determine the possibility of red's *real participation* in the final painting. Or consider a composition of molecular intensities. As eternal objects, that composition has a relational essence. An occasion of life, considered as a subjective aim, may also be thought of as an eternal object with a relational essence. Now Whitehead would say that the possibility of life's inhabiting that molecular composition will be determined by the *eternal relations* in God's nature of the eternal objects of that life and of that composition of molecular intensities. Thus the graduated order of appetitions in God's nature determines appetitions in the world; in this sense, heaven is immanent in reality.

It might well be asked if the notion of a realm of eternal objects (or appetitions) is meaningful or helpful. To begin with, the nature of a relationship between ideas would seem to depend not only on the nature of the related ideas, but on their manner of relatedness. What, for example, is the relation between '1' and '2'? It might seem that there is none, that instead, even in mathematics, these terms must be related by the introduction of a specific relation, such as plus, minus, and so on.

Whitehead does offer some help in working out this difficulty. He indicates that a particular eternal object, given its relational essence, can bear only some relations and not others. For example, a curve can intersect or be intersected by another curve (and this in determinate ways); it cannot murder and be murdered by another curve or by anything else. Thus an eternal object can only come together with other eternal objects in determinate ways as a result of their relational essences.

If the relations of ideas in God's nature were of this type only, there would be some determinancy of relations but certainly not enough. This limitation must apply to Whitehead's position that relations of an eternal object to all other eternal objects "stand determinately" in its essence. But Whitehead also believes that relations themselves are eternal objects.[62] Thus all ideas *could* be related to each other, if not directly, at least mediately. Accordingly, the ideas in God's primordial nature could all be related to any one idea realized in an actual entity. This is the "idealist" side of Whitehead's thought.

It should be pointed out that the relations so determined would be *merely* ideal; what is not explained at all is how the relations could be felt by an actual entity. For instance, red might be a relevant color in a painting, but how would the artist *know* that it is? It is possible that for Whitehead the explanation goes no further. Rather, Whitehead might be saying that the relevancy, or appetition, *is felt,* and that he is simply accounting for that feeling. Felt relevancy, or appetition, is after all direct evidence; the primordial nature of God is a construct.

But Whitehead also points out that an "actual entity has a status among other actual entities, not expressable wholly in terms of contrasts between eternal objects." [63] Thus God, as the realm of interrelated eternal objects, is not the world. There is also a need for a "physical side" to explain how ideas are related in the world.

The "physical side" is advanced by Whitehead's discussion of the role of the spatiotemporal continuum. Whitehead writes, "Fundamentally, the spatio-temporal continuum is the general system of relatedness of all possibilities." In the spatio-temporal relations between things, the ideas which have ingression in those things are related. Examples would be the relative positions of two particles in an atom or the position of two patches of color in a painting. Whitehead makes clear the status of such relationships when he says that "for the philosophy of organism the primary *relationship* of physical occasions is *extensive* connection." [64]

Whitehead is also clear that extensive relations are abstractions of *experiential* relations. The spatiotemporal continuum, he says, "provides the general scheme of extensive perspective which is exhibited in all the mutual objectifications by which actual entities prehend each other." Less technically, Whitehead denies that there is any other meaning of togetherness than "experiential togetherness" or a meaning abstracted from it. [65] Again, because a physical body is a result of the things which contribute data to it, the spatiotemporal positions of those things are intrinsic facts of its nature. This is the meaning of Whitehead's denial of simple location. It is also clear that the spatiotemporal continuum, defining the real relations among things, provides the transition from the ideal indeterminacy of relational essences to the *real* relations of ideas in the world. It is within this system of relatedness, the spatiotemporal continuum, that ideas are realized together, and the values of the organism emerge.

It should also be noted that relational essences fail to express this system of relatedness. If the spatiotemporal positions of things are intrinsic facts of their natures, such natures are not expressible wholly in terms of relational essences. What is being expressed is the utter singularity of real facts, which, as Whitehead himself points out, the universality of ideas is not adequate to express. This is the "physical side."

Thus Whitehead is in difficulty when he indicates that the ideas he is talking about are vectoral and scalar intensities, such as an electron. [66] For an electron is a *specific* entity in the world. Considered as an abstraction, it is still an abstraction *from there.* It is not the classic Platonic idea in the sense of a free-floating quality, and yet Whitehead often refers to ideas in this way.

Much of what Whitehead says about ideas seems relevant, however, to ideas considered as abstractions from a particular actual occasion or entity. In a conversation with A. H. Johnson, Whitehead remarked ruefully that he could not see how Charles Hartshorne and others could get along without eternal objects. Whitehead defended eternal objects by claiming it as evident that "a quality exemplified at one place can be exemplified at another," which, he said, could only be stated in terms of eternal objects.[67] But there seems nothing in a theory of ideas as abstractions which would rule this out. Another solution of the problem is suggested by Whitehead in his theory of the consequent nature of God (see Chapter V).

POTENTIALITY AND THE PRIMORDIAL NATURE OF GOD

The problem with Whitehead's concept of a realm of eternal ideas is that it may not explain anything. Consider the intensities in a stable atom. Whitehead's theory of relational essences and the realm of ideas would appear to say this: if the eternal ideas expressing these intensities do in fact go together well in the atom, they must go together well in possibility. If this is all the theory says, it might well be dispensed with. But Whitehead does go further: he states that in some way the eternal relations of the eternal ideas *determine* the stability of the atom. Again, it may be asked why it is necessary to conceive of ideas as independent of their place in experience. Why "eternal relations"? [68] Why not mere "relations"?

James leans toward regarding ideas as mere abstractions. But, with Whitehead, he also emphasizes their independent determinate interrelations, almost as if these did not require the real world for their existence:

"it is endlessly serviceable to be able to talk of properties abstractly and apart from their working, to find them the same in innumerable cases, to take them "out of time," and to treat of their relations to other similar abstractions. We thus form whole universes of platonic ideas *ante rem,* universes *in posse,* tho none of them exists effectively except *in rebus.* Countless relations obtain there which nobody experiences as obtaining . . . The music of the future sleeps now, to be awakened hereafter. Or if we take the world of geometrical relations, the thousandth decimal of π sleeps there, tho no one may ever try to compute it." [69]

James, unlike Whitehead, makes no agent responsible for the sleeping music of the future or the thousandth decimal of π. It is simply a question which James does not take up. He is quite content to refer to "necessary and eternal" relations among fixed ideas within a nominalist point of view.

But Whitehead believes that anything must have an agent, must exist *somewhere.* Where do potentialities exist, he asks, *which are not yet representing* the physical facts about real things? These potentialities, if they are "relevant," come to appear as the final causes of things, and they guide their concrescences to novelty. Where do they reside before they are realized? Whitehead asks; and what is it that makes them particularly relevant to those things?

Whitehead's answer is that they reside in God's primordial nature. And he says that the particular *relevance* of the potential ideas to the ideas actualized in the physical things is their *relation* to the actualized *ideas.* This relation is in the mind of God. In Whitehead's words, "Thus 'proximate relevance' means 'relevance as in the primordial mind of God.' " [70] God is thus necessary to explain novelty.

Because this relevance is based on the eternal relationships of ideas in God's primordial nature, it would be eternally prefigured. However, there is something static about this idea which Whitehead might well reject, although it is not clear from his writing how he would avoid the implication (see Chapter V). In any case, what God "explains" is the direct evidence for Whitehead that the occasions of the universe opt for organizations which produce for them greater richness of experience.

BETWEEN PHYSICAL AND MENTAL

For Whitehead, every organic physical occasion has a form for itself; this form is its mentality. He also maintains that physical occasions have forms as they are realized causally or perceptually by other organisms. In this analysis, the physical and mental aspects of existence do not operate in causal independence of one another. This position goes some of the way toward avoiding the problem of incompatibility between the mental and physical inherent in the positions of Descartes and Kant (see Introduction).

Whitehead further maintains that the creation of high-level abstractions, such as 'green', or of subjective aims is the production of conceptual novelty. Such productions, as they direct the concrescence of organisms, are responsible for new facts in the world. Isn't this then simply another way of describing how the soul can independently doubt, understand, affirm, deny, and will, and so influence the world, as Descartes says it can? Does not Whitehead's analysis of conceptual novelty here raise the problems of incompatibility of the physical and mental?

Whitehead would say no. Mentality, in his view, is the focus of the physical field; the field is the entire universe; and without its relations to the physical field, mentality would not exist. The novelty it originates is that of the world as the conceptual possibilities lie immanent in it waiting for the spring of novel conditions. The independence of the soul is thus the specific energy of the organism, as the locus of its field, realizing its own possibilities. For Whitehead, God can be conceived as the symbol for such possibilities as they exist for all fact and the creative force or tendency whereby potentiality is realized as greater intensity of experience or complexity of organization. Although at times Whitehead abstracts ideas from physical facts, or God from the world, he often does not. Nor do I believe that separation in any ultimate metaphysical sense is necessary for the functioning of his system. This is not to nominalize or secularize Whitehead; it is merely to put ideas and God in the world, which is where Whitehead intended that they be.

V The Larger Relations

THE ORDER OF NATURE

In this chapter, I step back from the individual to some extent to consider the larger relations in which he participates. These are the order of nature, God, and civilization. But the individual is always the final reality with which James and Whitehead deal. Like the present in which past and future are contained, he is for them the focus of the entire world. Indeed, were this not true, there would be no source for the discussion. Reciprocally, these three topics—the order of nature, God, and civilization—all have their implications for personal life, in perception and thought, in religious experience, and in morality.

SOCIETIES AND THEIR ENVIRONMENTS

Conscious perception simplifies the world, placing significant individuals in the foreground against what Whitehead calls a background of "undistinguished occasions providing the environment with its vague emotional tone." This background environment, Whitehead maintains, is only discernible with sophisticated techniques; it is otherwise never seen, for like the poor, it is always with us.[1] Nor does it command our attention in our efforts to survive, for were it normally hostile, we should not exist. We see a tiger, but such pervasive elements as air pressure, gravity, or the character of the electromagnetic field go unnoticed.

According to Whitehead, the natural order is the general

expression of the existence of societies, some tight, some loose, with their characteristic modes of interaction. Now in general, when an individual belongs to a society, his relations with its members, Whitehead would say, are how he prehends the members, or, in other words, how they participate in his nature. (This participation must, of course, be such as not to destroy him.) As causal inputs, such participation will result in that member having modes of behavior or reactions characteristic of all or most members of the society.

In the physical world, for example, all bodies form a society, with gravitational attraction the common rule of behavior based on mutual prehensions. Each individual achieves a certain common character by virtue of its membership, that is, gravitational mass.[2]

In the social world, an army might be considered an example of a society. Soldierliness would be the common character (with its characteristic behavior) of each soldier, imparted to him by his perception of other soldiers. Another example is provided by James, that of cooperative societies, such as a government, a commercial system, or a ship. "A social organism of any sort whatever, large or small," James says, "is what it is because each member proceeds to his own duty with a trust that the other members will simultaneously do theirs."[3] In this case, the common element which is prehended is the abstraction 'everyone doing his duty'. The common character is trust and responsibility. This line of thought is very close to the social philosophy of John Dewey, who remarks that social arrangements "are means of *creating* individuals."[4]

LAWS OF NATURE

Whitehead's general analysis means that things in nature and society do not follow rules, they *make* rules. Laws are *immanent* in things. They are what things do when they prehend each other in causal and perceptual relations. Similar things will establish uniform laws, but if their differences affect their interrelations, the laws will be merely statistical, and if the things change, the laws will change.[5] For example, laws of chemical interaction vary with the chemicals.

But Whitehead perhaps claims too much when he says, "When we understand the essence of these things, we thereby know their mutual relations to each other." [6] Two sets of qualifications seem to be in order. First, the natures must be related, as in the spatiotemporal continuum, or, derivatively, in the field of consciousness, for such relations to be determinate. Second, our knowledge of the things will be based on their relations *to us;* it will be mediated by instruments and our bodies. The result is that our knowledge of their "essences" will be necessarily limited and selective. These qualifications do not in any way, however, derogate from the general notion that things make their own laws of behavior through mutual prehensions.

James maintains roughly the same doctrine of natural law as does Whitehead, although he has no theory of prehensions to explain it:

"The laws of Nature are nothing but the immutable habits which the different elementary sorts of matter follow in their actions and reactions upon each other . . . The habits of an elementary particle of matter cannot change (on the principles of the atomistic philosophy), because the particle is itself an unchangeable thing; but those of a compound mass of matter can change . . . That is, they can do so if the body be plastic enough to maintain its integrity, and be not disrupted when its structure yields . . . Each relatively stable phase of equilibrium in such a [plastic] structure is marked by what we may call a new set of habits. Organic matter, especially nervous tissue, seems endowed with a very extraordinary degree of plasticity of this sort." [7]

James's plasticity is structural change, not destruction. Such a change, for Whitehead, might be the alteration of the quantum state of a molecule due to the absorption of a high-speed particle.[8] James is referring to changes of a mechanical type in neurons, although he may also have molecular changes in mind.

James, like Whitehead, disavows an Absolute who orders all relations among things.[9] Belief in such an Absolute is a doctrine which Whitehead calls "the laws of nature as imposed." It implies self-sufficient entities, that is, substances enjoying simple location, which have merely *external* relations with each other. Because the internal natures of the entities are not involved, there is ultimately no reason for the laws. Accordingly, they must be attributed to a creator whose fiats, as they operate in the physical world, can only be discovered through scientific induction.[10]

When the deity is discarded as dubious metaphysics, positivism, the nineteenth-century idea of law as mere description, remains. Whitehead remarks:

"The modern assumptions differ from older assumptions, not wholly for the better. They exclude from rationalist thought more of the final values of existence. The intimate timidity of professionalized scholarship circumscribes reason by reducing its topics to triviality, for example, to bare sensa and to tautologies. It then frees itself from criticism by dogmatically handing over the remainder of experience to an animal faith or a religious mysticism, incapable of rationalization."

The problem with plain description, as with the doctrine of law as imposed, is that it gives no reason, other than statistics, *why* what is observed in the past should be repeated.[11] James remarks that an acceptable philosophy must adequately define expectancy. But with the empiricism of the Hume or Mill variety, as opposed to a philosophy of substance, the future is up for grabs.[12] What is demanded is a theory of agency and a theory of relations. The function of substance, according to Whitehead's theory, is performed by real things whose behavior is ordered by their prehensive interrelations. This is the doctrine of law as immanent.

INTERNAL RELATIONS AND SOCIETIES

The laws of nature are the rules of behavior of the various societies which compose the natural world. The regularities of organic behavior *within* the organism are also the result of its various constitutive societies. The intensity of interrelations within a high-grade organism, such as man, is unmatched in the physical universe. In comparison with the society of men, the intensity of experience of an individual man is equally unmatched, because, as Whitehead says, "each human being is a more complex structure than any social system to which he belongs." [13]

Man achieves this intensity of experience by his coordination of the various societies which compose him. This coordination, Whitehead believes, is the necessary condition for life. For man it is multileveled. There are societies of particles, of molecules, of cells, of organs, of systems, but all are ultimately under the control, in some part, of the presiding or central occasion. It is primarily here that novelty is introduced, and its effects coordinated throughout the organism.[14]

The presiding occasion itself is a *personal society,* passing on its identity or character to the next later member, and so on, through all the occasions of the individual's life. It is thus a society through time. In this way, Whitehead's theory of societies provides the basis for his agreement with James's theory of the self (see Chapter III).

EVOLUTION AND THOUGHT

The organization of a man is the product of a long evolution. Both James and Whitehead were evolutionists. Both accepted the major finding of Darwin that the complex structure of living things evolved from forms of minimal complexity. Indeed, the opening chapters of the *Psychology* can be seen as an attempt to reconcile what James knew of neurophysiology with the main ideas of evolution (James, in general, backed the idea that natural selection by "accidental variation" is the mode by which evolution takes place, as opposed to the method of habitual "adaptation," endorsed by Lamarck and Spencer).[15] James's thinking that mental phenomena are "explainable" by their function in aiding survival is thoroughly Darwinist. Again, his argument that thought is efficacious is based on its evolutionary development—if it doesn't fulfill a function why has it evolved?

Moreover, his explanations for *how* thought occurs have a Darwinist cast. One early explanation is that thoughts originate through random variation:

"the new conceptions, emotions, and active tendencies which evolve are originally produced in the shape of random images, fancies, accidental out-births of spontaneous variation in the functional activity of the excessively instable human brain, which the outer environment simply confirms or refutes, adopts or rejects, preserves or destroys,—selects, in short, just as it selects morphological and social variations due to molecular accidents of an analogous sort." [16]

Here, James has simply taken Darwin's theory of natural selection and transferred it to thought.

He has another explanation of the origin of thought which concerns specifically the creation of ideal ends or subjective interests. Proposed in opposition to Spencer, it is neither Darwinist nor Lamarckian. Spencer maintained that the mind conforms passively to the uniformities it encounters in the environment; this is what Spencer meant by the adjustment of the internal to the external orders.[17] For James, it was a one-sided explanation: "My quarrel with Spencer is not that he makes much of the environment, but that he makes nothing of the glaring and patent fact of subjective interests which cooperate with the environment in moulding intelligence. These interests form a true spontaneity." [18]

James's thinking contains the germ of Whitehead's theory of evolution. For Whitehead, interests appear as conceptually novel reactions to the environment. These reactions adapt the organism to the environment, and they usher in changes in the organism itself, changes which intensify its experience, that is to say, its mentality. In some manner, this phenomenon is reflected in an upward trend of evolutionary development.

Like James, Whitehead also believes thoughts can be spontaneous variations of the mind. "Reason," he holds, discriminates among the variations and selects those promoting intensity of experience. (This function, James believes, is performed in man by the "will.") For Whitehead, Reason is the "special embodiment in us of the disciplined counter-agency which saves the world." [19] However, he evades answering directly the question of whether such discriminations are transmitted in heredity, and thus the question whether Reason is the agency responsible for evolution, although he strongly implies that it is.

Whitehead does attempt to account for the formation of distinct species by a theory derived from aesthetics. According to it, only certain organic formations of elements, or "compatible groups," are possible. Between such groups, there will be discernible differences. Whitehead, however, gives no indication that he saw genetic mutation as the basis for new "compatible groups." Genetics looked too much like the ghost of the theory of simple location: "The analogy of the old concept of matter sometimes leads them [the geneticists] to ignore the influence of the particular animal body in which they [the genes] are functioning." [20]

For Whitehead, natural selection describes "external relations between portions of matter"; it is "purposeless and unprogressive." [21] This dismissal of natural selection may be based in part on ignorance, but it may also reflect Whitehead's tendency to exaggerate an ignored aspect in a problem. In any case, Whitehead does strike at the weakness in Darwinist thought, the preoccupation with variation and the neglect of the way an organism achieves integration. [22] The ability to survive, in Whitehead's view, simply does not explain why complex organisms evolved:

"In fact life itself is comparatively deficient in survival value. The art of persistence is to be dead . . . The problem set by the doctrine of evolution is to explain how complex organisms with such deficient survival power ever evolved. They certainly did not appear because they were better at that game than the rocks around them. It may be possible to explain 'the origin of *species*' by the doctrine of the struggle for existence among such organisms. But certainly this struggle throws no light whatever upon the emergence of such a general type of complex organism, with faint survival power." [23]

The problem, for Whitehead, is to explain not survival, but the creation of a higher order of life, with greater spontaneity and intellectuality. As for man, Whitehead says that within recorded history "it would be difficult to demonstrate that mankind has improved upon its inborn mental capacity." [24] But if man has not improved genetically, he has, according to Whitehead, organized his environment for the service of thought to the improvement of human life: "Successful organisms modify their environment. Those organisms are successful which modify their environment so as to assist each other." [25] This, of course, accords with Whitehead's theory of societies.

As for the wider problem, Whitehead talks of "some mysterious impulse" in the universe supplying its energy to run upward, an impulse which at one time formed "protons, electrons, molecules, and stars." These are, however, now decaying. But in the animal body, he says, "we can observe the appetition towards the upward trend, with Reason as the selective agency." [26]

Behind the upward trend, and the earlier formation of the physical world, Whitehead sees, as did Plato, the work of God, or, alternately phrased, Reason. [27] With Plato, Whitehead

seems to hold that at the outset the universe was chaotic, and
that starting from this totally bad situation, Reason, or God,
persuaded chaos into such order as it has attained. But God
has had only partial success in fulfilling His aim; the aim is
ongoing, and Reason, or God, is immanent in things. God
aims at intensity of experience, and it is with organic societies
that he cooperates in its fulfillment, or, in Whitehead's phrase,
"the creative advance."

GOD

WHITEHEAD'S VISION

According to Whitehead, the progress of the world is at
least partially dependent on God. In religion, however, more
than progress is usually wanted. Whitehead says that "religion
is the longing of the spirit that the facts of existence should
find their justification in the nature of existence." [28] In addition, religion must deal in some way with man's longing for
immortality.

The chapter which ends *Process and Reality* envisages a
relation between God and the world which grants all that most
men wish in religion. The writing is awesome, organizing its
metaphysical terms like planets in a system. In brief, the
system is this:

There is the primordial nature of God, holding within
itself the interrelation of all eternal objects and thus the
grounds of relevance of eternal objects to the many occasions
of the world. It is unified, omniscient, exclusively good, but
"deficiently actual," requiring the world for its concretion.

There is the world as feeling and physical fact.

And finally, there is what Whitehead calls the "consequent
nature of God." This is God's consciousness of the world, or,
put another way, the objectification of the world in God's
nature. (In this sense, our consciousness of a tree is the objectification of the tree in our nature.) By being transformed into
God's consequent nature, the occasions of the world become

immortal, as God is supposedly immortal, although why He is necessarily immortal Whitehead does not say.

According to Whitehead, God's consciousness of the world is the mental pole of the multiplicity of the world's physical objects in their concurrent "unison of becoming." Like human consciousness of the human body, God's consciousness of the world achieves an integration.[29] This is God's vision for the world. Whitehead believes that this vision is perfected by the eternal relationships of all eternal objects which form God's primordial nature, although how this takes place Whitehead does not say.

In any case, he maintains that God is immanent in each occasion, supplying it with its initial subjective aim as it begins its concrescence, instilling in it the desire for such perfection as, in its immediate situation, that entity is capable of. Moreover, the subjective aim which God instills in each occasion is part of His overall vision for the world. How, it may be asked, is God's vision of the world made accessible and relevant to the individual occasions? Whitehead offers little help here, except to say that the occasions feel its accessibility and relevance: the artist feels inspiration and feels that what he has painted is right; the same is true for the moralist or the statesman. In any case, Whitehead maintains that in making His vision relevant and accessible, God expresses His love of the world. "In this sense, God is the great companion—the fellow-sufferer who understands." [30]

Whitehead holds that the world, imperfect as it seems in fact, is somehow integrated into God's vision of perfection. In this way, according to Whitehead, the evil that is perceived by God is somehow "saved." He writes: "The revolts of destructive evil, purely self-regarding, are dismissed into their triviality of merely individual facts; and yet the good they did achieve in individual joy, in individual sorrow, in the introducton of needed contrasts, is yet saved by its relation to the completed whole." [31] This salvation is a form of immortality. (Like the immortality achieved by the transformation of occasions into God's consequent nature, it depends on the perhaps gratuitous ascription of immortality to God.)

Finally, Whitehead says, each occasion also achieves immortality by becoming part of history. This is called "objective immortality" by Whitehead, and is, in his language, how the satisfaction or completed thing becomes an efficient cause for occasions in its causal future. It is also what is meant by the conservation of matter and energy, and the contribution of facts to ongoing systems.

"The aim of religion for immortality or salvation is thus achieved: In this way, the insistent craving is justified—the insistent craving that zest for experience be refreshed by the ever-present unfading importance of our immediate actions, which perish and yet live for evermore." [32]

This theology, however triumphant, cannot be entirely sustained, for it would deny freedom and deal inadequately with the problem of evil. If God supplies the initial subjective aim of each occasion, and if He integrates all occasions into the perfection of His vision, how can evil persist in the world? And how can the individual occasions of the world have any freedom to do evil or any responsibility to do good? And yet the world, considered either atomically or totally, is imperfect—men are self-destructive and wars are fought. Some adjustment in Whitehead's theology is clearly necessary.

Whitehead himself supplies it, although he is notably inconsistent. As explained in Chapter III, he sometimes gives to the occasion itself a measure of responsibility for its subjective aim. With Plato, Whitehead maintains that all men seek the Good—this, I believe, is for Whitehead a reflection of God's immanence. But he also says that they have inherited factors and their previous history to overcome, and that what they desire is not always godlike—there is the problem of ignorance. He admits, in *Religion in the Making,* that the universe's "incompletion, and its evil, show that the temporal

world is to be construed in terms of additional formative elements which are not definable in terms which are applicable
to God." And in *Adventures of Ideas*, he maintains that the
disorder or evil in the world indicates that God has been only
partially successful in persuading the world through His ideas
of the perfections of which it is capable. "We must conceive
the Divine Eros as the active entertainment of all ideals, with
the urge to their finite realization, each in its due season.
Thus a process must be inherent in God's nature, whereby his
infinity is acquiring realization." [33] But then God's role in the
world is not a total one; the world is incomplete, stubborn
and ignorant, and not easily moved.

JAMES'S CRITIQUE OF THE ABSOLUTE

Compared with Whitehead, James has nothing to offer in
the field of theology but a welter of hypotheses and wishful
thoughts, some hard looks at the facts of the world, and some
bitter disclaimers. The anguish which James felt in this life
was not much relieved by his thoughts about God. The problem for James was not any infertility of thought, but lack of
belief.

James was clearer on what he did not believe; he was un-
willing to take a sop from philosophic absolutism. Many who
read "The Will to Believe" or *Pragmatism* felt, perhaps
rightly, that he was encouraging belief in anything which
gives comfort, provided only that it cannot be disproved. Why,
then, not believe absolutism with all its assurances? The difficulty was that for himself, James lacked the will to believe,
and he considered no arguments sufficiently strong to convince
him; for the most part, he would rather pay the price of doubt
than gain the ease of beliefs he could not substantiate. He
preached an easier game than he played.

The absolutism he knew was chiefly that of Royce, with
whom he fought philosophically for years.[34] In so doing,
James refined attitudes and opinions which are also applicable
to Whitehead.

For James, one difficulty with the Absolute is that from it one can deduce no existential facts. "You cannot enter the phenomenal world with the notion of it in your grasp, and name beforehand any detail you are likely to meet there." [35] Whitehead would reply that owing to God you must look for the tendency toward greater intensity or depth of experience.

Another complaint James makes against the Absolute is that it cannot be known. Whitehead's God, however, as Whitehead describes Him, can be known by each occasion as it senses the relevancy of God's ideas or vision for itself.

Nor is Whitehead guilty of the absolutist belief, which James severely criticizes, that each particular exists because it is a thought in the mind of God.[36] In Whitehead's scheme, actual things exist in their own right; God merely persuades the world and has conceptions of it.

Whitehead's God is also immune to James's criticism of the God of Christianity, that he can do nothing to help us and is "on the side of our enemies as much as he is on our own." [37] Whitehead's God is at work in the present moment. His aim at intensity of experience puts Him "on our side" to the extent that we also have that goal. Whitehead said to Lucien Price:

"God is *in* the world, or nowhere, creating continually in us and around us. This creative principle is everywhere, in animate and so-called inanimate matter, in the ether, water, earth, human hearts. But this creation is a continuing process, and 'the process is itself the actuality,' since no sooner do you arrive than you start on a fresh journey. Insofar as man partakes of this creative process does he partake of the divine, of God, and that participation is his immortality, reducing the question of whether his individuality survives death of the body to the estate of an irrelevancy. His true destiny as cocreator in the universe is his dignity and his grandeur." [38]

In His relation to evil, Whitehead's God, as qualified, is different from the Absolute. The absolutists believe that the entire world is in some way a manifestation of God's nature. Accordingly, evil is part of a perfected whole. James asks: How can the whole be perfect if the parts are imperfect? "When, for example, I imagine such carrion as the Brockton murder, I cannot conceive it as an act by which the universe, as a whole, logically and necessarily expresses its nature without shrinking from complicity with such a whole." [39] But, for Whitehead, the world has evil, and God is only partially successful in persuading it to achieve the good of which it is capable.

The aspect of Whitehead's God which looks most like the Absolute is His primordial nature. James cites the "old metaphysical fallacy of looking behind a fact *in esse* for the ground of the fact, and finding it in the shape of the very same fact in *posse.*" Whitehead would reply that the ground of the fact is the real world, including God's immanence, or, alternatively phrased, the real world *and* God, neither having preeminent existence. He would agree with James that there is "no 'how' except the constitution of the fact as given." [40]

Still, James would be uneasy with Whitehead's concept of the primordial nature of God. At bottom, it would seem too much like another edition of the world commanding the interest and loyalty which James felt for this one:

"The essence of my system is that there is really growth . . . The world exists only once, in one edition, and then just as it seems. For the usual philosophies it exists in two editions, an eternal edition, complete from the start, in which there is no growth or novelty; and an inferior, side-show, temporal edition, in which things seem illusorily to be achieving and growing into that perfection which really preëxists. This reduplication of the same is absolutely irrational, in whatever way it be considered; and incompleteness and pluralism, in spite of their aesthetic scurviness, are intellectually to be preferred." [41]

Whitehead's God avoids the criticism, in part at least, which James levels against the Absolute that it is static, "complete from the start." The consequent nature of Whitehead's God, that is, His consciousness of the world, is dependent on the world from moment to moment. Only God's primordial nature seems somehow static, but this is deficiently actual, an abstraction from God's total nature which, for Whitehead, is active in the world in creating intensity of experience.

James might have still another objection to Whitehead's primordial nature of God. This aspect of God, according to Whitehead, consists of the entire multiplicity of eternal objects. James might well ask: Is it not better to think of ideas as being secularly invented, rather than as having their existence in God's nature? Are not the accidental collocations of nature, the creation of subjective aims, or the fusion of ideas in consciousness more understandable means? Referring to different mathematical systems, James wrote:

"Yet if . . . we assume God to have thought in advance of every *possible* flight of human fancy in these directions, his mind becomes too much like a Hindoo idol with three heads, eight arms and six breasts, too much made up of superfoetation and redundancy for us to wish to copy it, and the whole notion of copying tends to evaporate from these sciences. Their objects can be better interpreted as being created step by step by men, as fast as they successively conceive them." [42]

Nevertheless, James does speak of belonging to an "unseen region" where his ideals originate, a region which actually works upon our "finite personality." [43] Here he seems very close to Whitehead. James differs from him, however, in generally tending toward an exclusively "secular" interpretation of phenomena.

For Whitehead, God is the cause of certain phenomena which he otherwise finds difficult to designate. God fulfills an ontological role: what happens or what exists must be assigned to some actual entity which acts as an agent. Thus God is explanatory of the order of the universe, the complexity of organic forms, and the sense in life of rightness and immortality. But most of these things Whitehead also explains as secular effects, as the result of the internal relations between the real things of the world, with their emotions and conceptions playing their real roles. By this explanation, the laws of nature are the habits of such things in their interrelation; the formation of organisms is the result of the interrelation of their parts; and the sense of rightness and immortality (which, for Whitehead, are perhaps the same) is an aesthetic feeling accompanying organic formation. Expressed this way, Whitehead's philosophy, it seems to me, does not stand or fall on the existence of the primordial nature of his God.[44]

I would not here question the notion of the consciousness and the creativity of the world, nor their possible effects on process. But I do question the need for the a priori and metaphysically independent character, however deficiently real, of God's primordial nature. I would thus question whether the internal relations of ideas as they control real or potential process depend on the eternal relatedness of these ideas in God's primordial nature.

Such thoughts are, I believe, in the spirit of William James. In any case, James's criticism of an "edition de luxe," a universe in potential standing over a universe in being, certainly applies to Whitehead's God, although Whitehead's scheme is at least not clearly deterministic. That the Absolute necessarily meant a deterministic world was the heart of James's objection to absolutism. But, for Whitehead, God's dependence on the world and the limitations of His influence leave the question of determinism at least seriously in doubt.

A GOD OF NATURE

Whitehead's God, because He is immanent in all occasions, is the creative force in nature. He is at least partially responsible not only for the consciousness of man, but for such phenomena as the order of astronomical movements and the synthesis of proteins. Dylan Thomas perhaps expresses this thought when he writes, "The force that through the green fuse drives the flower / Drives my green age." [45]

Unlike Whitehead, James disavows the idea of a God of nature because nature does not elicit the sympathy and respect befitting God. The solar system, James says, is the result of a "local accident"; the universe is a dead wilderness; living forms, according to Darwinism, are produced and destroyed by chance:

"It is impossible, in the present temper of the scientific imagination, to find in the driftings of the cosmic atoms, whether they work on the universal or on the particular scale, anything but a kind of aimless weather, doing and undoing, achieving no proper history, and leaving no result. Nature has no distinguishable ultimate tendency with which it is possible to feel a sympathy." [46]

Where Whitehead emphasizes the real order in nature, James stresses, with Kant, that man's concepts make nature orderly for thought. Where Whitehead recurs to romantic poetry to emphasize aspects of nature ignored by science,[47] James reads nature out of his philosophy.

For nature itself, James had the greatest love, and when he became overwrought in Cambridge, he would long for the country; and when he could break away from responsibilities and actually go, he would return calmed and refreshed. But for once James distrusted his own experiences, and these formed no part of his philosophy. Taking the scientific description of nature at face value, James concluded that nature was "all plasticity and indifference" and that to "such a harlot" he owed no allegiance.[48]

ORTHODOX CHRISTIANITY

James also rejected orthodox Christianity. He saw it at its worst, struggling to defend itself against modern science, asserting doctrines out of temper with the age, oriental, despotic, even "savage":

"The theological machinery that spoke so livingly to our ancestors, with its finite age of the world, its creation out of nothing, its juridical morality and eschatology, its relish for rewards and punishments, its treatment of God as an external contriver, an 'intelligent and moral governor,' sounds as odd to most of us as if it were some outlandish savage religion. The vaster vistas which scientific evolutionism has opened, and the rising tide of social democratic ideals, have changed the type of our imagination, and the older monarchical theism is obsolete and obsolescent." [49]

Whitehead was, if anything, even more vehement. He had a deep love for the earliest Christianity; it introduced the gentle and tender elements into religion; it was based on the life of a man who had naive, imagistic insight into the nature of things; it was productive of supreme ideals for civilized life.[50] But after Paul, he believed, Christianity relapsed into barbarism: "The old ferocious God is back, the Oriental despot, the Pharaoh, the Hitler; with everything to enforce obedience, from infant damnation to eternal punishment." [51] The words are Whitehead's, but they might equally have been James's.

JAMES'S MYSTICISM

When one comes to James's positive thoughts, one finds that speculation, wishful thinking, and belief are too mixed up to be sorted out with any authority. It is doubtful that James could have sorted them out himself.

There are, however, two strands of thought in which at various times he seemed to have had some belief, the mystical and theistic. Underlying James's mysticism was the suspicion that so-called normal experience fails to reveal the functioning of the real powers in the world. Perhaps in states of mind induced by drugs, in insanity, dreamlife, psychical phenomena, and in religious exaltation and mystical enlightenment, a man communicated with these superior powers more directly than in normal, conscious life.

Whitehead did not disavow mysticism. He wrote, "If you like to phrase it so, philosophy is mystical. For mysticism is direct insight into depths as yet unspoken. But the purpose of philosophy is to rationalize mysticism: not by explaining it away, but by the introduction of novel verbal characterizations, rationally coördinated." [52] In the deepest sense, Whitehead cannot be understood without realizing the mystical basis for his thoughts, particularly those concerning the relations of God and the world.

But Whitehead's is a mysticism under the tightest discipline. In religion, Whitehead would credit superior persons, people who realized continuously what ordinary men achieved only in their best moments; but into the "demonic" area he refused to go: "Religious truth must be developed from knowledge acquired when our ordinary senses and intellectual operations are at their highest pitch of discipline. To move one step from this position towards the dark recesses of abnormal psychology is to surrender finally any hope of a solid foundation of religious doctrine." He did not dismiss emotional religious experience, and, with James, he credited religious experience as such, but he insisted that emotion endangered the "authority" of religious testimony. Hence the need for metaphysics.[53]

James, on the other hand, turned excitedly from one thing to the other. His experiments on himself with drugs convinced him of the limitations of the normal state; other significant types of mentalities, he believed, lay waiting at the touch of the proper stimulus.[54] The similarities between insanity and religion were so close as to suggest that they ultimately dealt with the same phenemona. Delusional insanity, with its texts and voices and external powers, seemed a "religious mysticism turned upside down"; both seemed to spring "from that great subliminal or transmarginal region of which science is beginning to admit the existence." [55]

His long interest in psychical research suggested the same kind of connections.[56] Such phenomena as mediums and clairvoyance led him to feel that we may "all have potentially a 'subliminal' self, which may make at any time irruption into our ordinary lives." [57]

But James was totally ambivalent about what lay beyond our normal consciousness. A secular interpretation was that "the 'more' with which in religious experience we feel ourselves connected is on its *hither* side the subconscious continuation of our conscious life." This suggestion is developed in a late article (1910) in which "memories, concepts and connotational states" are put into subliminal consciousness, and mystical experience is then explained as a sudden connection with this otherwise inaccessible area of the mind. [58]

But elsewhere, he takes a radically different tack. In referring to psychotic and "psychic" experiences, James expresses doubt that

"we shall ever understand some of them without using the very letter of [Gustav Theodor] Fechner's conception of a great reservoir in which the memories of earth's inhabitants are pooled and preserved, and from which, when the threshold lowers or the valve opens, information ordinarily shut out leaks into the mind of exceptional individuals among us . . . I think it may be asserted that there *are* religious experiences of a specific nature, not deducible by analogy or psychological reasoning from our other sorts of experience." [59]

James calls this the "transmission theory," in which the brain transmits impulses from the great consciousness which lies beyond. [60] And in an article dated 1909, James writes about a "continuum of cosmic consciousness, against which our individuality builds but accidental fences." "Our 'normal' consciousness," he says, "is circumscribed for adaptation to our external earthly environment, but the fence is weak in spots, and fitful influences from beyond leak in." [61] The idea that cosmic consciousness could only communicate in the "weak spots" supplied the connection with insanity, drugs, and unusual mental states. However, whether James ever did anything more than merely entertain the "transmission theory" one cannot say.

JAMES'S THEISM

The other theory, about which James was undoubtedly quite serious, was theism. The problem for James with traditional theism was that it denied any intimacy between God and man.[62] Because such a God is completely formed from eternity; because He is self-sufficient; because what He creates, including man, is foreign to His nature; because, finally, He is not basically affected by anything that happens here, He is, in the words of the poet Pierre Emmanuel, "infinitely absent" and "infinitely elsewhere."[63] The charm of pantheism would thus lie in obliterating this distance by having God dwell within creation.[64]

But, for James, companionship was close enough, and the God he wanted had to be "finite, either in power or in knowledge, or in both at once"; He had to be in time and work out a history like ourselves; and suffer and care, as we do, for the values we fight for. In this way, "he escapes from the foreignness from all that is human, of the static timeless perfect absolute."[65]

By making God a personalization of values, James made God's anthropomorphism merely symbolic: " 'God,' in the religious life of ordinary men, is the name not of the whole of things, heaven forbid, but only of the ideal tendency in things, believed in as a superhuman person who calls us to cooperate in his purposes, and who furthers ours if they are worthy. He works in an external environment, has limits, and has enemies."[66] Here is a God that fit His creator's personal needs. James believed that God should be dignified; but he treasured His intimacy and did not want to destroy it with an abstract theology.

The functions that James would have God perform are fulfilled by Whitehead's God, although the distance, grandeur, and infinite qualities remain. The companion, the fellow-sufferer, is also the multiplicity of eternal objects and the conceptual valuation of each occasion. James's phrase "the ideal tendency in things" comes close to hitting the mark as a description of Whitehead's God. Professor Hartshorne writes, "Whitehead does not simply brush aside as valueless the work of the classical theists, but rather he sets forth a higher synthesis of the more extreme tendencies of recent theism (as seen, for example, in James) and the older conceptions." [67] But the "higher synthesis" is "high church" in emotional tone; James would have his God more emotionally accessible even at the price of philosophic grandeur.

REAL ADVENTURE

The ideal impulses and values which for James originate from an "unseen region," Whitehead held to originate, in part at least, from God. Were James to share Whitehead's view, this would unify his entertainment of the transmission theory with his theism, but the notion is only implied. In any case, the point of existence, for James, is the furtherance of values. But there are no guarantees the values will win out. "If this life be not a real fight, in which something is eternally gained for the universe by success, it is no better than a game of private theatricals from which one may withdraw at will." James gives up personal immortality for the success of his values.[68] Elsewhere he would have only those things survive, in the words of Rudolf Lotze, "whose continuance belongs to the meaning of the world, and so long as it does belong; whilst everyone will pass away whose reality is justified only in a transitory phase of the world's course." [69] This means that there will be "real losses and real losers, and no total preservation of all that is." Life is a "real adventure," a "social scheme of cooperative work genuinely to be done." [70] It is a religion lacking great assurances, but challenging the will: modest as it was, it was all that James could believe in.

CIVILIZATION

Civilized life requires a philosophy to purify its ideals and define its purposes. Whitehead states this in terms of James's theory of attention and the self:

"Every epoch has its character determined by the way its populations re-act to the material events which they encounter. This reaction is determined by their basic beliefs—by their hopes, their fears, their judgements of what is worth while . . . How they act depends partly on their courage, partly on their intellectual grasp. Philosophy is an attempt to clarify those fundamental beliefs which finally determine the emphasis of attention that lies at the base of character." [71]

JAMES'S MORAL COURAGE

James spent most of his life defining *how* beliefs are achieved, not the beliefs themselves. That is why, in the final analysis, he is primarily a cognitive psychologist, or, philosophically, an epistemologist. His popular philosophy, pragmatism, is essentially a technique for arriving at belief, and a justification, *faute de mieux,* for keeping going with what beliefs one has.

One sees in James a profound loneliness. Surrounded by friends and loved ones, in correspondence with an ever-widening circle of colleagues in Europe and in America, he still felt a terrible isolation. It was not alienation, although the vulgarities of the America of the late nineteenth century for the most part repelled him,[72] but rather a sense that individual life was all that really counted. The curious mixture of love and isolation that one senses in the Puritan fathers, such as John Winthrop, seemed to be James's as well.[73] Perhaps it was the feeling that salvation is individual, that the joys of this life, even the most profound, such as love, are fleeting. And when that salvation itself is so terribly in doubt, then the night closes in on the spirit, and it is left with its naked courage, flashing like a

sword or piece of gold from the recesses of a Rembrandt painting, more lovely for its conflict with the darkness.

For the darkness was all about; James carried with him
throughout his life a sense of impending horror, of madness,
illness and suicide. He was, in his own phrase, a "sick soul,"
one whose awareness of evil was intensely painful, who felt it
at the very core of existence. Pain, and death, and sin, and
wrong—some might be "ministerial to higher forms of good,"
but not all; there was evil which could not be gainsaid. Philosophy had to deal with it; the "healthy-minded," by refus-
ing to recognize it, were denying the existence its most profound elements.[74] James wrote out of personal suffering; the
victim was himself. His flights of confidence, as in *Pragmatism*
and *The Will to Believe,* have the desperate courage of a man
whistling past a graveyard. His sermons are as much for himself as for his audience.

The loneliness he felt was increased by the threat and oppression of evil. He reached out to his audiences, but for him
life was an individual affair. What one could show was courage
in the face of it, one's will in overcoming obstacles. From
groups, one could expect little. They were pompous, self-
righteous, brutal; all the finest elements of life were to be
found in the workings of individuals. James wrote to a lifelong
friend:

"As for me, my bed is made: I am against bigness and greatness in all their forms, and with the invisible molecular moral
forces that work from individual to individual, stealing in
through the crannies of the world like so many soft rootlets, or
like the capillary oozing of water, and yet rending the hardest
monuments of man's pride, if you give them time. The bigger
the unit you deal with, the hollower, the more brutal, the more
mendacious is the life displayed." [75]

Thus, although James talked from time to time about coopera-
tion, he ultimately saw morality as a private affair, not merely
because group efforts seemed unlikely to effect a moral pur-

pose, but, more basically, because morality itself was based on individual conscience.

The agent of morality for James was the individual will. For himself, he was a strictly moral man within the Victorian code, although he was always open to what others might believe, even, in Santayana's phrase, "the intellectual cripples and the moral hunchbacks." [76] While he had principles for which he fought, he would not impose his standards on others. It somehow mattered less to him what the will was exercised for than that it was there.

For James, the man with will was the heroic man, the "worthy match and mate" of the world: "the effort which he is able to put forth to hold himself erect and keep his heart unshaken is the direct measure of his worth and function in the game of human life." [77] This was so because the consents and non-consents which man exercises are his freedom, his "underived and original contribution."

James was interested more in the controlled will than in willfulness. There was something flagrant, perhaps uncouth, even pathological, in the way a Napoleon or a Luther so quickly translated his impulses into action. James's heroes were of another stamp: "Your parliamentary rulers, your Lincoln, your Gladstone, are the strongest type of man, because they accomplish results under the most intricate possible conditions." [78] Such men often appear dangerously close to paralysis; they know much, think hard, and let fall between thought and act the shadow of doubt. But they recover and act.

James does not appear to be sure why. He likens their acts to the extensor muscles guided and steadied by the flexors.[79] There is control, to be sure, but without some new source of strength, one wonders, with all the inhibitions introduced by the arguments "against," why his statesmen ever act "for."

James does speak, in *The Varieties of Religious Experience,* of the wider religious experiences from which his ideals flow.[80]

And elsewhere he writes: "There are resources in us that naturalism with its literal and legal virtues never recks of, possibilities that take our breath away, of another kind of happiness and power, based on giving up our own will and letting something higher work for us, and these seem to show a world wider than either physics or philistine ethics can imagine." But James is unsure of these resources: "There is at any rate one side of life which would be easily explicable if those ideas were true . . ." [81] The language is hypothetical and personally elusive. James is mainly still in the dark.

If mysticism did not offer a sure foundation for a wider morality, still less did the "survival of the fittest." In a state of doubt, many of James's contemporaries turned to evolution as a standard: in Social Darwinism, what succeeded or survived was right.[82] But for James, things succeeded because people *wanted* them to and *worked* for them. If their motives determined the effect, the effect could not be used to determine the motives. "If what prevails and survives does so by my help, and cannot do so without that help; if something else will prevail in case I alter my conduct,—how can I possibly now, conscious of alternative courses of action open before me, either of which I may suppose capable of altering the path of events, decide which course to take by asking what path events will follow?" [83] Accordingly, for James, Social Darwinism offered a specious basis for morality.

Without a sure mysticism, without an evolutionist ethic, James ends up basing morality directly on the individual. James talks of people's "total character" and "personal genius," of their "personal aptitude or incapacity for moral life," and of the "dumb willingness and unwillingness of their interior characters." [84] There is a mysticism in this final defense of character beyond which one cannot go. Even James's most deeply felt values, such as intellectual excellence or what he calls "conscious completeness," [85] are for him simply private values.

Values are private, for one reason, because the perspectives of different individuals are personal, and so their conceptions of the world must also be: "The facts and worths of life need many cognizers to take them in. There is no point of view absolutely public and universal . . . The practical consequence of such a philosophy is the well-known democratic respect for the sacredness of individuality,—is, at any rate, the outward tolerance of whatever is not itself intolerant." [86] This mode of thinking thus implies a willingness to allow individuals their "quiet and peaceful enjoyment" of their private lives. In short, James's doctrine of special truth is the basis for political democracy of the classical liberal sort.[87] James's thinking is not an argument against socialism, but it is an argument against narrow-minded planning of institutions which do not allow for pluralism. His doctrine of special truth is a challenge to social planners to widen their view to the diversity of human life, rather than to constrain human life to the limits of their vision.

When James considers the ultimate basis of morality, he looks not to the needs of society or of particular classes, but to the needs of individuals. Believing as he does in special truth, he holds that there can be no common standard. Therefore, James must look to individuals who place their demands, of *whatever* kind, upon the universe. That something is desired or demanded is its own warrant, and unless it conflicts with other demands, James believed it should be satisfied.[88] The result is a type of utilitarianism.[89] What James sought was the greatest good for the greatest number. But goods are what people want or demand. "Since everything which is demanded is by that fact a good, must not the guiding principle for ethical philosophy (since all demands conjointly cannot be satisfied in this poor world) be simply to satisfy at all times *as many demands as we can?*" [90]

But James has left us with a problem, for clearly some integration must be effected. All the demands can simply not be satisfied. Territories, goods and services, particular times and spaces, all the resources of the world, must be allotted. And they must be allotted according to some standard, else how are conflicting demands to be weighed? Thus what James has presented is a beginning of a philosophy, but only that.

WHITEHEAD'S INTENSITY OF EXPERIENCE

Whitehead agrees with much that James has to say. And yet the tone is curiously different. Whitehead talks as if, in some mysterious way, his ship had come into harbor. It is hazy at this dawn of understanding, the outlines are not clear, but there is the feeling that the ship is home.

Whitehead generally seems to believe that things in themselves are good, and that evil is a question of destructive relationships.

"Evil, triumphant in its enjoyment, is so far good in itself; but beyond itself it is evil in its character of a destructive agent among things greater than itself. In the summation of the more complex fact it has secured a descent towards nothingness, in contrast to the creativeness of what can without qualification be termed good. Evil is positive and destructive; what is good is positive and creative." [91]

Thus the bullet that killed Robert Kennedy was not in itself evil, but was evil in its relations to the organism it fatally disrupted.

There is no doubt that much evil can be explained by a positive agent having a negative effect on others. But it seems to me that both James and Whitehead ignore here the kind of evil which comes from self-destructiveness, as depicted, for example, in the novels of Dostoevsky and as analyzed by Freud. The thief and the neurotic are not necessarily good in themselves: they may sit wrapped up in their own self-imposed limitations and misery. There is concealed in the thinking of James and Whitehead on this point a reversion to an eighteenth-century model of human nature, that of the positive autonomous man pursuing his own interests. Whitehead and particularly James realized that men frequently do not know their own interests and that even when they do, they often cannot pursue them, but rather seek their own destruction. But the realization of this fact is not reflected in their doctrine of evil.

In any case, James and Whitehead attempt to find a standard to be used in the promotion of greater good. James's standard is demands—what demands do the individuals make and what adjustment can be effected so that as many demands as possible can be met? Whitehead uses the standard of intensity of experience—how can intensity of experience be promoted by the adjustment and coordination of individuals? This standard is clearly less pluralistic and relativistic than James's, because of any individual it can be said that he enjoys more or less richness of experience, and so is more or less valuable for himself. The standard would cover the case of self-destructiveness, since self-destructive men would be less valuable for themselves, as well as for others. An aim of society would then be to promote behavior in such men which was self-fulfilling. This supposedly would be the aim of therapy, although it could not always be clear what was self-fulfilling and what was not.

In any event, the aim of society would be the promotion of its individuals. With James, Whitehead emphasizes the importance of the individual over the social system. Whitehead believes that the individual is more important because he is more complex; he is alive, whereas the social system is not; and thus he enjoys an experience which simply does not characterize society. (Totalitarian regimes which claim the life of the state are, for Whitehead, simply "barbarous.") Accordingly, he writes, "The worth of any social system depends on the value experience it promotes among individual human beings." [92]

The possibilities which the universe provides are options only for individuals who can experience them. In the primordial nature of God, these possibilities are relevant to each individual in a graded way; these possibilities are the source of aspiration as it comes from the divine nature. To this spread of possibilities, society, lacking sentient experience, is necessarily dead. And each particular society, manifesting only one in the infinite range of societal types potentially available, is necessarily limited and limiting. This would, in part, seem to be what Whitehead means when he says:

"Render unto Caesar the things that are Caesar's. But beyond Caesar there stretches the array of aspirations whose coordinating principle is termed God. It is not to be found in any one simple community life, either economic or knit by aim at domination. Even a religious community is inadequate. There always remains *solus cum solo*. We have developed a moral individuality; and in that respect we face the universe—*alone*." [93]

Accordingly, a wise government provides for alternative modes of community life and for an international life as well. The aim is to provide opportunities for individuals, not enforce conformity to social type.

But like Ruth Benedict, Whitehead would seem to hold that each society has its particular integrated type of perfection.[94] This view could conflict with the ideal just stated of providing a framework of opportunity for pluralism. But perhaps not. A particular society, such as a Zuni village, furnishes value experience for its individual members. Some integration around an ideal type—in the case of the Zuni, what Ruth Benedict calls the "apollonian" type—may be necessary, however limiting, for the village to function at all. However, these considerations would apply more to primitive societies, much less to present-day cosmopolitan Western culture.

In any case, Whitehead's reasoning leads him, with James, to disavow any absolute moral code. Whitehead puts it: "Thus the notion that there are certain regulative notions, sufficiently precise to prescribe details of conduct, for all reasonable beings on Earth, in every planet, and in every star-system, is at once to be put aside . . . All realization of the Good is finite, and necessarily excludes certain other types." [95] The ideal, or the good, rises from all the particulars of the case. It is necessarily restricted to that case, and to similar cases.

A disavowal of an absolute moral code is not, of course, the same thing as a disavowal of a good in itself. Nevertheless, Whitehead writes: "History can only be understood by seeing it as the theatre of diverse groups of idealists respectively urging ideals incompatible for conjoint realization. You cannot form any historical judgment of right or wrong by considering each group separately. The evil lies in the attempted conjunction." [96] Here Whitehead seems to have lapsed into carelessness: Clearly, some ideals, say, the glorification of the ruler, will promote less intensity of experience among the members of a particular society than other ideals. Some ideals are thus better than others. But what Whitehead is perhaps saying here is that *conflict* among available social ideals may promote less richness of experience than any one such ideal given free reign. Present-day South Vietnam (1970) might be an illustration.

TOWARD THE GOOD

In his review of the history of the West, Whitehead notes a "slow drift of mankind towards civilization." The drift is not inevitable. Societies, such as Byzantium, can more or less stop at some level, repeating their patterns in art and social life over the centuries, until they are swept away by more vital civilizations.[97] But for Whitehead the West illustrates this drift. Although different ages show different patterns, the general trend is toward greater value experiences for society's members.

Some theory of melioristic social change is required to explain this trend. James speaks of the "invisible molecular forces" and the "forces of truth," which work from individual to individual and which finally are vindicated by historical realization. For Whitehead, and most likely for James as well, these forces are of two types.

The first type is at a low level, what Whitehead calls the "slow growth of mutual respect, sympathy, and general kindliness." [98] These, he says, result in the improvement of behavior systems of human beings in their intercourse with each other.

The second type of force is at a higher level: it is that of ideas in their adventures in history. Ideas, such as the dignity of the human soul, have a "vague feeling of importance" derived from their superior generality.[99] They are rarely stated explicitly, but because they are implicit in human institutions, as possibilities if not as actualities, they haunt mankind, driving it to actions by reason of their appeal to an uneasy conscience.

In contrast to ideas and other persuasive forces, such as kindliness, Whitehead speaks of "senseless forces, floods, barbarians, and mechanical devices," which also effect social change. These, like causal forces in the physical world, are morally indeterminate and so do not tend to advance social progress.[100]

James and Whitehead also stress the need for routine in a society. Social life is founded on it; consequently, unless the social innovations attributable particularly to ideal forces are in some way routinized, they are in danger of being lost. Whitehead writes: "So many sociological doctrines, the products of acute intellects, are wrecked by obliviousness to this fundamental sociological truth." [101]

Ideals are always novelties. James writes that "there must be *novelty* in an ideal,—novelty at least for him whom the ideal grasps. Sodden routine is incompatible with ideality." [102] It is the purpose of philosophers and religious leaders to introduce these novelties into civilization, relying on the facility with which they are expressed, their generality, and the conscience of mankind to render them effective.[103]

It must then be asked: Where do the general ideals come from? And why does Whitehead put such emphasis on their generality; does such generality have moral value?

Whitehead says, "Habits of thought and sociological habits survive because in some broad sense they promote aesthetic enjoyment." [104] This indicates that in some ultimate way, aesthetics is behind the effectiveness of ideals. Now, for Whitehead, the teleology of the universe is directed to the production of beauty. Discord, such as pain, confusion, and conflict, is created when subjective forms or purposes, which may be beautiful in themselves, clash with one another. But wide purpose will coordinate the aims of smaller bits of included experience.

"Wide purpose," Whitehead says, "is in its own nature beautiful by reason of its contribution to the massiveness of experience." [105] This is a qualification of Whitehead's doctrine that beauty is finite. Beauty can result from the intensity of integration of a particular organic system. And it can also result from the adequacy of an idea to effect coordination of a wide spectrum of experience. The latter is much closer to what Kant refers to as the "sublime." [106] In any case, general ideas, such as the dignity of the human soul, can thus come from wide experience, and reciprocally achieve moral value by their ability to *coordinate* large areas of experience. Such coordination might be the dedication of one's life to the promotion of intensity of experience of mankind, that is, in the wider sense, mankind's aesthetic enjoyment.

Now, according to Whitehead, conceptual novelties which lead to a greater richness of values need not come directly from past experience; Whitehead believes God's purpose is to achieve richness of experience in the members of a society, and that such richness can come through the coordination effected by general ideas. Accordingly, these ideas, Whitehead says, may come from God. "God," he says, "is that function in the world by reason of which our purposes are directed to ends which in our own consciousness are impartial as to our own interests." [107]

Reciprocally, the process by which religious ideals achieve their breadth can also be seen as a widening of interest. At first a man is concerned only for his family or for his tribe. Then his consciousness expands to an attentive regard to his nation and finally to the world. The universe as a whole lays a claim on him which he must answer. "Religion," Whitehead says, "is world loyalty." This idea is at the heart of Whitehead's religion:

"The spirit at once surrenders itself to this universal claim and appropriates it for itself. So far as it is dominated by religious experience, life is conditioned by this formative principle, equally individual and general, equally actual and beyond completed act, equally compelling recognition and permissive of disregard."

"This principle is not a dogmatic formulation, but the intuition of immediate occasions as failing or succeeding in reference to the ideal relevant to them. There is a rightness attained or missed, with more or less completeness of attainment or omission."

"This is a revelation of character, apprehended as we apprehend the characters of our friends. But in this case it is an apprehension of character permanently inherent in the nature of things." [108]

What religion gives man then is an insight into each occasion or individual so that he discerns what ideals are relevant for it. Thus, as his vision and his loyalty widen to all reality, man achieves a God-like vision; he too judges all occasions not only by what ideals are relevant to them individually but by what ideals are relevant to them as members of larger societies and the world. (Or man can alternately be seen as an *agent* through whom God makes His vision relevant to individual occasion.) Like Plato with his Phaedrus, man persuades those occasions or individuals with the conceptual ideals relevant to them to rise to their opportunities by realizing ideals in practice which will fulfill them in their world. This is man's vision and his ministry.

The problem of evil remains: Why isn't good completely effective? Plato has an answer which Whitehead seems to presuppose throughout. There are two related reasons: lack of knowledge of the good and lack of inclination to do it. While a man's condition in the world does indicate the value of men for each other, a man may not understand his condition, and specifically, the need for service to his fellow men. Again, he may understand it in a distant, abstract way, but not intimately so as to have it dominate his thoughts. The solid, immediate comforts of his indulgent life may be more persuasive than this distant general ideal. James says that any idea, good or bad, which gains ascendency forms the content of otherwise unmediated action. The obstacle is that when men are in a condition of evil, their ideas will conform to their condition. The good of humanity, or social service, as an ideal, must be the novelty, and can gain ascendancy only by the widening of a man's knowledge of his condition beyond his limited case to include the wider conditions to which the ideal relates. Once this occurs, the ideal can coordinate both the individual and others, say, the poor, in a larger social conception. Thus the adjustment of claims of which James speaks and Whitehead's coordination of aims can come through the persuasive effects of facts and general ideas. Here the work of philosophy in the social field is defined.

Whitehead writes that larger religious conceptions came from men who traveled beyond their immediate group. This widening of acquaintance with the condition of others promoted both an extension of loyalty and a generalization of conceptions to fit the larger conditions to which they had to relate. But the point indicates a limitation of general ideas as persuasive agents by themselves. Loyalty is usually dependent upon affection, and affection usually comes through intimate knowledge.

Moreover, a principle of virtue is not some specific act. The individuals who make up the world require special care. There is a need for parents and wives and nurses, as well as philosophers. There is thus a need for love or affection in the universe which is not usually promoted by philosophic generality. Whitehead's analysis of love takes in James's idea of "claim" or "demand." But Whitehead transfigures the idea into the ideal relevant for the individual, for the "beautiful result." This is the claim—perhaps the individual must be persuaded even to have it—which must be adjusted to the world as it is:

"But some closeness of status, such as the relation of parent to child or the relation of marriage, can produce the love of self-devotion where the potentialities of the loved object are felt passionately as a claim that it find itself in a friendly Universe. Such love is really an intense feeling as to how the harmony of the world should be realized in particular objects . . . It is the passionate desire for the beautiful result, in this instance. Such love is distracting, nerve-racking. But, unless darkened by utter despair, it involves deep feeling of an aim in the Universe, winning such triumph as is possible to it." [109]

Philosophy, which extends beyond the individual case, is what coordinates such love, including self-love,[110] with the wider claims of the social order. There is a common standard for philosophy to use, intensity of experience. Philosophy can also judge social systems by assessing how they promote intensity of experience among individuals. And the individual can be rated "on the intrinsic strength of its own experience, and partly on its influence in the promotion of a high-grade type of order." [111]

Thus the individual and the society are connected in a common morality. They are also connected by analogy, because the individual *is* a society in his own right. The individual has fleeting appearances in the conscious field which are analogous to a society's "ripples of social efforts, harmonizing and clashing in their aims at ways of satisfaction." Beneath all are the deeper routines, those of the animal body and analogously, those of the basic economy. Low-grade cultures, like stones, endure without change, but men and brilliant cultures are fleeting.[112]

PEACE

The double role of the individual, for himself and for the high-grade social order, provides the framework for his morality. Personality must be surpassed—one must lose his life to gain it;[113] there are the high-grade orders which the individual must serve, principally his culture and his world, but really the *possibilities* for them.

And with the widening of concern, the paralysis of too much knowledge is avoided. Instead, distractions subside; a new source of energy is found. There flood back a God-like vision and a faith in beauty, "where reason fails to reveal the details."[114]

The result is a "wider sweep of conscious control," which Whitehead calls peace. "Thus Peace is self-control at its widest,—at the width where the 'self' has been lost, and interest has been transferred to coordinations wider than personality."[115]

This wider sweep of conscious control is perhaps the coordination that James was reaching for, what he felt and could not altogether find in religion, and what he saw a glimmer of in the careers of the great statesmen, the Lincolns and the Gladstones. But he would ask, thinking of them, and maybe not a little of himself: How, with so much tragedy and failure in the world, with the missed opportunities, social and political, the decay of standards, the cruelty, personal pain, frustration and loss, how can one find consolation? Whitehead's answer is a sense of tragedy, the catharsis of the man who is both audience and actor—James might have called it "courage":

"Amid the passing of so much beauty, so much heroism, so much daring, Peace is then the intuition of permanence. It keeps vivid the sensitiveness to the tragedy; and it sees the tragedy as a living agent persuading the world to aim at fineness beyond the faded level of surrounding fact. Each tragedy is the disclosure of an ideal:—What might have been, and was not: What can be. The tragedy was not in vain. This survival power in motive force, by reason of appeal to reserves of Beauty, marks the difference between the tragic evil and the gross evil. The inner feeling belonging to this grasp of the service of tragedy is Peace—the purification of the emotions." [116]

Conclusion

At the base of James's thought is what he calls a "methodical postulate":

"Nothing can be admitted as fact, it says, except what can be experienced at some definite time by some experient; and for every feature of fact ever so experienced, a definite place must be found somewhere in the final system of reality. In other words: Everything real must be experienceable somewhere, and every kind of thing experienced must somewhere be real." [1]

This "methodical postulate" expresses James's belief, a belief which Whitehead shared, that all reality is experiential. James and Whitehead hold further that the universe is not opaque, that it is all of the same stuff as we are, and so is open to thought.

The task of philosophy, as they see it, is to put men into the most vital relations with reality. It is to make most intensely subjective what was objective, that is, independent of us. Thus James's concept of truth is living reality, experiencing it, and so verifying it.

James and Whitehead are subjectivists to this extent, that the nature of the experience will depend as much on the knower as on the real things he experiences. Indeed, in the final moment in which the knower and its known unite, they are annihilated, and what emerges as a unique fact in the universe is the knower unifying his world. Alternately phrased, what emerges is the unity of the experienced world of that knower.

Whitehead's doctrine of reenaction means that, at the lowest levels, an organism will simply reenact the forms of its own inputs. But he and James also maintain that as the knower increases in complexity, his final subjective forms will be abstractions and distortions of his basic inputs. The task of philosophy is to make the abstractions conscious, to correct the distortions, and to unify experienced and experienceable fact under adequate generalizations. The final aim is the truth about the universe. And truth must be approached with childlike openness combined with the most refined sophistication.

For James and Whitehead, the epiphenomenal aspect of thought disappears. Ideas are efficacious in the world; they are real things in the universe, not just a gloss on them. They are the forms of experienced fact; they are also the incitement for changes in the future, the very soul of the organisms they seem to control. In this sense, a suffering, intending fact is the ultimate fact in the universe.

Whitehead and James both use the word "feeling" to describe this ultimate fact. But feeling, as James hints and Whitehead maintains, is an activity. There are two phases of its existence, creativity and transmission. Creativity is the act of unification out of the data of existence. For James, it is seen in its conscious phase, in the making of the total object of thought, that is, the unified conscious field or "perspective interest." More deeply, it is conceived as the making of the self and its products. For Whitehead, creativity is viewed as the process of concrescence as the organism rises from its data, guided by the unifying subjective aim.

The other phase is transmission. James's analysis of felt transition in consciousness anticipates Whitehead's theory of prehensions, or, in other words, feelings in the mode of causal efficacy. This is the aspect of transmission from the past to the present. Transmission is also the act of imparting influences to other entities, including the subject itself, in its causal

future. For James, this is the continuity of ideas in the conscious mind and the transmission of the self to its future occasions; it is also the experience of purpose guiding future
actions. For Whitehead, it is all of these; and conceived from
the physical standpoint, it is also how energy, in whatever
form, is transmitted by the organism to entities in its causal
future.

The effect of this philosophy is a feeling of closeness with
the world. The world is within us as we are in the world; our
acts of mentality are not epiphenomenal comments on the real
things of the world, but rather our final acts of unification. To
be sure, we may think well or badly; but however it goes,
there is always the ideal of harmonious issuance into truth, a
truth which is the form of existence itself within us.[2] Thus the
end of mysticism, the unification with existence, is achievable
at the height of consciousness.

But, as the mystics maintain, consciousness carries with it
inherent distortions. One reason is that conscious thought is a
learned tradition, and need bear little relation to the deeper
aspects of existence. Such considerations are behind Whitehead's fight against "clear and distinct ideas" and James's
affinity for Bergson. But both also maintain that physics and
physiology are necessary to tell us about the many events in
our immediate environment which do not otherwise come into
conscious experience.

Mysticism characteristically has a discipline for achieving
closeness with the world. Whitehead and James offer suggestions to the same purpose. One is an openness to all evidence.
A second is a willingness to let the data, including our previous existences, issue forth into their own ideas, and a corresponding willingness to discard traditional, mental structures.
A third is a sense of rigor in scrutinizing the way in which
ideas are combined, that is, a sense for logic. A fourth is a
sense for organic combination, that is, a sense for aesthetics.
This implies an understanding of the role of ideas in one's own

process of unification and in the unification of other organisms; reciprocally, it implies an understanding of the instrumental nature of abstraction. A fifth is an openness to inspiration as it may come from the source of all order (this suggestion is more peculiarly Whitehead's). And the last is a dedication to the process of achieving a harmony with the universe *through* conscious thought.

Another effect of this philosophy is an attempt to grasp the form of the experiences of other things. The doctrine that all the universe is composed of experiencing facts leads the philosopher to attempts to imagine or reenact those experiences. The chemist George Wald writes: "I tell my students to try to feel like a molecule. If they can reach the point of saying to themselves, when up against some problem of molecular behavior, 'What would I do if I were that molecule'—then things are going well." [3] James illustrates this approach perhaps best in *The Varieties of Religious Experience,* in which he tries to reenact sympathetically the whole range of religious experience, from that of madmen to that of saints. For Whitehead, this approach is the way in which man's understanding becomes God-like; it is the way "we apprehend the characters of our friends." It rests on the belief that although each occasion is unique in time and space, its mental content, that is, its form of experience or its "abstract essence," is not. It thus relies on a theory in which ideas "exemplified at one place can be exemplified at another," and, if exemplified, will aesthetically and logically interact with other ideas in similar ways. Thus although our grasp of the experience of other occasions is hazardous, it is not impossible.

James's discussion of the organization of the conscious field and the structure of the self opens up new fields of research which are just now being explored. What is the relation between cognitive schemes and the organization of new information, memory, and language? What are the relations between the deep layers of the conscious field, that is, the self, and the superficial layers, for example, the perceptual field? What are the various structures of the conscious field, and what are their relations to learning, awareness, purpose, dreams, and the various forms of art and psychopathology? Whitehead's thinking raises the same kinds of questions. In addition, his view that aesthetics and logic are intimately related, and that they are at the heart of the organic process, provides philosophic support for the attempt to understand intelligence through computer models and information theory. And, at the biochemical level, his theory of the production and role of organic purposes stands as a guide to research.

The idea of a suffering, experiencing fact clears away the quality of blank opacity which has clung to the concept of matter, particularly as this concept has been applied to the physical aspects of existence. Whitehead and, for the most part, James maintain that the laws of nature are the ultimate responsibility of the real things of the world; and that these things establish the laws according to the various inputs which they reenact or perceive, including themselves, from their immediate pasts. Their notion breaks down the artificial distinction between the laws of nature and the laws of social behavior, since both rely on mutual perception and the socialization of character.

The philosophy of James and Whitehead represents a reassertion of romanticism.[4] Romanticism faded in the nineteenth century because it seemed intellectually shoddy in comparison with the exact sciences. Characteristically, the romantic attributed to all existence the emotions he felt in himself; the result was clearly a great deal of falsehood. The scientific reaction was to explain away in energetic terms such emotions as were admitted.

The essence of romanticism is the belief that ideas stir the depths, that, for example, the words 'I love you' can move the beloved. For Whitehead and James, this is an example of the efficacy of ideas in the processes of the world. Even more basically, Whitehead attributes emotional feeling to all existence. Whitehead is careful not to attribute complex emotions to nexus, such as stones or thunderstorms. But all existence is emotional in some way. The intimate relation between the heart and the head of which traditional romanticism spoke is reestablished. A scientific knowledge of the emotional nature of all fact removes the obstruction of intellectual shoddiness and enables man once again to extend his sympathy and love to all existence.

In ethics and politics, the notion of sympathetic understanding provides an ultimate foundation. James talks of needs, Whitehead of intensity of experience, but both look to the value of all organisms for themselves as the first ethical demand. Although Whitehead's formulation gives him a method of adjusting conflicting demands which James's lacks, and is perhaps ultimately more life enhancing, both philosophers see the transition from personal morality to social ethics as a process of coordinating such demands for the benefit of all individual members. The uniqueness of the individual's experience, requirements, and potentialities is the basis for pluralistic democracy; the need in a social order for coordination is the basis for social justice.

Finally, James and Whitehead seek the source of values which quicken existence to rise to its higher potentialities. Theirs is an effort to implicate God in existence, and so remove the immense distance which separates man from God in conventional theism. (Whitehead's attempt is the more complete and assured of the two.) A seeming alternative is the existentialist one of making man altogether responsible for his own values.

But if God is immanent in things, as Whitehead holds, or if He is the "ideal tendency in things," as James maintains, then man, as a locus for the entire universe, *is* responsible for his own values. In any case, James and, particularly, Whitehead offer the insight that the aesthetics and logic which underlie all existence also form the basis for the adjustments and compositions of man's consciousness, and derivatively, his morality, art, and statesmanship. The egocentricity of much of modern philosophy is thus avoided. Man participates directly in the basic processes of the universe or sets up within himself and his society a sympathetic parallelism.

The religious beliefs of Whitehead and James rest on insights into the nature of things which are ultimately mystical. James talks of "an altogether other dimension of existence from the sensible and merely 'understandable' world." And for Whitehead, God and the world flow and ebb like the sea on the strand, rhythmic like consciousness and cause, value and fact. And there is on the farther shore, for him and for James, the sense of participation, of implication in what is eternal. Whether these are true insights or not depends on the answer to metaphysical questions whose very formulation lies on the margin of human thought.

Abbreviations Used in the Notes

WORKS BY WILLIAM JAMES

Essays	*Collected Essays and Reviews* (New York: Longmans, Green and Co., 1920)
Human Immortality	*Human Immortality* (Boston and New York: Houghton Mifflin and Co., 1898)
Letters	*Letters of William James,* edited by his son Henry James, 2 vols. (Boston: Atlantic Monthly Press, 1920)
Memories	*Memories and Studies* (New York: Longmans, Green and Co., 1912)
Pragmatism	*Pragmatism* (London, Bombay, and Calcutta: Longmans, Green and Co., 1907)
Psychology	*The Principles of Psychology,* 2 vols. (New York: Henry Holt and Co., 1890)
Radical Empiricism	*Essays in Radical Empiricism* (New York: Longmans, Green and Co., 1912)
Some Problems	*Some Problems of Philosophy* (New York: Longmans, Green and Co., 1911)
Talks	*Talks to Teachers* (New York: Henry Holt and Co., 1900)
Truth	*The Meaning of Truth: A Sequel to "Pragmatism"* (New York and London: Longmans, Green and Co., 1909)
Universe	*A Pluralistic Universe* (New York and London: Longmans, Green and Co., 1909)
Varieties	*The Varieties of Religious Experience* (New York: Random House, 1929)
Will	*The Will to Believe* (London, Bombay, and Calcutta: Longmans, Green and Co., 1912)

WORKS BY ALFRED NORTH WHITEHEAD

Adventures   *Adventures of Ideas* (New York: Macmillan Co., 1933)

Aims   *The Aims of Education* (New York: Macmillan Co., 1929)

Dialogues   *Dialogues of Alfred North Whitehead,* as recorded by Lucien Price (Boston: Little, Brown and Co., 1954)

Modes   *Modes of Thought* (New York: Macmillan Co., 1938)

Natural Knowledge   *An Enquiry Concerning the Principles of Natural Knowledge,* 2nd ed. (London: Cambridge University Press, 1925)

Nature   *The Concept of Nature* (London: Cambridge University Press, 1920)

Process   *Process and Reality* (New York: Macmillan Co., 1929)

Reason   *The Function of Reason* (Princeton: Princeton University Press, 1929)

Religion   *Religion in the Making* (New York: Macmillan Co., 1926)

Science   *Science and the Modern World* (London: Cambridge University Press, 1925)

Science and Philosophy   *Essays in Science and Philosophy* (New York: Philosophical Library, 1947)

Symbolism   *Symbolism: Its Meaning and Effect* (London: Cambridge University Press, 1928)

Notes

PREFACE

1. See Ralph Barton Perry, *The Thought and Character of William James,* 2 vols. (Boston and Toronto: Little, Brown and Co., 1935), hereafter called Perry.

2. *Science,* p. 199.

3. *Ibid.,* particularly chaps. 6–9. See A. d'Abro, *The Rise of the New Physics,* 2 vols. (New York: Dover: Dover Publications, 1951). The earlier title of this work is *The Decline of Mechanism.*

4. *Will,* pp. 323–324.

5. *Essays,* p. 449.

6. See Perry, I, 491.

7. James's last works, particularly *Some Problems of Philosophy* (1911), show some but not much influence of the new physics.

8. *Dialogues,* p. 238.

9. "Whitehead's Philosophical Development," in *The Philosophy of Alfred North Whitehead,* ed. Paul Arthur Schilpp (New York: Tudor Publishing Co., 1951), p. 41. Of these developments, the most important for Whitehead were probably vector physics and field theory. For the influence of mathematics, see pp. 24–25.

10. *Science,* pp. 212–213.

11. See Edmund Husserl, *Cartesian Meditations: An Introduction to Phenomenology,* trans. Dorion Cairns (The Hague: Martinus Nimhoff, 1969); Martin Heidegger, *Being and Time,* trans. John Macquarrie and Edward Robinson (New York: Harper & Row, 1962) and Maurice Merleau-Ponty, *Phenomenology of Perception,* trans. Colin Smith (London: Routledge & Kegan Paul, 1962). An introduction to logical positivism with a bibliography is provided in A. J. Ayer, *Logical Positivism* (New York: Free Press, 1959).

12. Whitehead's unpublished manuscripts and notes were destroyed after his death. Those few papers which still exist are

presently (June 1970) in the care of Professor Victor Lowe of Johns Hopkins, who is preparing a biography.

13. Victor Lowe remarks that "Whitehead's account of the field of perception is James', not Hume's." "The Development of Whitehead's Philosophy," in *The Philosophy of Alfred North Whitehead,* p. 64. Even more to the point, Lowe says that "James's unmatched psychological observations provide the chief outside evidence to show that Whitehead's theory of prehensions is not a castle in the air." *Understanding Whitehead* (Baltimore: Johns Hopkins Press, 1962), p. 263.

14. Letter to Mrs. Henry Whitman, August 22, 1903, in *Letters,* II, 199.

15. *Dialogues,* pp. 337–338.

16. In this study, I have assumed that the great mass of James's thought can be assimilated into such a system, and, accordingly, I have used all his principal works. As for Whitehead, I have conceived his earlier nonmathematical work as preparation for his more mature works in philosophy, and have referred to it only occasionally. For an analysis of chronological movement in James's thought, see Perry; for Whitehead, see Victor Lowe, "The Development of Whitehead's Philosophy," and Nathaniel Lawrence, *Whitehead's Philosophical Development* (Berkeley and Los Angeles: University of California Press, 1956).

17. *Adventures,* p. 353.

INTRODUCTION

1. *Pragmatism,* pp. 35–36.

2. *Identity: Youth and Crisis* (New York: W. W. Norton and Co., 1968), pp. 24–25.

3. Both standard biographies of James contain an immense amount of personal material. The orientation of Perry's *Thought and Character of William James* (1935) is philosophical rather than psychological or novelistic. Gay Wilson Allen's *William James: A Biography* (New York: Viking Press, 1967), is the first major biography to appear after Perry's. It draws heavily upon previously unavailable family papers and presents a wealth of new personal data. Unfortunately, Allen hardly deals with James's ideas. There is clearly a need for a biographic work which connects the personal data with James's psychology and philosophy.

A brilliant unpublished paper by Howard M. Feinstein, "William James on the Emotions," delivered to the Group for Applied Psychoanalysis at Harvard University in 1968, takes exactly this approach.

It can only be hoped that Mr. Feinstein will take the success of his paper as encouragement to discuss the whole body of James's work.

To date, there has been no biography of Whitehead published. The biography in preparation by Professor Lowe will soon fill the gap.

4. *Dialogues*, p. 232. Whitehead was referring to the period between 1880 and 1910.

5. *Science and Philosophy*, p. 115.

6. *Character and Opinion in the United States* (New York: Charles Scribner's Sons, 1920), pp. 43–44.

7. Perry, I, 149.

8. Letter of April 17, 1904, to James Henry Leuba, in *Letters*, II, 211. James's letters, however, are full of attempts to argue himself into a belief. See the letter to Thomas Davidson, January 8, 1882, quoted in Perry, I, 737.

9. August 29, 1944, *Dialogues*, p. 296.

10. *The Autobiography of Bertrand Russell* (Boston and Toronto: Little, Brown and Co., 1967), p. 190.

11. See the transmission theory in *Human Immortality;* see also *Pragmatism*, lectures 2, 3, and 8.

12. *Religion*, p. 85.

13. *Pragmatism*, p. 95.

14. *Science*, pp. 263–264.

15. James to Mrs. Henry Whitman, June 7, 1899, in *Letters*, II, 90; *Process*, part V, chap. 2.

16. Russell indicates that the Whitehead of this time at least may have had a more temperamental nature than most people thought: "Whitehead appeared to the world calm, reasonable, and judicious, but when one came to know him well one discovered that this was only a facade. Like many people possessed of great self-control, he suffered from impulses which were scarcely sane." *Autobiography*, p. 226.

17. *Ibid.*, p. 188.

18. *An Enquiry Concerning the Principles of Natural Knowledge*, 1919; *The Concept of Nature*, 1920; *The Principle of Relativity* (Cambridge University Press, 1922).

19. *Dialogues*, pp. 131, 150.

20. *Process*, p. 4. Whitehead maintains that philosophers who do not uphold a system fall "prey to the delusive clarities of detached expressions which it is the very purpose of their science to surmount" (*Adventures*, p. 287).

21. *Science*, p. 122.

22. The evolution of Whitehead's ideas from these sources can be

seen in the works on nature written after World War I. See Victor
Lowe, "Whitehead's Philosophical Development" in *The Philosophy
of Alfred North Whitehead,* ed. Paul Arthur Schilpp (New York:
Tudor Publishing Co., 1951).

23. *Identity: Youth and Crisis,* p. 151.

24. Gay Wilson Allen, *William James: A Biography* (New York:
Viking Press, 1967), pp. 163–167. According to William's son Henry,
the traumatic experience of a "Frenchman" in *The Varieties of Religious Experience* (pp. 157–158) is that of James himself.

25. The definition is from the second *Essais,* which in his diary of
April 30, 1870, James recorded he had been reading. James was later
to dedicate *Some Problems of Philosophy* to Renouvier, stating "but
for the decisive impression made on me in the seventies by his mas-
terly advocacy of pluralism, I might never have got free from the
monster superstition under which I had grown up." A year before,
James had professed belief in a completely determined universe. See
his letter of March 1869, in *Letters,* I, 152–153.

26. Allen, *William James,* pp. 180 and 168. The doctrine became
the basis of James's central essay, "The Will to Believe."

27. Quoted in *Ibid.,* p. vii.

28. Letter of September 28, 1909, to Theodore Flournoy in *Letters,*
II, 327–328; *Psychology,* II, 458–459.

29. Diary entry of April 30, 1873, quoted in Perry, I, 343.

30. *Science,* p. 281.

31. James is generally credited with founding the first laboratory
for experimental psychology in the United States. See Allen, *William
James,* pp. 193–194; also Perry, II, 9–10, which quotes James's letter to
G. Stanley Hall admonishing him for claiming this achievement for
himself. Of German experimental psychology, James wrote: "This
method taxes patience to the utmost, and could hardly have arisen in
a country whose natives could be *bored*" (Psychology, I, 192). In any
case, as soon as he could James turned the Harvard laboratory over
to Hugo Munsterberg, a former pupil of Wilhelm Wundt.

32. *Pragmatism,* p. 19; see also *Universe,* pp. 51 and 126.

33. James's critique of Hegel, Bradley, and Royce spares nothing.
See *Will,* pp. 263–298; *Pragmatism,* pp. 29–31, 42–43; *Essays,*
chaps. 22 and 38; *Universe,* lectures 2 and 3.

34. James recalls a German philosophy professor saying, "Yes, we
philosophers, whenever we wish, can go so far that in a couple of sen-
tences we can put ourselves where nobody can follow us." James
remarks, "The professor said this with conscious pride, but he ought
to have been ashamed of it." *Universe,* p. 18.

35. From "The Good Anna" in *Three Lives* (New York: Random House, 1933).

36. *Modes*, p. 4.

37. *Science*, p. 122–123.

38. "What Psychical Research Has Accomplished" in *Will*, pp. 362–327. James was for two years president of the Society for Psychical Research, an activity which cost him the respect of some of his more conservative colleagues.

39. *Religion*, p. 67.

40. *Varieties*, p. 13. See Chapter V, below.

41. See *Psychology*, II, 370–371. In the nineteenth century, the unusual, the odd, the *outré* were "examined" by the scientist and written up as "findings." The phenomena were measured exhaustively; the scientist might even be his own subject; his efforts of patience were heroic. He attended meetings of his societies, such as James's Society for Psychical Research; his colleagues were bearded and grave; the world was being examined piece by piece; it was better that the women, in their innocence, remain ignorant. As for the insane, they were classified and measured, and referred to in Latinate phrases; otherwise they were ignored. (The German art movies after World War I, such as *The Cabinet of Dr. Caligari*, evoke the weirder aspects of this image.)

42. See *Dialogues, passim*.

43. For a study of nineteenth-century historicism, see Albert Schweitzer's *The Quest of the Historical Jesus*, trans. W. Montgomery (New York: Macmillan Co., 1948).

44. *Autobiography*, p. 247.

45. December 15, 1939; *Dialogues*, pp. 133–134.

46. *Memories*, p. 211.

47. Letter to George H. Palmer, April 2, 1900, in *Letters*, II, 123.

48. Perry writes, "He had queer ideas, but *he* was not queer. With all his philosophical detachment he knew instinctively how to meet the world on its own terms, how to make himself understood, and how to be free and spirited without ever transgressing the accepted norms of convention or polite intercourse" (I, 129). Even his bitterest fights with the absolutists were generally accompanied by personal friendliness.

49. See *Process*, p. v and part II.

50. See *The Philosophical Works of Descartes*, trans. Elizabeth S. Haldane and G. R. T. Ross, 2 vols. (Cambridge: At the University Press, 1931). All citations of Descartes are to this edition.

51. David Hume, *A Treatise of Human Nature* (London: Oxford

University Press, 1888) [hereafter referred to as Hume's *Treatise*], bk. I, pt. iv, sec. 6.

52. *The Principles of Philosophy*, pt. I, par. 52.

53. *Ibid.*, par. 63.

54. *Ibid.*, pt. IV, par. 198.

55. *Meditations on First Philosophy*, Meditation II.

56. *Science*, p. 24.

57. *The Principles of Philosophy*, pt. I, par. 51.

58. *Adventures*, pp. 201–202; see also *Nature*, pp. 158–159.

59. *Nature*, p. 171.

60. Whitehead, however, and, to some extent, James, would have some ideas result from God, which introduces an element of uncertainty into the explanation (see Chapters III–V).

61. Hume's *Treatise*, bk. I, pt. i, sec. 1.

62. *Ibid.*, pt. i, sec. 2; pt. iii, sec. 5.

63. *An Inquiry Concerning Human Understanding* (Chicago: Open Court Publishing Co., 1907), pp. 28–29; see also pp. 43–44, 46–47.

64. *An Essay Concerning Human Understanding*, 2 vols. (New York: Dover Publications, 1959), hereafter referred to as Locke's *Essay*.

65. *Ibid.*, bk. I, chap. xxiii, par. 32.

66. *Ibid.*, bk. II, chap. vii, par. 8; chap. viii, par. 8; bk. IV, chap. ii, par. 14; chap. xi, par. 2.

67. *Ibid.*, bk. IV, chap. xi, par. 8.

68. *Ibid.*, bk. II, chap. xxvii, par. 5.

69. *Ibid.*, bk. IV, chap. vi, par. 11.

70. Hume's *Treatise*, bk. I, pt. iv, sec. 6; Appendix

71. James wrote in 1892, "There is nothing but the old psychology which began in Locke's time, plus a little physiology of the brain and senses and theory of evolution, and a few refinements of introspective detail" (*Talks*, p. 7).

72. Perry, I, 543.

73. *Science*, p. 206.

74. *Psychology*, I, vi; see also "A Plea for Psychology as a 'Natural Science'" (1892) in *Essays*, pp. 317–318, 323–324.

75. Cited without reference in *Psychology*, I, 131.

76. Locke's *Essay*, bk. IV, chap. iii, par. 28.

77. *Psychology*, I, 81–82.

78. Contained in *The Origin of Psycho-Analysis*, ed. Marie Bonaparte, Anna Freud, Ernst Kris; trans. Eric Mosbacher and James Strachey (New York: Basic Books, 1954).

79. Note of 1873, quoted in Perry, I, 500.

80. See, for example, J. S. Mill, *An Examination of Sir William Hamilton's Philosophy* (London: Longman, Green, Longman, Roberts and Green, 1865), and his *System of Logic* (New York: Longmans, Green and Co., 1959). The classic statement of associationist psychology is James Mill's *Analysis of the Human Mind,* ed. J. S. Mill (London: Longmans, Green, Reader and Dyer, 1869).

81. Hume's *Treatise,* bk. I, pt. i, sec. 4.

82. *Psychology,* I, 1–2.

83. *Ibid.,* p. 604.

84. *Process,* p. vi.

85. *Essays,* pp. 436–437. In the same passage, James remarks, "Kant's mind is the rarest and most intricate of all possible antique bric-a-brac museums, and connoisseurs and dilettanti will always wish to visit it and see the wondrous and racy contents. The temper of the dear old man about his work is perfectly delectable. And yet he is really—although I shrink with some terror from saying such a thing . . . at bottom a mere curio, a 'specimen.' "

86. *Immanuel Kant's Critique of Pure Reason,* trans. F. Max Müller (New York: Macmillan Co., 1949), "Preface to the Second Edition of 1787," p. 694.

87. *Process,* p. 236.

88. *Immanuel Kant's Critique of Pure Reason,* "Transcendental Analytic," bk. II, chap. 1.

89. Immanuel Kant, *The Critique of Judgement,* trans. James Creed Meredith (London: Oxford University Press, 1952), pt. II, sec. 4.

90. *Science and Philosophy,* p. 7.

91. Richard J. Herrnstein and Edwin G. Boring, *A Source Book in the History of Psychology* (Cambridge, Mass.: Harvard University Press, 1965), p. 148, list Johannes Müller, Ewald Hering, Carl Stumpf, and R. H. Lotze (with qualifications) as nativists; Hermann von Helmholtz and Wilhelm Wundt as empiricists.

92. *Autobiography,* p. 247.

93. *Dialogues,* pp. 132 and 344–345.

I. THE KNOWING OF THINGS TOGETHER

1. Perry, I, 176.

2. Hume's *Treatise,* bk. I, pt. i, sec. 1; Kant's *Critique of Pure Reason,* "Transcendental Analytic," bk. I, chap. 2, sec. 3, p. 98.

3. Locke's *Essay,* bk. II, chap. viii, par. 12.

4. *Psychology*, I, 224.

5. *Process*, p. 480. Kant would probably not object to either this statement or that of James above. But, James and Whitehead might ask, if this were so, why do sensations have the central place they have in Kant's system?

6. *Psychology*, I, 487.

7. *Ibid.*, II, 82. See Wolfgang Köhler, *Gestalt Psychology* (New York: Liveright Publishing Corporation, 1947), and Kurt Koffka, *Principles of Gestalt Psychology* (New York: Harcourt, Brace and World, 1935).

8. *Psychology*, I, 488.

9. Hans-Lukas Teuber, "Somatosensory Disorders Due to Cortical Lesions, Preface: Disorders of Higher Tactile and Visual Functions," *Neuropsychologia*, III (1965), 287–294, and personal conversations with Dr. Teuber.

10. For a similar doctrine, see George Berkeley's *Essay towards a New Theory of Vision* (1709), par. xlvi, contained in Richard J. Herrnstein and Edwin G. Boring, *A Source Book in the History of Psychology* (Cambridge: Harvard University Press, 1965), pp. 170–171.

11. Hume, however, did not deny relations in the mind, as James accused him of doing. See *Psychology*, I, 487; Hume's *Treatise*, bk. I, pt. i, sec. 5.

12. *Psychology*, I, 245; *Radical Empiricism*, p. 95.

13. *Adventures*, p. 201. This position is not, however, consistently held. Cf. *Process*, p. 295.

14. *Mind*, IX (1884), 18–19.

15. *Adventures*, pp. 290–291.

16. *Process*, p. 239.

17. *Psychology*, I, 225–226. James comments that even in split personalities thoughts in each fragment are grouped in a personal way.

18. *Ibid.*, p. 162.

19. "On Some Omissions of Introspective Psychology," *Mind*, IX (1884), 18.

20. *Process*, p. 246.

21. *Process*, p. 349; *Modes*, p. 81; *Adventures*, pp. 339–340.

22. *Adventures*, pp. 347–349.

23. *The Interpretation of Dreams*, trans. and ed. James Strachey (New York: Science Editions, 1961).

24. *Psychology*, I, 288–289. The transformation of higher experi-

ences from data offered by lower faculties is called "transmutation" by Whitehead, and will be discussed in Chapters II and III.

25. *Psychology*, I, 285; see also *Modes*, lecture 4. This thinking comes close to the Tichener context theory (see Herrnstein and Boring, pp. 193–197) or Dewey's variant of it (see *Logic: The Theory of Inquiry* [New York: Henry Holt and Co., 1938], p. 67).

26. *Psychology*, I, 402. James here overemphasizes conscious control, as he frequently does. What one notices and what one agrees to are two different classes, though overlapping. Pain, for example, is something which we involuntarily attend to; to speak of an "agreement" to attend to it is plainly wrong.

27. Along similar lines, Merleau-Ponty remarks that "normal functioning must be understood as a process of integration in which the text of the external world is not so much copied as composed." *Phenomenology of Perception*, trans. Colin Smith (London: Routledge & Kegan Paul, 1962), p. 9.

28. See *Psychology*, I, 343.

29. *Ibid.*, pp. 176–177. It should be noted, however, that in later works, such as "Does Consciousness Exist?" and *A Pluralistic Universe*, James generally abandons the effort to establish the physical basis for experience.

30. *Ibid.*, II, 638.

31. *Universe*, pp. 390–391.

32. *Process*, p. 341. The similarity between concrescence and Kant's "synthesis" has already been noted.

33. *Hume's Treatise*, bk. I, pt. ii, sec. 3.

34. *Kant's Critique of Pure Reason*, "Transcendental Aesthetic."

35. See Locke's *Essay*, bk. II, chaps. iv, xiii and xiv.

36. *Psychology*, I, 240.

37. *Ibid.*, p. 620.

38. The doctrine, James points out, is taken from S. H. Hodgson's *Philosophy of Reflection*, 2 vols. (London: Longmans, Green and Co., 1878), I, 248–254, cited in *Psychology*, I, 608. Hodgson, the well-known English empiricist, was a close friend of James, and a major influence on him. See Perry, I, pp. xxxviii–xl. The phrase "specious present" was coined by E. R. Clay, an obscure American, in his work *The Alternative: A Study in Psychology* (London: Macmillan and Co., 1882), p. 167, cited in *Psychology*, I, 609. The basis for the notion can be found in Locke's *Essay*, bk. II, chap. xiv. See also Edmund Husserl, *The Phenomenology of Internal Time-Consciousness* (1905), trans. James S. Churchill (Bloomington, Ind.: Indiana

University Press, 1964), especially p. 23; and Merleau-Ponty, *The Phenomenology of Perception,* p. 275.

39. *Psychology,* I, 606–607. Husserl suggests that the mental materials must be "continuously modified from moment to moment" for succession to be established (*The Phenomenology of Internal Time-Consciousness,* p. 32).

40. "The Anatomy of Some Scientific Ideas" in *Aims,* pp. 190–191.

41. *Psychology,* I, 611. James states that larger units, minutes, days, and years, have to be conceived symbolically, and constructed by addition. Cf. *Adventures,* p. 233.

42. *Psychology,* I, 639–641.

43. *Ibid.,* pp. 643, 635, 646–647. Ulric Neisser speculates that the primary memory of James may correspond to his "echoic memory," a cognitive mechanism that stores information for up to a few seconds so that it can actually be heard. (Neisser has a corresponding mechanism for visual information, called the "iconic memory.") Neisser seems to rule out the correspondence because "echoic storage can substantially exceed the specious present; it may last for seconds and include several segments of speech." But this is quite within the span of time which James maintains the "specious present" includes. See Neisser's *Cognitive Psychology* (New York: Appleton-Century-Crofts, 1967), p. 200.

44. *Radical Empiricism,* p. 50; *Universe,* p. 326. See Victor Lowe, *Understanding Whitehead* (Baltimore: Johns Hopkins Press, 1962), chap. 13.

45. *Psychology,* I, 631.

46. *Ibid.,* pp. 630–631.

47. *Ibid.,* pp. 624–625.

48. *Psychology,* I, 649, 234.

49. *Ibid.,* p. 235. James writes, *"A permanently existing 'idea' or 'Vorstellung' which makes its appearance before the footlights of consciousness at periodical intervals, is as mythological an entity as the Jack of Spades"* (p. 236). The view of the associationists is accordingly called the "reappearance hypothesis" by Neisser (*Cognitive Psychology,* pp. 280–284), who also links Freud, the behaviorists, and even the Gestalt psychologists to the idea. Neisser lays much more emphasis upon the construction of memories than does James, who stresses more the changing moment of the stream in which the idea is remembered. The "reappearance hypothesis" in its original and strictest form can be found in the early dialogue of Plato, such as the *Meno* and *Phaedo.*

50. *Psychology,* I, 654.

51. *Ibid.*, p. 563.

52. *Time and Space,* p. 266, cited by James, *Psychology,* I, 572.

53. *Psychology,* I, 578.

54. *Ibid.*, pp. 281 and 279.

55. *Ibid.*, p. 253. Cf. *Adventures,* pp. 233–235, and *Process,* p. 197.

56. See F. C. Bartlett, *Remembering* (Cambridge: Cambridge University Press, 1932), and *Thinking* (New York: Basic Books, 1954); Jean Piaget, *The Construction of Reality in the Child,* trans. Margaret Cook (New York: Basic Books, 1954); J. S. Bruner, J. J. Goodnow, and G. A. Austin, *A Study of Thinking* (New York: John Wiley and Sons, 1956); J. S. Bruner *et al., Studies in Cognitive Growth* (New York: John Wiley and Sons, 1967); Ulric Neisser, *Cognitive Psychology;* George A. Miller, Eugene Galanter, and Karl H. Pribram, *Plans and the Structure of Behavior* (New York: Henry Holt and Co., 1960).

57. See Noam Chomsky, *Syntactic Structure* (The Hague and Paris: Mouton and Co., 1957).

58. *Psychology,* I, 255.

59. *Pragmatism,* pp. 177–178.

60. "Space, Time and Relativity" (1915) in *Aims,* p. 243. The theories of space contained in Whitehead's later writings are discussed in Chapters II–IV.

61. *Psychology,* II, 31–32. Cf. Locke's *Essay,* bk. II, chap. 13. James says that he "has derived most aid and comfort from the writings of Hering, A. W. Volkmann, Stumpf, Leconte, and Schön," and also renders homage to Hodgson. *Psychology,* II, 282.

62. *Cognitive Psychology,* p. 88.

63. *Psychology,* I, 426–427.

64. *Ibid.*, II, 35, 39, 269, and 36. Here, as so often elsewhere, James slips into regarding sensations as basic units.

65. *Ibid.*, pp. 145, 150, 152.

66. Kant's *Critique of Pure Reason,* "Transcendental Aesthetic," p. 16.

67. *Psychology,* II, 144, 275.

68. R. H. Lotze, *Medicinische Psychologie, oder Physiologie der Seele,* (Leipzig, 1852), bk. II, chap. 4, par. 289, in Herrnstein and Boring (translation by Don Cantor), p. 136.

69. For a discussion of local sign theory, see Hermann von Helmholtz, *Popular Scientific Lectures* (1867), trans. P. H. Pye-Smith in Richard M. Warren and Roslyn P. Warren, *Helmholtz on Perception: Its Physiology and Development* (New York: John Wiley and Sons, 1968), p. 111.

70. *Psychology,* II, 196.

71. *Ibid.,* p. 206.

72. *Ibid.,* pp. 158–159, 177.

73. *Ibid.,* p. 171. Compare the "Phi phenomenon" of Max Wertheimer, *"Experimentelle Studien über das Sehen von Bewegung"* (1912), in Herrnstein and Boring (translation by Don Cantor), pp. 163–168. For analogous ideas of Whitehead, see Chapter II.

74. *Psychology,* I, 621–622.

75. *Ibid.,* II, 146–147.

76. Such possibilities of psychological space are explored more thoroughly in the literature of phenomenology. See, for instance, Merleau-Ponty, *Phenomenology of Perception,* pp. 141, 156, and part II passim.

II. CAUSALITY, PERCEPTION, AND SELF

1. *Process,* p. 239, already quoted.

2. *Radical Empiricism,* pp. 12–24. See Edmund Husserl, *Cartesian Meditations: An Introduction to Phenomenology,* trans. Dorion Cairns (The Hague: Martinus Nimhoff, 1969), pp. 25–26, for the identical position.

3. *Radical Empiricism,* p. 15.

4. Letter to Charles Renouvier, September 30, 1884, quoted in Perry, I, 799.

5. *Radical Empiricism,* pp. 27–34.

6. Perry, I, 498. Cf. Maurice Merleau-Ponty, *The Phenomenology of Perception,* trans. Colin Smith (London: Routledge & Kegan Paul, 1962), p. 82.

7. *Radical Empiricism,* pp. 88–89.

8. *Universe,* p. 372.

9. *Process,* p. 243.

10. A modern variant, which James cites, is the mathematical idea of function: "Mathematicians make use, to connect the various interdependencies of quantities, of the general concept of function. That A is a function of B . . . means that with every alteration in the value of A, an alteration in that of B is always connected"(*Some Problems,* p. 207).

11. *Immanuel Kant's Critique of Pure Reason,* trans. F. Max Müller (New York: Macmillan Co., 1949), "Transcendental Doctrine of Method," chap. 1, sec. 2, p. 614. Hume himself suggests the Kantian solution. Cf. Hume's *Treatise,* bk. I, pt. iii, sec. 14.

12. *Process*, p. 265.

13. *Ibid.*, p. 267.

14. *Ibid.*, pp. 187, 267.

15. *Adventures*, p. 275. The feeling of "withness" is much less pronounced in sight, owing to the delicacy of the eye, than in touch. The preoccupation of philosophers with sight has tended to obscure the kind of experience Whitehead is talking about.

16. *Process*, pp. 99–100, 390.

17. *Ibid.*, p. 268.

18. *Ibid.*, p. 91.

19. *Varieties*, p. 492.

20. *Truth*, p. 69; *Psychology*, II, 7.

21. *Truth*, pp. 70, 174; see also *Some Problems*, pp. 208–209.

22. *Symbolism*, p. 25. By emphasizing sensations rather than objects, Whitehead is here adopting the sensationalist description of perception, which he rejects. James frequently falls into the same error.

23. *Essay*, bk. II, chap. viii, par. 8.

24. *Process*, p. 272. For James's agreement with this view, see *Truth*, p. 70.

25. See *Natural Knowledge*, pp. 25–26.

26. There are numerous instances where James seems to be supporting Whitehead's three-dimensional view of perception, in which the perceived enters into the constitution of the perceiver. See *Will*, pp. 269–271; *Universe*, pp. 258–259; *Radical Empiricism*, pp. 149–151. But at other times, James endorses the more traditional "representational" theory: "Yet the cosmic objects, so far as the experience yields them, are but ideal pictures of something whose existence we do not inwardly possess but only point at outwardly" (*Varieties*, p. 489).

27. *Process*, p. 220.

28. *Ibid.*, p. 351.

29. *Ibid.*, pp. 32, 34–35.

30. *Ibid.*, pp. 362–363.

31. *Ibid.*, p. 133; cf. p. 182. See also pp. 479–480.

32. The problem of isomorphism, which this discussion raises, is taken up by Wolfgang Köhler, *Dynamics in Psychology* (New York: Liveright Publishing Corporation, 1940).

33. *Symbolism*, p. 35.

34. *Process*, p. 182.

35, *Adventures*, p. 335.

36. *Process*, p. 362.

37. "Whitehead on Mind and Nature," in *The Philosophy of*

Alfred North Whitehead, ed. Paul Arthur Schilpp (New York: Tudor Publishing Co., 1951), p. 397.

38. *Process*, pt. IV, chap. 4. This section is extremely difficult to follow, and my interpretation is not sure.

39. *Adventures*, p. 278. Whitehead points out that strains are the ordering principle behind fundamental equations in physics, such as Maxwell's electromagnetic equations (*Process*, p. 474). (Whitehead's concept of strain would appear to be a generalization of these equations.) If strains are also a part of the perceptual process, perception may offer a more direct insight into fundamental physics than nineteenth-century thinkers suspected. See *Process*, pp. 498–499.

40. Both James and Whitehead emphasize the brain's independence of its outside data in creating what we may actually perceive. *Process*, pp. 493–494.

41. While this is the subject of Whitehead's *Symbolism*, the account in *Process and Reality* (particularly pt. II, chap. 8) is far more rigorous, and succeeds in avoiding several confusions found in the earlier work.

42. *Symbolism*, p. 68; see also *Process*, pp. 99, 273.

43. *Psychology*, II, 301; *Process*, p. 272.

44. *Process*, pp. 482–483.

45. *Symbolism*, p. 50.

46. *Process*, pp. 497–498.

47. *Ibid.*, p. 96.

48. *Ibid.*, p. 189. The presented duration is the "spatialized world in which the physical object is *at rest*, at least momentarily for its occasion *M*" (p. 488). This is why Whitehead can say that "an actual entity never moves; it is where it is and what it is" (p. 113). Whitehead explains that "*M* itself lies in many durations; each duration including *M* also includes some portions of *M's* presented duration" (p. 191). In this study, however, such factors can be ignored, because as Whitehead himself goes on to point out, in "human perception practically all the important portions are thus included." See *Nature*, chaps. 5–6. In any case, the difference of time systems between two or more objects can psychologically be more easily handled as relative motion; as it effects changes in time systems, relative motion must be at some significant fraction of the speed of light.

49. *Process*, p. 489.

50. *Ibid.*, 273.

51. *Ibid.*, 271.

52. *Symbolism*, p. 41.

53. *Process*, pp. 166, 164, 211.

54. *Psychology*, I, 162–176.

55. *Ibid.*, pp. 168, 174.

56. *Ibid.*, p. 304. Cf. Merleau-Ponty, *The Phenomenology of Perception*, p. 424; Edmund Husserl, *Cartesian Meditations*, pp. 25–26.

57. *Psychology*, I, 427, 249–250.

58. For the same reasons, James's differences with Freud may also be explained as largely semantic. Nevertheless, James is generally taken as denying the kind of unconscious, causative experiences which are at the heart of the Freudian theory. As has been pointed out, however, his concept of associational activity is closely parallel to Freud's. Even more to the point, in a review of Pierre Janet's *État mental des hystérique* and *L'amnésie continue* in the *Psychological Review*, I (1894), 195–199, he seems to accept the whole theory of the unconscious. While it is true that James is merely reviewing Janet's ideas, he does so with enthusiasm, and without disagreement. What is lacking of the Freudian theory is Freud's dream symbolism (which James rejected), infant sexuality, and constructive trauma. In the same issue, James reviews Josef Breuer's and Freud's *Ueber den psychischen Mechanismus hysterischer Phänomene* with equal enthusiasm.

59. *Psychology*, I, 339.

60. *Modes*, p. 160.

61. See *Psychology*, I, 340–360.

62. *Radical Empiricism*, pp. 3–4.

63. Hume's *Treatise*, appendix. See also bk. I, pt. iv, sec. 6.

64. *Psychology*, I, 239, 339–340.

65. *Ibid.* This is probably what Whitehead means when he says, "No actual entity can be conscious of its own satisfaction" (*Process*, p. 130). See Chapter III.

66. *Psychology*, I, 340–341.

67. "Thus our experience in the present discloses its own nature as with two sources of derivation, namely the body and the antecedent experiential functionings. Also there is a claim for identification with each of these sources" (*Modes*, p. 220).

68. *Psychology*, I, 341.

69. *Adventures*, p. 243; *Process*, p. 117.

70. See *Psychology*, I, 331, 335.

71. *Ibid.*, pp. 297–298, 301–302.

72. James's thinking on this entire topic is a maze of confusion, contradiction, and insight (see chap. 10 of the *Psychology*). One treads here with extreme caution.

73. *Psychology*, I, 291. James groups these into (a) the material self (body, wife, house); (b) the social self (the valued opinion of others, reputation, honor); and (c) the spiritual self (ability in argument, morality).

74. For the replacement of object cathexis by identification, and the contribution of this phychic process to "character," see Freud's *Ego and the Id*, trans. Joan Riviere (London: Hogarth Press, 1949), p. 35.

75. *Psychology*, I, 319. The connection between the basic instinctual gratifications and the body is thus another reason, in addition to immediate perceptual derivation, that James identifies the self with the body (see Chapter III).

76. *Ibid.*, p. 322.

77. See *Process*, pp. 87, 211. This idea must be used with care. Between the boy and the man little "identity" remains. If a complex eternal object is what is passed on from moment to moment in the life of a man from infancy to dotage, we must look for continuity of change, with the momentary complex eternal object connected by like to like, or, in Ludwig Wittgenstein's phrase, "family resemblances." See his *Blue and Brown Books* (New York and Evanston: Harper & Row, 1965).

78. *Psychology*, I, 332.

79. *Ibid.*, p. 341.

80. See *Psychology*, I, 307–308; also Chapter III. See also George A. Miller, Eugene Galanter, and Karl H. Pribram, *Plans and the Structure of Behavior* (New York: Henry Holt and Co., 1960), chap. 2.

81. *Psychology*, I, 427. See Ulric Neisser's *Cognitive Psychology* (New York: Appleton-Century-Crofts, 1967), pp. 225–226, for an interpretation similar to James's.

82. *Psychology*, I, 304; *Radical Empiricism*, p. 13. This analysis ignores the feelings of direct continuity, as suggested by both Whitehead and James, which hold for all items, whether derived from the preceding central occasion or from the body.

83. See Miller, Galanter, and Pribram, *Plans and the Structure of Behavior*, chap. 2.

84. *Cognitive Psychology*, chap. 11.

85. *Psychology*, I, 253, 339, 334.

86. *Ibid.*, pp. 319–320, 323.

87. *Radical Empiricism*, pp. 36–37.

88. *Immanuel Kant's Critique of Pure Reason*, "Transcendental Analytic," bk. I, chap. 2, sec. 2, par. iii, p. 87; "Transcendental Dialectic," bk. II, chap. 1, pp. 282–283.

89. *Radical Empiricism*, pp. 88–89.

90. *Religion*, p. 100.

91. *Varieties*, pp. 489–490.

92. *Modes*, p. 149.

93. *Ibid.*, pp. 160–161.

94. *Psychology*, I, 304.

95. *Modes*, p. 13.

96. *Universe*, p. 380.

III. ORGANIC PURPOSE

1. *Human Immortality*, p. 40.

2. *Process*, p. 156.

3. *Reason*, pp. 9–10.

4. *Some Problems*, pp. 210, 208. See also *Universe*, p. 390.

5. *Reason*, p. 11. "From this point of view (which is currently accepted by many physiologists), the psychological correlates of these reflexes, the urges and pleasures of hunger and satiety, are epiphenomena of the regulation of food intake; they accompany regulation but do not cause it." Philip Teitelbaum, *Physiological Psychology* (Englewood Cliffs, N. J.: Prentice-Hall, 1967), p. 97.

6. *Universe*, p. 259.

7. *Science*, p. 111. James's position is identical: "Using sweeping terms and ignoring exceptions, *we might say that every possible feeling produces a movement, and that the movement is a movement of the entire organism, and of each and all its parts*" (*Psychology*, II, 372).

8. *Modes*, p. 50.

9. *Psychology*, I, 5.

10. *Truth*, pp. 185–186. The word "definable" avoids the nominalist-realist controversy over the role of ideas (see Chapter IV).

11. *Some Problems*, p. 213.

12. *Process*, pp. 128–129.

13. *Reason*, p. 12. In an early review, James noted "how much of ontology is contained in the 'Nature,' 'Force,' and 'Necessary Law' " of science. From *Mind*, IV (1879), 334, quoted in Perry, I, 501. Kant also warned of these dangers; see *The Critique of Judgement*, trans. James Creed Meredith (London: Oxford University Press, 1952), pt. II, sec. 17.

14. The implication of mentality in action evokes Dewey. However, Dewey would reject the implied connection with Aristotle, because Aristotle's final causes are too static, too little influenced by

the reciprocity between organism and environment. These are the elements of Aristotelian thought which Whitehead and James also reject.

15. *Reason*, p. 26; *Process*, pp. 47, 48. When the urge is primarily conceptual, Whitehead substitutes the term "vision."

16. James points out that learning is connected with physical modification or growth. See *Psychology*, I, 10–12.

17. *Ibid.*, II, 551.

18. *Process*, pp. 155–156; *Reason*, pp. 26–27.

19. "Remarks on Spencer's Definition of Mind as Correspondence" in *Essays*, pp. 64–65; *Psychology*, I, 141. It may be argued that "survival" is not the experienced end, but food, shelter, a mate, and so on.

20. At a higher level, Whitehead measures the difference between men and animals by the extent that ideal ends rise above bodily inheritance. See *Modes*, pp. 37–38.

21. *Natural Knowledge*, p. 14.

22. "The Sentiment of Rationality" (the section quoted was delivered as a lecture in 1880) in *Will*, p. 84.

23. "Reflex Action and Theism" (1881) in *Will*, p. 114; "The Physical Basis of Emotion" (1894) in *Essays*, p. 350.

24. It might well be argued that the example of the bear is too complicated to fit the reflex scheme. But the bear example points up one of the major difficulties with the scheme: most real situations are too complicated, and a "pure" reflex by itself is almost impossible to find. At best, it is a useful abstraction from a greatly more complicated psychological and physiological situation.

25. *Psychology*, I, 24.

26. *Ibid.*, p. 26.

27. See I. M. Sechenov, "Reflexes of the Brain" (1863), and I. P. Pavlov, *Lectures on Conditioned Reflexes* (1904), selections in Richard J. Herrnstein and Edwin G. Boring, *A Source Book in the History of Psychology* (Cambridge, Mass.: Harvard University Press, 1965), pp. 308–321 and 564–569, respectively.

28. John Dewey, "The Reflex Arc Concept in Psychology" (1896), in *Ibid.*, pp. 321–325.

29. *Psychology*, I, 76. Compare William McDougall's view: "We may then define an instinct as an inherited or innate psycho-physical disposition which determines its possessor to perceive, or pay attention to, objects of a certain class, to experience an emotional excitement of a particular quality upon perceiving such an object, and to act in regard to it in a particular manner, or at least, to experience an impulse to such an action." From *An Introduction to Social Psychol-*

ogy (1908), cited in Edward J. Murray, *Motivation and Emotion,* (Englewood Cliffs, N. J.: Prentice-Hall, 1964), p. 5.

30. *Psychology,* II, 394. James also had a theory very much like the "imprinting" of current-day ethologists, such as Konrad Lorenz and Niko Tinbergen: *"When objects of a certain class elicit from an animal a certain sort of reaction, it often happens that the animal becomes partial to the first specimen of the class on which it has reacted, and will not afterward react on any other specimen."* James's examples, a favorite hole, a traumatic fear, and so forth also suggest Freudian fixation.

31. *Ibid.,* p. 383. James tests for the existence of instincts by asking if at one time the behavior could have been useful for survival.

32. *Ibid.,* p. 384.

33. *Ibid.,* pp. 487, 550. James makes clear that pleasure and pain are only some of the ideas that have impulsive power. They do not instigate instinctual or emotional action. A hen does not sit on eggs for the pleasure of it, according to James, nor, for that reason, does a man smile or frown.

34. *Ibid.,* p. 392.

35. *Ibid.,* p. 402.

36. *Ibid.,* p. 429. James maintains that starving the instincts of objects in early life will create "gaps" in the psychic constitution "which future experience can never fill," and perhaps may even give rise to perversions. *Ibid.,* p. 441. His theory suggests, as does Freud's, that nonfulfillment of early instinctual needs creates a likelihood of reversion to those earlier forms of instinctual expression. This, for Freud, is a primary basis for perversion.

37. *Ibid.,* I, 108, 118. This analysis suggests that James viewed habitual actions as essentially servo-mechanisms.

38. *Ibid.,* pp. 115, 122. As a philosophy of education, this runs the risk of making habitual actions and modes of thought which are false or inept. But an emphasis on continual voluntary choice, such as is found in Dewey, runs an opposite risk: the plethora of choice and lack of reliable skills may render the student indecisive and ineffectual.

39. See particularly chap. 2, "The Rhythm of Education," in *Aims.*

40. See particularly *Talks,* p. 151, and *Aims,* p. 60.

41. *Psychology,* II, 449–450.

42. James himself did not claim that the perception of bodily changes accounts for all the emotional feeling. He wrote to Charles Renouvier: "I feel sure that some part of our emotions is covered by this account; whether the whole of them is so covered is a question

about which I am still doubtful." Letter of September 30, 1884, quoted in Perry, I, 698.

43. *Psychology*, II, 493, 518-519.

44. *Ibid.*, p. 505. Helmholtz himself was aware of the difficulties of proving that feelings of innervation were experienced. He remarked that "we know of these impulses in no other form, nor by any other definable characteristic except for the fact that they produce the intended observable effect; thus this effect alone serves for the discrimination between the different impulses in our own consciousness." From "The Facts of Perception" (1878) in Richard M. Warren and Roslyn P. Warren, *Helmholtz on Perception: Its Physiology and Development* (New York: John Wiley and Sons, 1968), p. 214. James was not arguing against the existence of innervation; he was only denying that the command signal or the discharge is consciously felt.

45. *Psychology*, II, 558-559.

46. *Adventures*, p. 347.

47. *Psychology*, I, 434, 439.

48. *Ibid.*, pp. 442, 444.

49. *Ibid.*, p. 219. The language in brackets is mine.

50. See Ullric Neisser, *Cognitive Psychology* (New York: Appleton-Century-Crofts, 1967), pp. 103, 300-302.

51. *Talks*, p. 92. James also says that distinct gestalts arouse our "aesthetic interest."

52. *Psychology*, I, 417.

53. See John von Neumann, *The Computer and the Brain* (New Haven: Yale University Press, 1958).

54. Gerald Guthrie and Morton Weiner, "Subliminal Perception or Perception of Partial Cue for Pictorial Stimuli," *Journal of Personality and Social Psychology*, III (1966), 619-628, cited in Neisser, *Cognitive Psychology*, p. 28.

55. Some animals, such as the frog, have high object specificity already built in. J. Y. Lettvin's work indicates correlation between the factors in the visual environment which the frog's perceptive mechanism is set for and the factors in the environment necessary for its survival. Thus, a "net convexity detector" in its perceptive machinery is its "bug perceiver." J. Y. Lettvin *et al.*, "What the Frog's Eyes Tell the Frog's Brain," *Proceedings of the Institute of Radio Engineering*, XLVII (1959), 1940-1961, and private conversations with Dr. Lettvin.

56. *Psychology*, I, 324.

57. *Ibid.*, p. 319.

58. James's view of dreams is different: They are the "capricious play" of associations as the currents of the mind "run—'like sparks in burnt-up paper'—wherever the nutrition of the moment creates an opening" (*ibid.*, p. 594). James could "make nothing" of Freud's dream theories and found symbolism "a most dangerous method."

59. *Ibid.*, II, chap. 21 *passim*. For a discussion of the concept of truth, see Chapter IV, below.

60. *Adventures*, p. 313 and chap. 16 *passim*.

61. See *Process*, part III, chap. 5, secs. iii–v; also *Adventures*, chap. 18.

62. *Psychology*, II, 296.

63. *Ibid.*, p. 393.

64. *Ibid.*, p. 561. Whether the act itself follows depends, of course, on whether what is willed is possible, or, in James's words, a "live option." We cannot will to fly, or even to sneeze, but we *can* will to stand up.

65. *Ibid.*, I, 451. Several garbles in the original text have been corrected.

66. *Ibid.*, II, 528; *Universe*, pp. 390–391. James speculated that physical energy might not be involved, but in his day a physiological explanation of conscious decision making was not possible; perhaps it still is not. See *Psychology*, I, 142.

67. *Psychology*, I, 584.

68. An exception must always be made for the strong sensory experiences and distinct gestalts which compel attention sui generis.

69. *Psychology*, II, 568–569.

70. *Ibid.*, I, 298. See also pp. 302–303.

71. The ideo-motor theory assumes, perhaps gratuitously, that a kinesthetic response to various objects will be present ideationally in the mind. Such an action may be regarded as a subplan under the "object" or a larger plan. See George A. Miller, Eugene Galanter, and Karl H. Pribram, *Plans and the Structure of Behavior* (New York: Henry Holt and Co., 1960).

72. *Psychology*, II, 531.

73. *Ibid.*, I, 288. These were the kinds of decisions which James with his prolonged identity crisis was particularly sensitive to (pp. 309–310).

74. James's concept of the self seems remarkably close to Erik Erikson's "ego identity." With Erikson, James would put more emphasis on characterological decisions of late childhood and adolescence than does Freud's general theory, where early sexual development has almost complete sway in determining future character.

Again, James's emphasis on will, on decisions based on character, gives to his concept of the self a strength and independence in the psychic life which Freud's ego generally lacks. See Erikson's *Childhood and Society* (New York: W. W. Norton and Co., 1950).

75. *Adventures*, p. 59.

76. *Modes*, p. 231.

77. *Reason*, p. 21.

78. James sometimes says that mentality does *not* create but only operates on what is created for it. Along these lines, James argues (a) that all things which we can imagine are based on the sensations we experience, and the parts of other objects we have seen, as in the case of a winged horse; and (b) that all actions which we perform are *based* on our original endowment of impulsive or reflexive actions. *Psychology*, I, 138. See also *Psychology*, II, 584. Cf. Locke's *Essay*, bk. II, chap. 2, par. 2.

79. *Psychology*, I, 453.

80. *Ibid.*, p. 448; *ibid.*, II, 572.

81. See "The Will to Believe" in *Will*.

82. *Psychology*, I, 594.

83. "The Dilemma of Determinism" in *Will*, p. 158.

84. See *Truth*, p. 252. Whitehead puts the matter simply: "We treat the past merely as material for dissection, something settled and obvious, and we have no intimate feeling for the wavering steps of its advance . . . We treat our novelties of to-day as though it were a novel fact that there should be novelty. History is the drama of effort. The full understanding of it requires an insight into human toiling after its aim." From "Historical Changes" in *Science and Philosophy*, p. 203.

85. *Dialogues*, pp. 192–193.

86. The qualifications which Whitehead puts on this freedom by virtue of the relevance of God's nature will be discussed below. See also *Adventures*, pp. 255–256.

87. The distinction between purpose and accident can be found in Plato's *Timaeus* as the distinction between persuasion and force. Ideas "persuade" the universe to achieve what order it attains; force reduces the world to atomic chaos. The role of ideas as persuader may also be found as the theory of rhetoric in the *Phaedrus*.

88. *Modes*, p. 40.

89. *Some Problems*, pp. 150–152.

90. *Universe*, pp. 391–392.

91. *Immanuel Kant's Critique of Pure Reason*, "Method of Transcendentalism," chap. 1, sec. 2.

92. See B. F. Skinner, *Science and Human Behavior* (New York: Free Press, 1965), chap. 17, for a highly qualified defense of the behaviorist position.

93. *Process*, p. 234; see also *ibid.*, p. 228.

94. *Aims*, p. 23.

95. *Process*, p. 447.

96. *Ibid.*, pp. 445–446.

97. *Psychology*, II, 653. Whitehead himself points out that different geometries can characterize the same space equally well. The choice of which to use depends on the practical choice of the user. Further, Whitehead says that transmutation is the ability to simplify the multiplicity of the data into single characterizations of the sensory field. Again, objective mathematical relations need not be maintained.

98. *Process*, pp. 103, 118.

99. *Ibid.*, p. 36.

100. "Whitehead's Philosophical Development" in *The Philosophy of Alfred North Whitehead*, p. 53. Lowe cites Whitehead's article "La Théorie relationniste de l'espace," delivered at an international congress in 1914, and printed in *Revue de métaphysique et de morale*, XXIII (1916), 429–430, as the first expression of this view. See also *Process*, p. 470, for a later expression.

101. *Process*, pp. 470–471, 474.

102. *Ibid.*, p. 323.

103. *Ibid.*, pp. 447–448.

104. The extensive continuum is explained in *Process and Reality*, pt. IV, and in *An Enquiry Concerning the Principles of Natural Knowledge*, *The Concept of Nature*, and *The Principle of Relativity*.

105. Whitehead also explains this effect differently, as a manifestation of the fact that contemporary events function in causal independence of each other owing to the time needed for the transmission of causal inputs. But if the organism is a product only of its immediate past, it would appear to lack freedom. Accordingly, the organism's integrative processes must be taken into account, as Whitehead himself generally assumes. See *Adventures*, pp. 251–253.

106. *Science*, p. 148.

107. Cf. *ibid.*, pp. 148 and 177, with *Process*, p. 434.

108. *Modes*, p. 157.

109. *Natural Knowledge*, p. 3.

110. *Some Problems*, p. 185. In both *Psychology* (I, 622) and *Universe* (p. 235), James follows Bergson in arguing that life is continuous, and is only cut up into artificial moments by our intellect. But in the latter work (pp. 231–232), he also maintains that our

perceptions are in quanta, and argues that quanta are necessary to avoid the "Zenonian paradoxes." For Whitehead's discussion of Zeno, which looks to James for support, see *Process*, pp. 105–107.

111. *Adventures*, pp. 261–262.

112. *Process*, p. 81; see also p. 444.

113. *Ibid.*, p. 66. Whitehead's own definition of negative prehension overspecializes his use of the term.

114. See *Science*, chap. 8.

115. *Process*, pp. 155–156.

116. *Ibid.*, pp. 158–160.

117. The similarities with Irwin Schrödinger's *What Is Life?* (Cambridge: At the University Press, 1951) are striking.

118. *Process*, pp. 165, 161.

119. Whitehead gives transmutation as an example of a negative prehension. In his description, a fairly simple eternal object is "projected" onto a region; thus there is an elimination of the bewildering detail of the data (*Process*, p. 154). It can be argued, however, that what is felt as central experience is the result in some way of what energy is actually available for such experience. The elimination of the detail of the incoming data is effected by the nervous system. Thus, from the standpoint of the central experience, detail is simply not experienced, at least not detail of the same type or order of magnitude as that of the incoming data.

120. *Process*, p. 166.

121. *Ibid.*, p. 324.

122. *Psychology*, I, 162, already quoted; see also I, 148.

123. *Pragmatism*, pp. 286–287.

124. *Process*, p. 164.

125. *Varieties*, p. 506.

126. *Process*, pp. 315, 73.

127. See *Adventures*, p. 64. While Plato generally stresses the divine origin of the soul, he characteristically gives the other side its hearing. In the *Phaedo* (85e), Simmias of Thebes likens the soul to the attunement of a musical instrument. This is essentially Whitehead's first answer. With such thinking, one could construct a Whiteheadian philosophy without theology.

128. *Adventures*, p. 86. See Chapter V.

129. *Process*, p. 160; *Adventures*, p. 341.

130. See *Reason*, pp. 21–22. The parallel with Freud's eros is very close (Whitehead, following Plato, uses the same term in *Adventures in Ideas*). "Eros aims at complicating life by bringing about a more and more far-reaching coalescence of the particles into which living

matter has been dispersed, thus, of course, aiming at the maintenance of life" (*The Ego and the Id,* trans. Joan Riviere [London: Hogarth Press, 1949], p. 55). Freud also makes eros responsible for the integration of the ego (p. 64).

131. Statement of 1879 or 1880, quoted in Perry, I, 489.

132. *Process,* p. 315.

133. See *New Introductory Lectures on Psychoanalysis,* trans. James Strachey (New York: W. W. Norton and Co., 1965), p. 61; also *Civilization and Its Discontents,* authorized translation under the supervision of Joan Riviere (London: Hogarth Press, 1951), chap. 7.

134. *Adventures,* p. 341.

135. *Process,* p. 424.

136. What follows is my highly interpretive rendering of *Process and Reality,* pp. 420–428. The section is unrelievedly abstract.

137. Whitehead offers no explanation of why this occurs; it is for him simply what happens. Whitehead phrases it: "Thus the conceptual valuation now closes in upon the feeling of the nexus as it stands in the generic contrast, exemplifying the valued eternal object" (*ibid.,* p. 422).

138. See *Science,* p. 187.

139. *Adventures,* p. 340.

140. *Adventures,* pp. 346, 271.

141. *Psychology,* II, 672–673.

142. *Process,* pp. 281, 395.

143. *Ibid.,* p. 326.

144. See *ibid.,* pp. 342–343, 284.

145. See *ibid.,* pp. 401–402.

146. *Ibid.,* p. 284.

147. *Ibid.,* p. 245, 286.

148. *Ibid.,* pp. 132–133.

149. *Ibid.,* p. 370.

150. *Ibid.,* p. 245.

151. *Ibid.,* p. 294.

152. *Radical Empiricism,* p. 25, previously quoted.

153. "My present field of consciousness is a centre surrounded by a fringe that shades insensibly into a subconscious more . . . Which part of it properly is in my consciousness, which out? If I name what is out, it already has come in" (*Universe,* p. 288). Cf. Freud's description: "the conscious idea comprises the concrete idea plus the verbal idea corresponding to it, whilst the unconscious idea is that of the thing alone." *Collected Papers,* authorized translation under the

supervision of Joan Riviere (New York: Basic Books, 1959), IV, 138.

154. *Universe*, pp. 283–284.

155. See *Psychology*, I, 221.

IV. CONCEPTS AND CONCEPTUAL OPERATIONS

1. *Some Problems*, pp. 79–80.

2. *Psychology*, I, 477.

3. *Ibid.*, p. 460.

4. *Ibid.*, p. 480.

5. *Ibid.*, p. 506.

6. *Universe*, p. 237.

7. See *ibid.*, pp. 249–250.

8. *Ibid.*, p. 340. Whitehead traces the idea of "static existences of time-less interrelations" to Greek science. Philosophy, he says, was left with the "problem of deriving the historical world of change from a changeless world of ultimate reality" (*Modes*, pp. 111–112).

9. *Modes*, pp. 256–258. Lest these thoughts be attributed exclusively to Bergson's influence, see "On Some Hegelisms" (1882) in *Will*, pp. 167–168, where identical views are expressed. Nevertheless, Bergson's influence is strong in the later period. James said, "Reading his works is what has made me bold" (*Universe*, p. 214).

10. *Some Problems*, pp. 85–88. Some of these criticisms seem directed as much against traditional empiricism as against rationalism.

11. *Universe*, p. 212.

12. "But the rationality yielded is so superbly complete in *form* that to many minds this atones for the loss, and reconciles the thinker to the notion of a purposeless universe, in which all the things and qualities men love, *dulcissima mundi nomina*, are but illusions of our fancy attached to accidental clouds of dust which the eternal cosmic weather will dissipate as carelessly as it has formed them" (*Psychology*, II, 667).

13. *Adventures*, p. 287.

14. *Truth*, p. 295.

15. *Pragmatism*, p. 133.

16. *Process*, p. 407.

17. *Pragmatism*, p. 222.

18. *Truth*, pp. 82, 104–105.

19. *Psychology*, II, 293.

20. *Will*, pp. 15, 82; *Varieties*, pp. 426–427.

21. *Psychology*, II, 335. James points out that it is man's varied instinctual interests that enable him to dissociate so many aspects of things.

22. *Will*, p. 70.

23. *Psychology*, II, 329. This thinking forms the theme of much of Dewey's work.

24. *Radical Empiricism*, pp. 63–64; cf. *Science*, p. 37; Dewey's *Logic: The Theory of Inquiry* (New York: Henry Holt and Co., 1938), pp. 124–125.

25. The phrase is J. S. Bruner's. See his "On Perceptual Readiness," *Psychological Review*, LXIV (1957), 124.

26. *Pragmatism*, pp. 209–210; *Psychology*, II, 644–645, 661–669.

27. *Aims*, pp. 243, already cited, and 157–158.

28. According to James, the opening statement of pragmatism was Peirce's article "How to Make Our Ideas Clear," in the January 1878 issue of *Popular Science Monthly*. See *Collected Papers of Charles Sanders Peirce*, ed. Charles Hartshorne and Paul Weiss (Cambridge, Mass.: Harvard University Press, Belknap Press, 1960). Peirce was a lifelong friend of James and, without doubt, exercised a major influence on his thought. In the pragmatic movement, James also associated himself with F. C. S. Schiller and John Dewey. See James's review of Schiller's *Humanism: Philosophical Essays* in *Essays*, pp. 448–452; see also Dewey's *Logic: The Theory of Inquiry*, pp. 3–4.

29. *Some Problems*, p. 60. With such emphasis on action, James drew the criticism that pragmatism was uninterested in theory, or, worse, was a philosophical justification for money getting: "It is usually described as a characteristically American movement, a sort of bobtailed scheme of thought, excellently fitted for the man on the street, who naturally hates theory and wants cash returns immediately." "The Pragmatist Account of Truth and Its Misunderstanders" in *Truth*, p. 185.

30. *Pragmatism*, p. 53.

31. *Universe*, p. 342; *Pragmatism*, pp. 56–58.

32. *Will*, p. 20.

33. *Ibid.*, p. 11.

34. *Will*, pp. 59, xi–xii.

35. *Ibid.*, p. 22.

36. *Ibid.*, p. 24.

37. *Pragmatism*, pp. 256–257. For a similar statement, see *Some Problems*, pp. 214–215.

38. *Process*, pp. 93–94; see also *Modes*, p. 64.

39. "Whitehead as Teacher and Philosopher," *Philosophy and Phenomenological Research*, XXIX (March 1969), 362.

40. *Process*, p. 21.

41. *Ibid.*, pp. 16–17; *Nature*, p. 171.

42. "Immortality" in *Science and Philosophy*, pp. 95–96.

43. While this distinction between organic and inorganic things seems implied by Whitehead, it is not made explicitly.

44. "Mathematics and the Good" in *Science and Philosophy*, p. 106; see *Process*, p. 66.

45. See *Process*, pp. 383–389.

46. *Ibid.*, p. 359. When Whitehead comes to defining what a subjective aim is, he is often incurably vague. But he does avoid the implication which seems to inhere in James's notion that the abstraction itself is teleological. This notion seems sometimes to be in James's mind when he implies that the salient idea in the field itself brings forth the action.

47. *Reason*, pp. 56–57; *Science*, chap. 2.

48. *Modes*, pp. 112, 125, 126.

49. "Mathematics and the Good" in *Science and Philosophy*, pp. 106, 109.

50. *Modes*, p. 84. Whitehead traces the connection between aesthetics and mathematics to Plato and Pythagorus with their theories of proportion in music and architecture. He also cites the feeling of mathematicians that proofs are "beautiful." See *Adventures*, pp. 190–191; see also "Analysis of Meaning" in *Science and Philosophy*, pp. 129–130.

51. *Modes*, p. 85. Whitehead might have altered this statement had he had more experience of abstract art.

52. *Science*, p. 26, and *Process*, p. 315, previously cited.

53. *Science*, p. 281.

54. *Radical Empiricism*, p. 115. The language in brackets is James's.

55. *Process*, p. 30.

56. *Ibid.*, pp. 341–342, 202.

57. *Science*, pp. 221–223.

58. *Pragmatism*, p. 284.

59. *Science*, p. 223. Whitehead's language here is highly abstract (cf. *Science*, chap. 10, *passim*), and my interpretation is not altogether sure.

60. See *Immanuel Kant's Critique of Pure Reason*, trans. F. Max Müller (New York: Macmillan Co., 1949), "Transcendental Dialectic," bk. II, chap. 3, sec. ii.

61. *Science*, p. 223.

62. *Process*, 295.

63. *Ibid.*, p. 350.

64. *Science*, p. 226; *Process*, p. 441.

65. *Process*, pp. 118, 288.

66. *Nature*, p. 171. Whitehead here specifically refers to an electron as an eternal object.

67. "Whitehead as Teacher and Philosopher," p. 358.

68. *Science*, p. 230.

69. *Truth*, p. 203.

70. *Process*, p. 73.

V. THE LARGER RELATIONS

1. *Adventures*, p. 362; *Modes*, p. 101.

2. *Process*, pp. 314–315; *Adventures*, p. 142. For Whitehead's technical definition of a "society," see *Adventures*, p. 261.

3. *Will*, p. 24.

4. *Reconstruction in Philosophy* (New York: Henry Holt and Co., 1920), p. 194.

5. *Process*, pp. 141–142; *Adventures*, p. 143.

6. *Adventures*, p. 142.

7. *Psychology*, I, 104–105. Whitehead uses the same term: "People make the mistake of talking about 'natural laws.' There *are* no natural laws. There are only temporary habits of nature" (*Dialogues*, p. 294).

8. See Irwin Schrödinger, *What Is Life?* (Cambridge: At the University Press, 1951), chap. 4.

9. *Universe*, p. 61; see also *Pragmatism*, p. 56.

10. *Adventures*, pp. 144–145.

11. *Ibid.*, pp. 147–148, 151, 158.

12. See *Will*, pp. 79–82.

13. From "An Appeal to Sanity," March 1939, in *Science and Philosophy*, p. 65.

14. *Adventures*, p. 266–267.

15. *Psychology*, II, 626–632. Darwin himself endorsed Lamarck's view as an alternative, but subordinate, mode of evolution.

16. "Great Men and their Environment" (1880) in *Will*, p. 247. In the same article, James proposes that great men are biological mutants that the society accepts or rejects. Such extreme examples of Darwinist thought do not generally appear in James's later writings.

17. Herbert Spencer, *The Principles of Psychology* (London, 1885), pt. 4, chaps. 2 and 3, in Richard J. Herrnstein and Edwin G. Boring, *A Source Book in the History of Psychology* (Cambridge, Mass.: Harvard University Press, 1965), pp. 380–388.

18. Letter to Henry Holt, November 22, 1878, quoted in Perry, II, 35.

19. *Reason*, p. 28.

20. *Process*, p. 225; *Modes*, p. 189.

21. *Science*, p. 152.

22. See Loren Eisely, *Darwin's Century* (Garden City, N.Y.: Doubleday & Co., 1958), p. 336.

23. *Reason*, pp. 2–3. Whitehead is here being just a bit sophistic, as the evolutionists conceive survival not as mere persistence, but as the maintenance of life.

24. *Adventures*, p. 60. There was, no doubt, the example of the Greeks to give him pause.

25. *Reason*, p. 48; *Science*, p. 288. Cf. Dewey, *Logic: The Theory of Inquiry* (New York: Henry Holt and Co., 1938), pp. 25–27.

26. *Reason*, p. 19.

27. *Ibid.*, p. 21. Cf. *The Timaeus* in *Plato: The Collected Dialogues*, ed. Edith Hamilton and Huntington Cairns (New York: Bollingen Foundation, 1961), pp. 1151–1211.

28. *Religion*, p. 85.

29. *Process*, p. 523. See also "Immortality" in *Science and Philosophy*, p. 90.

30. *Process*, p. 532.

31. *Process*, p. 525. The burden of this passage is partially contradicted by Whitehead in a conversation summarized by his student A. H. Johnson. "There is always elimination when things are objectified in God. That is the tragedy which even God does not escape." Johnson also gives as Whitehead's view that evil does not lose its character in God's nature. From "Whitehead as Teacher and Philosopher," *Philosophy and Phenomenological Research*, XXIX (March 1969), 371.

32. *Process*, p. 533.

33. *Religion*, p. 96; *Adventures*, p. 357.

34. See Josiah Royce, *The World and the Individual*, 2 vols. (New York and London: Macmillan Co., 1900–1901).

35. *Universe*, p. 126. See also *Pragmatism*, p. 19.

36. *Universe*, pp. 36–40.

37. *Varieties*, p. 512. This somewhat heretical view is discretely attributed to a "friend."

38. Statement of November 11, 1947, in *Dialogues*, pp. 370–371.

39. "The Dilemma of Determinism" in *Will*, p. 177.

40. *Radical Empiricism*, pp. 118, 121.

41. Jottings of 1903–1904, quoted in Perry, II, 384.

42. *Truth*, p. 82. James's reference to the "Hindoo idol" suggests that Whitehead's primordial nature of God has its Indian analogies: "Then the son of Pandu [Arjuna] beheld the entire universe, in all its multitudinous diversity, lodged as one being within the body of the God of Gods." *Bhagavad-Gita*, trans. Swami Prabhavananda and Christopher Isherwood (New York: New American Library, 1954), p. 92. This scene in the *Bhagavad-Gita* compares with that of the voice from the whirlwind in the book of Job. In the latter, God speaks of his acts of creation and his power. In the former, Krishna speaks of his identity with the world, but also, like the primordial nature of God, of his transcendence of the world in time, space, and fecundity of forms.

43. *Varieties*, pp. 506–507, previously quoted.

44. For a different view, cf. Charles Hartshorne, "Whitehead's Idea of God" in *The Philosophy of Alfred North Whitehead*, ed. Paul Arthur Schilpp (New York: Tudor Publishing Co., 1951), pp. 535–541.

45. From "The Force That Through the Green Fuse Drives the Flower" in *The Collected Poems of Dylan Thomas* (New York: New Directions, 1953), p. 10.

46. *Varieties*, p. 841. The idea of nature as "aimless weather" comes from Chauncy Wright. Whitehead did hold that the loose societies of the physical universe, such as astronomical systems, lack intensities of value, and that it is in complex organisms, such as man, that the work of God's hand most impressively establishes His being.

47. See *Science*, chap. 5.

48. *Will*, p. 44.

49. *Universe*, pp. 29–30.

50. *Religion*, pp. 56–57; *Process*, pp. 520–521.

51. *Dialogues*, p. 176.

52. *Modes*, p. 237.

53. *Religion*, pp. 125, 123–124, 83.

54. *Varieties*, pp. 378–379. The note attached to James's article "On Some Hegelisms" (in *Will*, pp. 294–298), explores the relation between drug states and philosophic dispositions, in this case, between nitrous oxide gas intoxication and Hegelianism. James's modest piece might be considered a forerunner of the current massive research into the psychic effects of drugs.

55. *Varieties*, p. 417. The theory that insanity is related to religion is, of course, the most ancient of ideas.

56. See *William James on Psychical Research*, compiled and edited by Gardner Murphy and Robert O. Ballou (London: Chatto and

Windus, 1961), in which all of James's major writings on this topic are collected.

57. "Psychical Research" in *Will*, p. 321; see also "Frederick Myers' Service to Psychology" in *Memories*, p. 154.

58. *Varieties*, p. 502; see also p. 499 and "A Suggestion about Mysticism" in *Essays*, pp. 502–504.

59. *Universe*, p. 299. In the light of the work of Jean Charcot, Janet, and Freud, James's crediting a "great reservoir" and superior powers, rather than personal psychosis, with being the basis of insanity might have seemed dated even to some of James's contemporaries.

60. *Human Immortality*, p. 51.

61. "Final Impressions of a Psychical Researcher" in *Memories*, p. 204. However, James said in the same article that after twenty-five years of following psychic research, he was "theoretically no 'further' than I was at the beginning . . . The peculiarity of the case is just that there are so many sources of possible deception in most of the observations that the whole lot of them *may* be worthless, and yet that in comparatively few cases can aught more fatal than this vague general possibility of error be pleaded against the record" (p. 175).

62. *Universe*, pp. 24–28.

63. From "Nada" in *Mid-Century French Poets*, ed. Wallace Fowlie (New York: Grove Press, 1955), p. 272.

64. *Universe*, p. 30.

65. *Ibid.*, p. 318.

66. *Ibid.*, p. 124. Exactly the same view is expressed in *Varieties*, p. 515.

67. "Whitehead's Idea of God" in *The Philosophy of Alfred North Whitehead*, p. 516.

68. See *Universe*, p. 124; *Will*, p. 61; *Varieties*, p. 514. See also *Pragmatism*, pp. 297–298.

69. Quoted in *Psychology*, I, 349; see also *Varieties*, p. 515.

70. *Pragmatism*, pp. 296, 290.

71. *Adventures*, p. 125.

72. Henry Adams seems the quintessential case of an alienated man of James's class. See *The Education of Henry Adams* (Boston: Houghton Mifflin Co., 1961).

73. See Edmund S. Morgan, *The Puritan Family* (New York: Harper & Row, 1966) and *The Puritan Dilemma* (Boston: Little, Brown and Co., 1958).

74. *Varieties*, pp. 161, 158–159.

75. Letter to Mrs. Henry Whitman, June 7, 1899, in *Letters*, II, 90.

76. *Character and Opinion in the United States* (New York: Charles Scribner's Sons, 1920), p. 75.

77. *Psychology,* II, 578–579.

78. *Talks,* p. 180.

79. *Ibid.,* pp. 179–180.

80. See *Varieties,* p. 506, previously quoted.

81. *Universe,* pp. 305–308.

82. William Graham Sumner was perhaps the clearest American idealogue for this position. Frank Lester Ward held, in opposition, that biological forces had been superseded by social ones subject to human control. Their dispute, Perry Miller says, helped initiate serious social science in the United States. See *American Thought: Civil War to World War I,* ed. Perry Miller (New York: Holt, Rinehart and Winston, 1965), pp. xxvi–xxx.

83. *Will,* pp. 98–99; see also "Review of Spencer's *Data of Ethics*" (1879) in *Essays,* pp. 148–149.

84. From "The Moral Philosopher and the Moral Life" (1891) in *Will,* pp. 214–215.

85. *Essays,* p. 5.

86. *Talks,* p. v. James applies the same analysis to aesthetics: "Any abstract treatment of the 'Aesthetic Ideal' is inadequate to the innumerable different demands which different men (and the same men at different moments) are entitled to make upon the artist" (letter to Henry Rutgers Marshall, 1893, quoted in Perry, II, 256).

87. James opposed U.S. intervention in the Philippines on the grounds that we were imposing our system of beliefs on an alien culture. See Perry, II, 310–311.

88. From "The Moral Philosopher and the Moral Life" in *Will,* p. 195.

89. Pragmatism, like utilitarianism, was a "practical" philosophy, easily explained from the podium by men whose thought exceeded in range and subtlety their pet ideologies. James, in fact, dedicated *Pragmatism* to J. S. Mill, whom, he said, "my fancy likes to picture as our leader were he alive to-day." See Mill's *Utilitarianism* (London: Parker, Son, and Bourn, 1863).

90. *Will,* p. 205.

91. *Religion,* p. 95–96.

92. "An Appeal to Sanity" (1939) in *Science and Philosophy,* p. 64.

93. *Ibid.,* p. 65.

94. Ruth Benedict, *Patterns of Culture* (Boston: Houghton Mifflin Co., 1934). Cf. *Adventures, passim.*

95. *Adventures*, p. 375.

96. *Ibid.*, pp. 356–357.

97. *Ibid.*, pp. vii, 368.

98. *Adventures*, p. 127.

99. *Ibid.*, p. 5.

100. *Ibid.*, p. 21.

101. *Ibid.*, p. 114; *Psychology*, I, 121.

102. *Talks*, p. 292.

103. *Adventures*, pp. 29–30.

104. *Science and Philosophy*, pp. 129–130.

105. *Adventures*, p. 342.

106. *Critique of Judgement*, trans. James Creed Meredith (London: Oxford University Press, 1952), bk. II, "Analytic of the Sublime."

107. *Religion*, p. 158.

108. *Ibid.*, pp. 60–61.

109. *Adventures*, p. 373.

110. Whitehead's conception of personal succession (see Chapter II) means that regard for one's own future is the altruistic or sympathetic provision of a present occasion for another occasion in the future. In this way, it is like love of another person in the present. See Charles Hartshorne, "Whitehead's Philosophy of Reality as Socially Structured Process," *Chicago Review*, VIII (1954), 60–77. See also *Adventures*, pp. 275–276.

111. *Adventures*, p. 377.

112. *Ibid.*, p. 369. This line of thought is distinctly Elizabethan. See E. M. W. Tillyard, *The Elizabethan World Picture* (London: Chatto and Windus, 1950).

113. *Process*, p. 23.

114. *Adventures*, pp. 367–368.

115. *Ibid.*, p. 368.

116. *Ibid.*, p. 369.

CONCLUSION

1. *Universe*, p. 372.

2. See Ivor Leclerc, "Form and Actuality," in *The Relevance of Whitehead*, ed. Ivor Leclerc (New York: Macmillan Co., 1961).

3. Quoted in J. C. Speakman, *Molecules* (New York: McGraw Hill Book Co., 1966), p. vi.

4. This idea was suggested by the artist Galeyn Remington.

Index

Absolute, 14, 194, 202–206, 211–212. *See also* God

Abstract essences (Whitehead), 175–176, 232; as patterns, 179. *See also* Abstraction; Essences; Relational essences

Abstraction, 164, 177–178, 182, 230; as function of simple location, 22; and aesthetics and logic, 180; as electron, 186; as ideas, 187; as sensations, 189; of God and ideas from the world, 190. *See also* Abstract essences; Eternal objects; Ideas; Subjective aims; Universals

Actual entities (Whitehead), 97, 141; and enduring objects, 143; not self-contained, 176. *See also* Actual occasions

Actual occasions (Whitehead), 22–23, 34–35; as ultimate metaphysical ground, 153. *See also* Actual entities

Adams, Henry, 272n72

Aesthetics, 231–235; in concrescence, xii, 33, 144–145, 152–156, 179–180; of conscious field, 43; and limits of character, 131; and conformal propositions, 157; and logic, 179–180, 268n50; and genetic mutation, 197; in feelings of rightness or immortality, 206; in survival of social ideals, 223; and gestalts, 260n51; and special truth, 273n86. *See*

also Art; Beauty; Contrasts, multiple

Alexander, Samuel, 35

Anticipation, 162. *See also* Transitional feelings

Appearance (Whitehead), 70, 73, 79, 81; in Kantian thought, 32; and beauty, 155. *See also* Presentational immediacy, perception in the mode of; Sensationalism; Sensations

Appetitions (Whitehead), 103–104; as eternal ideas, 136; as negative prehensions, 145; in concrescence, 148–149, 154; and primordial nature of God, 149, 184; and nonconformal propositions, 157; as relevance, 185. *See also* Final causes; Ideals; Live options; Purposes; Relevance; Subjective aims

Appropriation, 89, 98. *See also* Identity; Self; Transitional feelings; Warmth and intimacy

A priori sciences, *see* Mathematics

Aristotle: on final causes, 102, 129, 257–258n14; on metaphor, 153; on ideas, 164

Art, 180, 233, 235; and consciousness, 44, 155–156; and interest, 120. *See also* Aesthetics; Beauty; Contrasts, multiple

Association: in construction of objects, 39; in spatial perception, 63; in education, 113; in

275